WOMAN'S ASTROLOGY

Tiffany Holmes
WOMAN'S ASTROLOGY
Your Astrological Guide to a Future Worth Having

E. P. DUTTON & CO., INC. / NEW YORK

Acknowledgment for permission to excerpt passages is made to the following: Evangeline Adams. From *The Bowl of Heaven*, by Evangeline Adams. Copyright 1926 by Dodd, Mead & Company, Inc. Copyright renewed 1954 by George E. Jordan, Jr. Reprinted by permission of Dodd, Mead & Company, Inc. From *Astrology for Everyone*, by Evangeline Adams. Copyright 1931 by Evangeline Adams Jordan. Copyright renewed 1959 by George E. Jordan, Jr. Reprinted by permission of Dodd, Mead & Company, Inc. Also from *Astrology: Your Place Among the Stars*, by Evangeline Adams. Copyright 1930 by Evangeline Adams Jordan. Copyright renewed 1958 by George E. Jordan, Jr. Reprinted by permission of Dodd, Mead & Company, Inc. / Ilya Chambertin. From *Astroanalysis*, by Ilya Chambertin. Reprinted by permission of Prestige Books, Inc. / Linda Goodman. From *Linda Goodman's Sun Signs*, by Linda Goodman. Reprinted by permission of Taplinger Publishing Company. / Morris C. Goodman. From *Astrology and Sexual Analysis*, by Morris Goodman. Copyright © 1972, Fleet Press Corporation, New York. Reprinted by permission of Fleet Press Corporation. / Frances Sakoian and Louis Acker. From *The Astrologer's Handbook*, by Frances Sakoian and Louis Acker. Reprinted by permission of Harper & Row Publishers, Inc.

Library of Congress Cataloging in Publication Data

Holmes, Tiffany.

Woman's astrology.

Includes bibliographical references.

I. Astrology. I. Title.

BF1729.W64H64   1977   133.5′02′4042   76-23391

ISBN: 0-525-23597-3 (cloth)

0-525-04775-1 (paper)

Published simultaneously in Canada by Clarke, Irwin & Company Limited, Toronto and Vancouver

FIRST EDITION

10 9 8 7 6 5 4 3 2 1

This book is lovingly dedicated to
Irene Frank Siegel and the late Joseph S. Siegel (my parents),
to my brother, Arthur M. Siegel,
to "Clark Kent" and to Lynne Palmer,
who taught me not only the houses
but the foundations.

ACKNOWLEDGMENTS

I want to thank as well Connie Clausen, Janet Kaplan, Sheri Safran, Barbara Seaman, Jody Ward—and everyone else who has nursed me through the "mean reds" of the creative process.

Contents

Introduction

Leos enjoy football and other sports. Leo girls are often cheerleaders.

The average Virgo woman believes that cleanliness is next to godliness.

A proud Leo woman dislikes asking her husband for money. Husbands of these women should always give them an ample allowance.

A man born in Aries with Aquarius rising, or vice versa, is nearly certain to be talented in research, mechanics, or invention.

Nineteen fifty-four fortune cookies? No—nineteen *seventy*-four space-fillers in a leading astrology magazine. And this is just a small sampling. The popularization of any good thing usually has drawbacks as well; in the case of astrology, a deluge of printed matter appeared perpetuating the male-female dichotomy and ancient antifeminist dogma, expressed in the now-popular jargon, Astrologese. No longer just women and men, but Virgos, Geminis, or what-have-you, we are grouped into eternal zodiacal races and will presumably continue the battle of the sexes in the same roles as ever before. Or will we? Astrological terms *can* be employed to guide in more contemporary ways. Any of the above items could be rewritten to encompass *all* of humanity without threatening astrological axioms in the least:

Leos enjoy football and other sports.

The average Virgo believes that cleanliness is next to godliness.

A proud Leo dislikes asking for money and should have ample pay.

Anyone born in Aries with Aquarius rising, or vice versa, is nearly certain to be talented in research, mechanics, or invention.

Similarly, in a reading for a specific client—for example, a teen-age girl—great variations often occur. The chart below shows how two different astrologers might interpret the same factors *and still be technically right*. The headings M (Masculinist) and F (Feminist) refer to attitudes, not the sex, of the astrologer.

BOTH

You have the Sun conjunct Neptune in the first house.

M

You'll have to conceal your ego and be more of a flatterer if you want to succeed with a man.

F

You're in danger of losing touch with your real feelings if you pretend and fake your way through relationships with the male sex.

BOTH

You have Mars in the second house.

M

You could spend money as though it's burning a hole in your pocket.

F

You may be a spendthrift. You're quick to "put your money where your mouth is." You could, though, bring money in through sports if you direct your competitive energies intelligently.

BOTH

You have the Moon conjunct Saturn in the fourth house.

M

Your father probably taught you the value of being dutiful about your housework.

F

Your father may have been old-fashioned and oppressive about housework, but the source of your energy may be ambition. Don't feel guilty; work toward your goal.

BOTH

You have Jupiter in the seventh house.

M

You'll probably get a rich husband, especially if you try to win him by being a good sport.

F

You may have a flippant attitude about marriage and not care whether you marry or not. If you *do* marry, the man will probably be generous and have a sense of humor. You may also find fulfillment as a doctor or lawyer.

BOTH

You have Uranus conjunct Pluto in the eleventh house.

M

Rebellious and peculiar friends could lead you astray.

F

You could find new, progressive-thinking friends in a group with a cause such as the women's liberation movement.

Both readings are correct in terms of the letter of astrological law, but only one is *right*. Only one shows real awareness. Only one is true to the spirit of astrology's aims: to help a client make the most of raw materials, not to stunt her growth. Astrology, if it is to help, cannot stay in an ivory tower.

If, in an encounter with an astrologer, you find the astrological terms bewildering and distracting, don't let that put you off. We're well-meaning people who intend to help, not intimidate, so don't hesitate to question either spoken or written advice that you believe is at odds with the ambitions and convictions of the woman you have become. Don't be awed by the language; if you think it's antiquated—damaging, even— speak up. Start a dialogue. You'll be glad you did.

Many "pop" astrology books are full of applause for "feminine" women and "masculine" men—which is a disservice to women and men who don't fit the stereotypes. I can't emphasize enough the fact that both "feminine" and "masculine" planets (that is, the Moon and Venus, and the Sun and Mars, respectively) are present in every chart regardless of the individual's sex. After all, the Moon and Venus aren't about to drop out of the universe just because a boy is born! I must emphasize, too, that the most neutral and cerebral planets, Mercury and Uranus, give intellectual energy to us all. Our common grounds are sadly underemphasized.

Also bear in mind that it is impossible to tell whether an unlabeled chart is female or male. You would, of course, be able to determine whether the personality is active or passive, but you cannot say, "That passive personality is a female's." To demonstrate this point in teaching, I gave students unidentified birth data to calculate during a lesson. After detailing the meanings of the planets, we set up the chart together. When we were done I asked a student to guess who the person was.

"I think it's a man," she said.

"Why?"

"The forcefulness and aggressiveness."

It was Patty Hearst—and my student will never make *that* mistake again!

Another point I'd like to bring out is that the advice for men in pop horoscopes varies dramatically from that aimed at women: How to score with her and How to get notions of a career out of her head so she'll want to come home to you, for men, *versus* How to get him to marry you and Don't try to change him—just consider yourself lucky you have him, for women.

I discovered, too, that the images of the male and the female of each astrological "species" are far from equal. In one contemporary women's magazine the male Aries is described as generous, while the female Aries makes a mess of the checkbook and needs a smart man to balance it. If the vast majority of horoscopes could be reduced to a word or two for each sign, male and female, this is what we'd have:

> Male Aries: go-getter
> Female Aries: aggressive
>
> Male Taurus: steadfast
> Female Taurus: bovine
>
> Male Gemini: verbal
> Female Gemini: gossipy
>
> Male Cancer: conservative
> Female Cancer: stubborn
>
> Male Leo: aristocratic
> Female Leo: bossy
>
> Male Virgo: discriminating
> Female Virgo: nit-picking
>
> Male Libra: attractive
> Female Libra: vain

Male Scorpio: sexy
Female Scorpio: nymphomaniac

Male Sagittarius: wanderer
Female Sagittarius: irresponsible

Male Capricorn: ambitious
Female Capricorn: social climber

Male Aquarius: spontaneous
Female Aquarius: unreliable

Male Pisces: visionary
Female Pisces: dreamer

Although it's crude, this list is uncomfortably close to the message within reach of all of us: how much of this can a woman really relate to? So I searched for a horoscope that could give even the remotest satisfaction to anyone with a liberated consciousness and found one paragraph hidden in 1975 horoscope booklets! It's a start, but it didn't wipe out the imperative I continued to feel: create a guide *now*.

This book is designed to help you choose a career if you haven't already done so; offer a booster shot of sisterly support; urge you to question astrological pronouncements that run counter to a woman's best interests; and shame colleagues of mine who may be reading this into rethinking their guidance. *No astrologer has the right to lock a client into a stereotype.* I urge the lay reader to question, and the astrologer to offer more thoughtful advice. The fault lies not in our stars—but in some of our interpreters.

In this book my feelings about astrology and about the new strength of women converge totally: the passive and helpless attitude of fatalism is self-destructive. As implied in the title, there are futures . . . and there are futures. To achieve that which is worth having, active collaboration on the individual's part is a vital necessity. There's so much more to shaping your future than just aging.

Astrology as a study for amateurs or as a profession spurs considerable soul-searching. It *has* to. And the most immediate issue is: what does astrology mean to you? What *can* it mean? What will I *let* it mean? What can I live with? Is it inevitable? Can I beat the system? I've come to realize that in my own life astrology is not a crutch or a cop-out, but rather a safety belt that helps me get over the bumps of life. The bumps are still there, but at least when you're prepared for them you don't go through the windshield. Most important of all: never doubt for a minute that *you* are in the driver's seat.

TIFFANY HOLMES
1976

PART ONE

1

Debunking the Myth:
Exposing Sexist Astrology

To make the most of a new, relevant astrology, we must first dispense with the old, sexist astrology that would have us cutting off our toes to fit the glass slipper. The following danger signals point out where I disagree most heatedly with traditional astrology.

1. Positive-Masculine-Negative-Feminine

Sexism in astrology begins at the elemental level: Fire, Earth, Air, Water. Visions of Mother Earth aside, the ruckus starts with the labels themselves. It's all well and good to say that Fire and Air signs have a positive electrical charge and Water and Earth signs a negative one. It's when the catch-phrases "positive-masculine" and "negative-feminine" are used that I start seeing red. These labels are usually accompanied by an embarrassed disclaimer of value judgments, asserting that they merely represent magnetic polarity, a physical fact. If that's really all it is, why not dispense with *masculine* and *feminine* altogether? Why not streamline the jargon to reflect the contemporary consciousness?

2. The Natural Zodiac Wheel

The positive-masculine signs alternating with the negative-feminine signs combine with the ruling planets and the houses they traditionally rule in an antiquated conceit known as the *natural zodiac wheel*. Aside from the sexism rampant in this natural zodiac wheel, I object to it on the grounds that it is confusing to astrologers and to students and clients alike. Dispense with what's theoretically "natural" and concentrate on the chart at hand. We each have only one chart—the one calculated from the moment of birth:

Aries: the first-house sign, positive-masculine, a Fire sign, represented by the ram and ruled by the planet Mars. Aries has all the boldness, ambition, impatience, and aggressiveness of its ruling planet, and forcefully demands the freedom and initiative of the house it is "naturally" allotted to, the first. When planets in this sign are discordant, having planetary distances of 45°, 90°, 135°, or 180°, egocentricity may be expected.

Taurus: the second-house sign, negative-feminine, an Earth sign, represented by the bull and ruled by the planet Venus. As Venus is the planet of beauty, and as the part of the body ruled by Taurus is the throat, persons born under Taurus are often gifted with beautiful voices as well as attractive appearances. The second-house association is the customary explanation for the materialistic streak in this "feminine" sign.

Gemini: the third-house sign, positive-masculine, an Air sign, represented by the twins and ruled by the planet Mercury. "Masculine" couldn't be more of a misnomer than it is here; Gemini is perhaps the most neutral sign of the lot and is the one most heavily represented in the charts of bisexuals and adolescents who like the unisex look. The Gemini personality, owing to its cerebral ruling planet, is quick-thinking, witty, and an articulate reporter. When a Gemini planet is under a discordant aspect, restlessness, nervousness, and an overly diverse scattering of interests may be expected.

Cancer: the fourth-house sign, negative-feminine, a Water sign. Cancer is ruled by the Moon, and this is where the plot thickens: the fourth house rules the home and family life and the Moon rules emotions and "maternal instincts." Since the Moon also rules Cancer, members of this sign typically have deep, heavy emotions which they direct at their homes and at members of their families. No wonder Cancer is represented by a crab!

Leo: the fifth-house sign, positive-masculine, a Fire sign. Represented by the king of beasts, Leo may be more beastly than most in throwing power around, and its planetary ruler, the Sun, reinforces this tendency. Without a creative outlet for Leo energies, a frustrated member of this sign concentrates on showing off, interfering in other people's lives, and passing the buck. Hence the Sophie Portnoys of the world. Leo's creative energies are powerful, and this personality should insist on work that is worthy of it.

Virgo: the sixth-house sign, negative-feminine, an Earth sign. This sign is also ruled by Mercury, but Mercury as the ruler of Virgo operates quite differently than as the ruler of the "masculine" Gemini: with Virgo Mercury becomes finicky, detail-minded, health-conscious, and often impresses others as being old maidish in its fanatic attention to trifles (this distinction applies mainly when talking of Mercury-in-Gemini *versus* Mercury-in-Virgo. As with any sign placement for a planet, the harmony or discord of the aspects can support or mitigate any of the above. My purpose here is to show the shift of connotation as we go from "masculine" to "feminine"). Virgo is often called the sign of service and is represented by a woman holding wheat, chaff and all. It is interesting to note that the 1970 Women's Strike for Equality took place on August 26 (the anniversary of the ratification of the women's suffrage amendment, which was subsequently proclaimed Women's Rights Day), a Sun-in-Virgo date. It was a large-scale unburdening for women all over the country; womanly service was at a standstill.

Libra: the seventh-house sign, positive-masculine, an Air sign, represented by the balancing scales of justice and ruled by the planet Venus. Venus as the ruler of Libra is different from Venus as the ruler of Taurus: with Libra it has a detached manner and a distinct fondness for abstractions on ethical questions, in contrast with its more personal influence over Taurus. People with Libra planets are scrupulously impartial when they have no vested interests at stake; for this reason they make excellent judges. Because Libra is so adept at weighing one value or interest against another and because it is the house associated with partnerships, it is known as the marriage sign. The Libran personality craves an ongoing dialogue—preferably debate—and enjoys playing the devil's advocate. Under discordant aspects the Libran tends to tire easily and to become lazy, indecisive, and vain (Venus's influence).

Scorpio: the eighth-house sign, negative-feminine, a Water sign, represented by the scorpion and ruled by the planets Mars and Pluto. Scorpio is one of the three most prevalent rising signs in the survey of feminist activists (Chapter 11), which is rather appropriate; this "feminine" sign is the only one to be symbolized by a creature that stings (ask any male chauvinist who's been stung). It is also the only "feminine" sign to be ruled by the "masculine," sexual planet, Mars. Harmoniously aspected Scorpio planets foster deductive skill, courage, persuasiveness, and healing ability. Scorpio's negative traits are vindictiveness, self-destructive sexual activity, morbidity, and hermitlike withdrawal.

Sagittarius: the ninth-house sign, positive-masculine, a Fire sign, represented by the centaur and ruled by the planet Jupiter. Sagittarians have a lively sense of humor—which may sometimes be at the expense of others. For example, one man with his Moon and ascendant in Sagittarius wrote "Betty Friedan wears a bra" on the wall of the men's room at the church where the National Organization for Women used to meet. This may be part of the reason NOW had to find new quarters. (I wasn't in the men's room myself. He told me.) Absolute and ingenuous honesty (which may be interpreted as a put-on), wanderlust, a strong feeling for fair play, and positive thinking also characterize Sagittarius.

Capricorn: the tenth-house sign, negative-feminine, an Earth sign, represented by the goat and ruled by Saturn. Discipline, practicality, ambition, and the ability to persevere for years before the goal is reached are the strongest Capricorn traits. Feelings of responsibility toward the older, more dependent people in the family will also influence life for the Capricorn personality. Capricorn would probably be the first to call attention to discrimination or oppression; she would work for years toward a payoff that is tangible, but would not hold still for thankless sacrifice. Parents and others often use accusations of selfishness to keep Capricorn in line. When this occurs, consciousness-raising and the support of people who really care are the best antidotes.

Aquarius: the eleventh-house sign, positive-masculine, an Air sign, represented by the boy carrying water, and ruled by Saturn and Uranus. Aquarius is gifted with inventive ability and foresight, and has the special talent of predicting the social effects of new institutions and politics. Aquarius is inquisitive, interested in people, iconoclastic, independent, and, under discordant aspects, often unreliable and unpredictable.

Pisces: the twelfth-house sign, negative-feminine, a Water sign, represented by two fish swimming in opposite directions, and ruled by the planets Jupiter and Neptune. In this dichotomy Jupiter represents the profitable and humanitarian direction, while Neptune is the futile and self-defeating one (and it is a consciousness-raising kick in the head that a sign associated with indecision and not knowing whether it's coming or going should be classed as negative-feminine!). Despite uncertainty of direction, however, Pisces is capable of being psychic, artistic, imaginative, and sympathetic. The ability to dissociate the self from its physical surroundings by means of mental legerdemain or wishful thinking can be either an asset or a liability.

To see even more clearly the sexism in the natural zodiac wheel, connect the positive-masculine signs with the traits of the houses they "naturally" rule, and do the same for the negative-feminine. The results look something like this:

POSITIVE-MASCULINE

1. The self and personal freedom (Aries)
3. The mind, short journeys, and written and spoken communications (Gemini)
5. Speculation and creativity of all kinds, sex (Leo)
7. Competition, partnership, public relations, advisory relationships (Libra)
9. The legal profession, religion, higher education, philosophy, publishing, broadcasting, long-distance travel (Sagittarius)
11. Friendships and fraternal groups, social concerns (Aquarius)

NEGATIVE-FEMININE

2. Material assets and the disposal of same (Taurus)
4. The home, domesticity, family life (Cancer)
6. Service, food, illness, pets (Virgo)
8. Debts, taxes, insurance, death (Scorpio)
10. Ambition, influence of one's mother, status, reputation (Capricorn)
12. Solitude and privacy, sorrows and limitations, self-undoing (Pisces)

3. "Male" and "Female" Planets

The Sun = male sex = importance, power
The Moon = female sex = trivia, service
Mars = male sex = aggressive pursuit
Venus = female sex = passive acceptance

These sexist fundamentals are so often worded as though they were mathematical verities that I have set them off in equation format to show you how ridiculous they are. We all have *all four* planets in our charts. Thus, as paradoxical and complex human beings will, we manifest contrasting behaviors—sometimes even in a single hour! The Sun gives everyone, women and men alike, hope for achieving a position of importance and power. The Moon gives everyone a capacity for giving service, plus a certain amount of unavoidable daily trivia. Mars gives us a desire to engage in aggressive pursuit every now and then. And we can all be passively accepting of other people on occasion. Ponder for a moment these words by the late Abraham Maslow: "Only recently have we become aware, fully aware, from our studies of healthy people . . . that every human being is both poet and engineer, both rational and nonrational, both child and adult, both masculine and feminine, both in the psychic world and in the world of nature."[1]

4. Man's Sun-Woman's Moon

In conversations with students and astrology buffs, pairings have been termed good when the woman's Moon was conjunct (i.e., in the same sign as) or otherwise harmoniously aspected to the man's Sun. The rationale behind this is that the woman needs to lean on and serve a man who will want to lead her, and that the man, in turn, needs the reassurance that the woman will be receptive to his forceful, presumably benevolent control. To this, I say: if a Moon-Sun contact between charts is good, *it can be just as good in reverse.* If you, as a woman, have the freedom and inclination to look for a man, watch what happens when you meet one whose Moon is conjunct or harmoniously aspected to *your* Sun! Then you, too, can know the joy of having someone hang on your every word. He will be truly receptive to the kind of woman you are without play-acting on your part.

5. The Attraction of Adjacent Signs "Because One Is Masculine and the Other Is Feminine"

As we have seen, the "masculine" and "feminine" signs alternate around the natural zodiac wheel. Dispensing with these labels, there are three simple, nonsexist reasons for the attraction of two neighboring signs: 1) each sign is so different in temperament from either of the two which flank it that any fascination arising between, for example, a Scorpio and a Sagittarius, must stem from the appeal of the unknown; 2) Mercury and Venus travel so close to the Sun that either or both may be in the same adjacent sign as the partner's Sun, thereby reinforcing the bonds of communication and affection respectively; 3) in the case of a partner whose Sun is in the sign *after* yours, you may have a progressed planet forming a conjunction to your partner's Sun (see Chapter 7 for details on how progressions work). The bond, then, would be particularly intense during the time of the progressed conjunction, when you are learning from the other person's example how to respond in ways other than your earlier pattern.

The appeal of the exotic is also at work in the much-publicized attraction of opposite signs. The combination of opposites, however, is a combination of sign pairs of the same "sex" group: Taurus-Scorpio, Cancer-Capricorn, and Virgo-Pisces are "feminine"; Aries-Libra, Gemini-Sagittarius, and Leo-Aquarius are "masculine." This unaesthetic circumstance is not mentioned in the lyrical texts on compatibility I've seen; there the "masculine" and "feminine" labels drop into quicksand—all the more understandable when you realize that homosexuality of any sort is never prescribed.

No astrological education is complete without a background course in the literature of the discipline, and so I offer you

ASTROLIT I
A consciousness-raising survey of post-1965 astrological literature. Prerequisite: intense interest.

The intention here is not to humiliate the perpetrators publicly—they know who they are—but to show all of you what not to believe and what not to accept. Hint: not one source is Godey's *Lady's Book*. Post-1965, remember.

You will find that sign descriptions written to enable you to recognize the sign species in general are decent enough ("Male or female, these people will fight what they feel is an injustice. . . ."), but once the subject of love comes up and the writers separate their readings of men and women, you will get the following:

1. "Make like the emancipated woman in front of his friends and he'll have one of two reactions . . . he's likely to give you a shove and a shaking, maybe even a good smack in the right place when you get home—or worse, before you get home."[2] Trade in emancipation for intimidation, and you, too, can have marital bliss.

2. "You're likely to choose a man who is weaker than you are, one whom you can—and will—dominate. This is the beginning of domestic tragedy."[3] When a man dominates, God's in His heaven, all's well with the world. When a woman dominates—domestic tragedy.

3. "She'll exert every effort and energy to make the marriage a success, placing her husband's welfare and interests *above her own.*"[4] (Italics added.) Now hear this: the new ideal is that the importance of the husband's welfare is *the same as* the wife's. No less, no more.

4. "A strong preponderance of planets in masculine signs indicates a self-propelling person with positive aggressive tendencies." (This should read ". . . planets in Fire and Air signs"—and stop there. But it goes on.) "In a man's chart, such a preponderance is favorable. However, in a woman's chart it can indicate an inclination to be *more aggressive than is traditionally considered appropriate for her sex.*"[5] (Italics added.) It is not for astrologers to wield sex discrimination—the universe doesn't. Our job is to point out constructive channels for energies that, "traditionally considered appropriate" or not, do exist.

5. "If a strong preponderance of planets occurs in negative passive signs, the person probably will not manifest himself aggressively but can possess great strength in terms of passive endurance. A grouping of negative signs in a woman's horoscope makes her more feminine and is considered appropriate for her sex. In a man's chart, it can encourage effeminacy and lack of aggressiveness."[6] If your astrologer stigmatizes you, where can you turn?

6. "The positive type of Gemini is, however, a reminder that this is a masculine sign. These people display much force and initiative."[7] In the negative types, then, masculinity is swept under the rug, so that we may mistake the haphazardness of the negative personality for the usual scapegoat, the female.

7. "As you know from the other Sun signs, few women are perfect."[8] A corollary could well be added for men—but I haven't found it.

8. "The notorious 'leather girl' of New Jersey represents the extreme of this type, who enjoys sadistic pleasures, beating men, satisfying their lusts in torturing the male and forcing him into satisfying her lusts with all kinds of weird and far-out acts of perversion. At the other end of the Taurus scale is the sadistic female who searches far and wide for a partner who will force her into sexual slavery, overpowering her into the lowest forms of obnoxious and disgusting acts—which she thoroughly enjoys."[9] Some scale—from sadistic to sadistic! The author's view of the Taurus male is perversion-proof: he may try something once but will not become addicted to any kinky practices. The astrological basis for this distinction is totally imperceptible to me!

9. "The Virgoan girl makes an ideal secretary."[10] I don't dispute that

tidiness and efficiency make Virgo desirable as a secretary—but "*girl*"?

10. "To avoid unwanted sexual approaches to her, the Gemini woman has an added dodge to that of a display of nervous hysteria. She has mother. . . . She will, if she marries, create a monstrous mother-in-law of her mother, who may well have started out as a nice plain woman."[11] The Gemini man, on the other hand, is merely a nice, mild square who is content to live with his mother if he doesn't happen to marry. By the way, the Gemini woman's dodge is news to me.

11. "Outwardly, Miss Gemini, you must maintain some show, some pretense of being free and independent. This does not necessarily mean that you must have extramarital affairs. Your desire to remain independent may be satisfied by something as simple as membership in a women's club.

"Your husband MUST see below this surface show and understand that you are essentially a dependent person."[12] See how simple it is! And if your husband doesn't see below the "surface show," he might let you wander alone into the wrong women's club. Like N.O.W.

12. "These characteristics [ardent, passionate, and selfish] are softened in the female."[13] If so, it's the result of programming, not nature, astrology, or whatever else you want to call it. This illustrates perfectly the essential point of this lesson: we must distinguish and conscientiously separate the wheat of astrological truths from the chaff of sexist programming.

13. "As a rule [the Moon in the fourth house] makes the natives fond of cooking and housekeeping; it is especially favorable in a woman's horoscope."[14] Speaking as a woman who has this placement, let me just say that I am fond of cooking and housekeeping—other people's.

14. "[Elliot] Richardson was born in Boston, July 20, 1920, under the sign of the Crab which, astrologers say, indicates a 'hard shell and an ability to nip,' and is a far more natural sign for women than men, standing for intuition and introversion."[15] Even nonastrological articles in nonastrological publications get lyrical about what sign is natural for what or whom. When in doubt, doubt.

15. "[Mars in the first house] is favorable for men because it makes them strong and masculine."[16] When you say that a given planetary position is favorable for one sex or the other, the message is merely that such a position makes it easier for the woman or man to conform to the long-held sexual stereotypes—stereotypes which should not still exist and which astrology should debunk.

16. "You may have to tame [Aries] a little, but she'll accept it with surprising docility if she really loves you."[17] This is but one sample of the "tame her" guides for the man in love. Women, on the other hand, are urged to accept resignedly men's foibles and adapt, or tame, themselves.

17. "The manliest male [Sagittarius] will become as hysterical as a woman. This manly guy will immediately manifest his latent femininity by importuning all the gods, seeresses and witches to get him out of his dilemma."[18] I'm astounded by this reaction to a sign inextricably linked with religion: when a male of this supposedly masculine sign importunes "all the gods," out comes his latent feminity! Logic like this would confound P. T. Barnum.

18. "In a woman's horoscope, Mars indicates the type of man she wishes to attract. In a man's horoscope, it represents the way he expresses his masculinity in attracting a woman."[19] Why separate the readings for the two sexes? How about replacing this with the more androgynous "Mars indicates the type of sexual relationships the person is likely to experience, and the assertiveness shown in getting any relationship started."

Now that we have exposed the sexist malignancy in astrology, we can excise it. From now on we can look forward to a healthy, androgynous astrology—with the planets bestowing their gifts upon women and men alike.

NOTES TO CHAPTER ONE

1. Abraham Maslow, *The Farther Reaches of Human Nature* (New York: Viking, 1971).
2. Linda Goodman, *Linda Goodman's Sun Signs* (New York: Bantam Books, 1968), p. 57.
3. Ilya Chambertin, *Astroanalysis* (New York: Lancer, 1970), p. 46.
4. *Ibid.*, p. 47.
5. Frances Sakoian, Louis S. Acker, *The Astrologer's Handbook* (New York: Harper & Row, 1973), p. 19.
6. *Ibid.*, p. 21.
7. Joan Quigley, *Astrology for Adults* (New York: Holt, Rinehart and Winston, 1969), p. 21.

8. Linda Goodman, *op. cit.*, p. 141.
9. Morris Goodman, *Astrology and Sexual Analysis* (New York: Fleet Press, 1972), p. 37.
10. Derek Parker and Julia Parker, *The Compleat Astrologer's Sun-sign Guide* (New York: Crown, 1973), p. 120.
11. Morris Goodman, *op. cit.*, p. 53.
12. Chambertin, *op. cit.*, p. 79.
13. Teri King, *Love, Sex and Astrology* (New York: St. Martin's Press, 1973), p. 14.
14. Sakoian, Acker, *op. cit.*, p. 110.
15. *The New Republic*, February, 1976.
16. Sakoian, Acker, *op. cit.*, p. 154.
17. Linda Goodman, *op. cit.*, p. 25.
18. Morris Goodman, *op. cit.*, p. 139.
19. Sakoian, Acker, *op. cit.*, p. 258.

2

Self-Awareness:
The First Steps

What's the first thing you look at in an astrology book or magazine? Probably your own sign. Know thyself is one bit of advice that we all get sooner or later, and is guidance we try all our lives to follow. Astrology has proved a fascinating tool in this pursuit; even nonbelievers look at their daily horoscopes (when nobody's looking) despite their better judgment. Critics of astrology are absolutely right when they point out that one sentence in a newspaper horoscope column can't possibly apply to the entire twelfth of the population born under any one sign—there are too many individual variations. It is for this reason that astrologers urge you to begin your study of astrology with your own timed birth chart.

The best way to get a timed birth chart is to consult a professional astrologer. I say this not because I'm trying to drum up business for myself—if Jupiter is all it's cracked up to be, I'll be too busy promoting this book—but simply because I believe it. If your *Yellow Pages* doesn't list astrologers, write to the American Federation of Astrologers, Post Office Box 22040, Tempe, Arizona 85282, for a listing from their membership files.

At this point a few definitions are in order:

Planet: A heavenly body that moves; as opposed to a *star*, which remains at a fixed point in terms of a degree of the zodiac and which does not enter into readings. For our purposes the Sı n and the Moon will be called planets, although technically they are luminaries.

Sign: A 30-degree arc in the ecliptic (the Sun's path), of which it is one-twelfth, indicating the location and the manner of expression of the planet between its limits (not to be confused with the constellation of the same name, as the signs and constellations no longer coincide one hundred percent). Throughout this book the sign-names Aries through Pisces will refer to the arc signs.

House: A department of life. The houses' demarcation lines, or cusps, are determined by the time of birth in relation to the day of the month and the longitude and latitude of birth.

Aspect: The distance between any combination of planets. It is in the computation of aspects that astrologers determine the harmony or discord of a planet.

Whether or not you have, or plan to have, a personalized chart calculated by a trained astrologer, I hope you'll find something of help in this guide. Self-recognition is merely a start. The exercise of free will—active participation in shaping your future—is the crucial difference.

Sun Signs

Any factor in a chart is bound to be grossly distorted when separated from the context of the whole picture. Each factor serves either to support or to qualify some other detail in the horoscope. The rising sign is at least equal in importance to the Sun sign. An Aries with Taurus rising is as different from an Aries with Gemini rising as a Sun-in-Taurus person is from a Sun-in-Gemini.

Your personality is the self you present when dealing directly with others. This is represented by the rising sign and may be modified by planets located in the first house. The Sun represents the true self that only you can know best, and this self may be widely divergent from the face you show to others. If the signs of the Sun and the ascendant (a synonym for rising sign) are compatible, or are the same, there is relatively little split in the personality.

If the natures of the Sun and rising signs are in conflict, it may result in a frequent feeling of being misunderstood. For example: someone with a Sagittarius Sun might see herself as a good sport with a sense of humor, but if Capricorn is rising she would have been trained from childhood to be proper and restrained, and thus would wonder why people shy away from the pal she knows she is capable of being; what others see is a shy, self-conscious conformist.

The function of the signs is somewhat akin to that of a filter through which energy passes. Each of the ten planetary energies—of which the

Sun is only one—has a sign at any given time. Those of you who were born *on the cusp*—that is, on one of the days when the Sun is expected to change from one sign to the next—should know your exact time of birth and have either a computer or a professional astrologer calculate which sign your Sun is in (it has to be in either one sign or the next, no matter how marginally).

It should help, particularly in questions of compatibility, to remember what the signs in each element-group have in common, and the ways in which they differ.

The Fire Signs—Aries, Leo, and Sagittarius—are said to be most compatible with one another and with Air signs. People with Fire-sign emphasis in their charts are enterprising, dynamic, often entertaining, and highly enthusiastic. Aries people have the strong ego-drive and courage that make pioneering possible—either as the first of a kind in an existing job or as creators of an entirely new kind of work. The first woman president may well be an Arien. Aries is impatient enough to break through barriers rather than tiptoe around them or take no for an answer. There is a crudity to the Aries approach that is seldom found with the other two Fire signs. Leo people are enormously proud, and almost always succeed in reaching positions where they can delegate the less interesting chores to others. Leo likes to be a benefactor and may be rather patronizing in the process. Like the other Fire signs, Leo's image is generally sincere and well-meaning. Loyalty is deep and genuine— and occasionally given to the wrong people. Sagittarius people have a strong sense of fair play and are known for being sporting, but this generosity of spi it sometimes tempts others to take unfair advantage of them. Sagittarius has higher aspirations toward law and religion than the other Fire signs.

The Earth Signs—Taurus, Virgo, and Capricorn—are excellent at work involving detail and careful planning. They blend well with one another and with Water signs. Professionalism is valued highly by these people, and they take pains to be thorough and meet deadlines. All three signs share a strong respect for the dollars and cents of reality. Taurus, because of the rulership of Venus, is the Earth sign most attracted to the arts and the finer things in life, and may achieve professional skill in sculpture, gardening, or metal work (earth materials). Virgo is famous (or notorious, depending on your attitude) for being incredibly painstaking about even the smallest detail. Virgo, more than any other sign, gets ego-gratification, and sometimes even an aesthetic kick, from devising efficient methods for doing things. Because Virgo personalities often have the additional gift of manual dexterity, they are typecast as highly desirable secretaries. Alternatives to this often dead-end work may be writing, designing, management consulting, editing, book production, or a health career (but care should be exercised to avoid hypochondria, which is Virgo's best-known neurosis). Capricorn has a natural flair for economics and budgeting, is tenacious and reliable, and likely to rise to a key position in any organization. Capricorn's worst drawback is the tendency toward pessimism, which undermines ambitions for career advancement.

The Air Signs—Gemini, Libra, and Aquarius—are the most fulfilled in careers involving communications and interaction with other people, especially Fire-sign and other Air-sign people. Gemini is both mentally and physically restless and thrives on the freedom to travel and report impressions. Journalism, editorial work, and selling are good occupational choices. The career is but a small part of the Gemini personality's life, however; new enthusiasms seem to come along at the rate of at least one a day, and the vitality may be worn out scattering itself over the many temptations that attract the Gemini mind. Libra prefers personal dealing to written or detached communication, and for this reason may be found in personnel or other advisory positions. Gemini and Libra have indecision problems in common. With Gemini the difficulty arises when it comes to choosing an activity or a career from several momentarily attractive possibilities. With Libra the struggle is more abstract and is centered between two opposing concepts. Aquarius is the most strongly individualistic and decisive of the freedom-loving Air signs. Deeply interested in people, Aquarius prefers a one-way street: to understand and be able to predict behavior, without being predictable. Aquarius is fond of doing the opposite of what is expected and enjoys the ego-satisfaction of keeping people guessing. Motivated by both a different drummer and a social conscience, Aquarius demands and needs plenty of leeway.

The Water Signs—Cancer, Scorpio, and Pisces—can be the most vividly emotional or dramatically callous signs of the zodiac, depending on the prompting of past experience. Compatibility is a highly individual matter for these signs. Water-sign personalities, more than any others, should have a planet-by-planet comparison when contemplating close partnership; the wrong companion in long-term intimate contact can seriously affect their physical as well as mental health. If their sympathies are unjustly exploited, Water signs can become relentless in tuning out (if they're lucky enough to make up their minds to do just that). Cancer is the sign most concerned with environmental conditions, and not necessarily just on the home front, either. Administration with a personal touch is Cancer's trademark. Cancer is also a genius at spatial relationships, and would as soon become an architect as rearrange the Rice Krispie collection in the kitchen cabinet. Scorpio is a skilled investigator and prefers to work with as little interference from others as possible. With Scorpio you have to deserve their trust in order to gain their cooperation; otherwise they would rather be loners, thank you. Pisces is an idealist, a utopian who can visualize future advantages for underdogs; given a cause that really engages them, they can be fierce fighters.

Rising Signs

The truth about one's personality is at the very least a blending of the Sun and rising signs. You can estimate your ascendant (rising) sign from the table below if you do not already have your personal chart. These estimates are admittedly sketchy, and your rising sign may in fact be the sign just before or after the one listed. If you are in doubt, read the profiles for all the signs in question and see which describes you best. The following physical clues may help narrow the choice:

ARIES: Bold eyebrows that seem to meet in a single line on the bridge of the nose; large, striding steps; red hair or red highlights.

TAURUS: Gap between the two front teeth; short neck; shoulders wider than hips; protruding eyes.

GEMINI: Quick movements, especially of eyes and hands; light, clear eyes; medium coloring.

CANCER: Wide, broad face; lines in face are pronounced, especially around eyes; pale coloring; may walk with elbows bent slightly.

LEO: Regal posture; large head; hair looks manelike in its thickness; hairline may recede at young age.

VIRGO: May have widow's peak; clear and sharp features; prominent chin.

LIBRA: Dimples—somewhere; either tall and elegant or short and plump.

SCORPIO: Steady gaze; muscular body; appears sexy, although not necessarily classically attractive.

SAGITTARIUS: Straight eyebrows; fleshy body, especially around the hips; square jaw.

CAPRICORN: Dark coloring; dark, opaque eyes; deliberate movements.

AQUARIUS: Light to medium coloring; elongated hands, arms, and legs; kinky or frizzy hair.

PISCES: Heart-shaped face; fleshy cheeks; eyes may frequently have far-away expression or seem on the brink of tears.

If you were born between 2 A.M. the last Sunday in April and 2 A.M. the last Sunday in October, or any of the following exceptions, deduct one hour from the recorded time of your birth before using the table that follows.

EXCEPTIONS

1918:   3/31-10/27
1919:   3/30-10/26
        2/9-9/30/45

Charts are calculated from Standard Time; thus Daylight Savings or wartime births must be adjusted by subtracting one hour.

ARIES

If your time of birth was:	Then your most likely rising sign is:
4-6 A.M. (sunrise)	Aries
6-8 A.M.	Taurus
8-10 A.M.	Gemini
10-12 noon	Cancer
12 noon-2 P.M.	Leo
2-4 P.M.	Virgo
4-6 P.M.	Libra
6-8 P.M.	Scorpio
8-10 P.M.	Sagittarius
10 P.M.-12 midnight	Capricorn
12 midnight-2 A.M.	Aquarius
2-4 A.M.	Pisces

TAURUS

If your time of birth was:	Then your most likely rising sign is:
4-6 A.M. (sunrise)	Taurus
6-8 A.M.	Gemini
8-10 A.M.	Cancer
10 A.M.-12 noon	Leo

TAURUS *(cont.)*

If your time of birth was: Then your most likely rising sign is:

12 noon-2 P.M.	Virgo
2-4 P.M.	Libra
4-6 P.M.	Scorpio
6-8 P.M.	Sagittarius
8-10 P.M.	Capricorn
10 P.M.-12 midnight	Aquarius
12 midnight-2 A.M.	Pisces
2-4 A.M.	Aries

GEMINI

If your time of birth was: Then your most likely rising sign is:

4-6 A.M. (sunrise)	Gemini
6-8 A.M.	Cancer
8-10 A.M.	Leo
10 A.M.-12 noon	Virgo
12 noon-2 P.M.	Libra
2-4 P.M.	Scorpio
4-6 P.M.	Sagittarius
6-8 P.M.	Capricorn
8-10 P.M.	Aquarius
10 P.M.-12 midnight	Pisces
12 midnight-2 A.M.	Aries
2-4 A.M.	Taurus

CANCER

If your time of birth was: Then your most likely rising sign is:

4-6 A.M. (sunrise)	Cancer
6-8 A.M.	Leo
8-10 A.M.	Virgo
10 A.M.-12 noon	Libra
12 noon-2 P.M.	Scorpio
2-4 P.M.	Sagittarius
4-6 P.M.	Capricorn
6-8 P.M.	Aquarius
8-10 P.M.	Pisces
10 P.M.-12 midnight	Aries
12 midnight-2 A.M.	Taurus
2-4 A.M.	Gemini

LEO

If your time of birth was: Then your most likely rising sign is:

4-6 A.M. (sunrise)	Leo
6-8 A.M.	Virgo
8-10 A.M.	Libra
10 A.M.-12 noon	Scorpio
12 noon-2 P.M.	Sagittarius
2-4 P.M.	Capricorn
4-6 P.M.	Aquarius
6-8 P.M.	Pisces
8-10 P.M.	Aries
10 P.M.-12 midnight	Taurus
12 midnight-2 A.M.	Gemini
2-4 A.M.	Cancer

VIRGO

If your time of birth was: Then your most likely rising sign is:

4-6 A.M. (sunrise)	Virgo
6-8 A.M.	Libra
8-10 A.M.	Scorpio
10 A.M.-12 noon	Sagittarius
12 noon-2 P.M.	Capricorn
2-4 P.M.	Aquarius
4-6 P.M.	Pisces
6-8 P.M.	Aries
8-10 P.M.	Taurus
10 P.M.-12 midnight	Gemini
12 midnight-2 A.M.	Cancer
2-4 A.M.	Leo

LIBRA

If your time of birth was: Then your most likely rising sign is:

4-6 A.M. (sunrise)	Libra
6-8 A.M.	Scorpio
8-10 A.M.	Sagittarius
10 A.M.-12 noon	Capricorn
12 noon-2 P.M.	Aquarius
2-4 P.M.	Pisces
4-6 P.M.	Aries

LIBRA *(cont.)*

If your time of birth was:	Then your most likely rising sign is:
6-8 P.M.	Taurus
8-10 P.M.	Gemini
10 P.M.-12 midnight	Cancer
12 midnight-2 A.M.	Leo
2-4 A.M.	Virgo

SCORPIO

If your time of birth was:	Then your most likely rising sign is:
4-6 A.M. (sunrise)	Scorpio
6-8 A.M.	Sagittarius
8-10 A.M.	Capricorn
10 A.M.-12 noon	Aquarius
12 noon-2 P.M.	Pisces
2-4 P.M.	Aries
4-6 P.M.	Taurus
6-8 P.M.	Gemini
8-10 P.M.	Cancer
10 P.M.-12 midnight	Leo
12 midnight-2 A.M.	Virgo
2-4 A.M.	Libra

SAGITTARIUS

If your time of birth was:	Then your most likely rising sign is:
4-6 A.M. (sunrise)	Sagittarius
6-8 A.M.	Capricorn
8-10 A.M.	Aquarius
10 A.M.-12 noon	Pisces
12 noon-2 P.M.	Aries
2-4 P.M.	Taurus
4-6 P.M.	Gemini
6-8 P.M.	Cancer
8-10 P.M.	Leo
10 P.M.-12 midnight	Virgo
12 midnight-2 A.M.	Libra
2-4 A.M.	Scorpio

CAPRICORN

If your time of birth was:	Then your most likely rising sign is:
4-6 A.M. (sunrise)	Capricorn

CAPRICORN

If your time of birth was:	Then your most likely rising sign is:
6-8 A.M.	Aquarius
8-10 A.M.	Pisces
10 A.M.-12 noon	Aries
12 noon-2 P.M.	Taurus
2-4 P.M.	Gemini
4-6 P.M.	Cancer
6-8 P.M.	Leo
8-10 P.M.	Virgo
10 P.M.-12 midnight	Libra
12 midnight-2 A.M.	Scorpio
2-4 A.M.	Sagittarius

AQUARIUS

If your time of birth was:	Then your most likely rising sign is:
4-6 A.M. (sunrise)	Aquarius
6-8 A.M.	Pisces
8-10 A.M.	Aries
10 A.M.-12 noon	Taurus
12 noon-2 P.M.	Gemini
2-4 P.M.	Cancer
4-6 P.M.	Leo
6-8 P.M.	Virgo
8-10 P.M.	Libra
10 P.M.-12 midnight	Scorpio
12 midnight-2 A.M.	Sagittarius
2-4 A.M.	Capricorn

PISCES

If your time of birth was:	Then your most likely rising sign is:
4-6 A.M. (sunrise)	Pisces
6-8 A.M.	Aries
8-10 A.M.	Taurus
10 A.M.-12 noon	Gemini
12 noon-2 P.M.	Cancer
2-4 P.M.	Leo
4-6 P.M.	Virgo
6-8 P.M.	Libra

PISCES *(cont.)*

If your time of birth was: Then your most likely rising sign is:

8-10 P.M.	Scorpio
10 P.M.-12 midnight	Sagittarius
12 midnight-2 A.M.	Capricorn
2-4 A.M.	Aquarius

Aries
(March 22-April 21)

Aries is ruled by Mars, the planet of drive and aggression. And although certain energies, such as Mars, are traditionally associated with one sex or the other, the fact is that everyone has *all* the planets—they differ only with regard to the degree of their influence.

Mars also represents courage, daring, competition, initiative, and the lusty side of sex. (Where Mars—or an Aries planet—is in harmonious aspect to Venus, there is a balance of lust and tenderness in the individual's love relationships. Under a discordant aspect the time spent in bed is either lusty *or* romantic—with the partners in conflict as to how it should be.) A male astrologer, Marc Edmund Jones, cautions:

> Since the ideograms of these two planets [Mars and Venus] are employed commonly in biological notation to represent male and female distinctions, special care is needed to keep the one from indicating a primarily feminine expression, and the other a specific masculine emphasis.*

When Mars or an Aries planet is harmonious, the energy level is high and so is the courage. Crusades you begin may win the support and enthusiasm of others, and the result of this combined fight for a beneficial cause may be a significant breakthrough, a new beginning, a historical first. It is with Mars-Aries energy that new and monumental changes occur and competitions are won.

When Mars or an Aries planet is discordant, your temper may easily be aroused and you may overreact violently. By other people's standards your reaction may seem inappropriate in relation to the apparent provocation; however, the observer can't always know the sequence of irritating events, of which the last is just the final straw. With discord you are more prone to friction and argument, hastiness, accidents, sexual frustration, and the emergence of long-suppressed hostility.

If you have an Aries birthday and know your time of birth within

*****Astrology: How and Why It Works**, Baltimore, Penguin Books, 1971.

approximately two hours, you can see the influences of your rising sign and the ways in which you are *most* Arien below:

Aries Rising or First-House Sun (Personality), 4-6 A.M.: You are alert, fast-moving, competitive, highly sexed, and enthusiastic. If Mars or your Aries Sun is harmonious, your muscular coordination is good and you find ego-gratification through athletic competition or prowess in self-defense. If Mars or the Sun is discordant, your nature is argumentative, angry, impatient, and impulsive. Watch out for rashes, fevers, burns, and fractures.

Pisces Rising or Second-House Sun (Money Managing), 2-4 A.M.: Your impulsive spending can mean trouble for years unless you have other factors in your chart indicating self-control or unless you force yourself to refrain from needless expenditures through sheer will power. Anger is likely to trigger off a spending spree—especially if you want to teach someone you're fighting with a good lesson. Spending won't solve anything, and it is the Pisces influence that makes you resort to melodramatic means to get your point across.

Aquarius Rising or Third-House Sun (Your Mind and Communications), Midnight-2 A.M.: You are a quick and incisive thinker (the tendency of *both* signs) and enjoy the mental stimulation of arguments keenly. Your telephone manner or style of correspondence is abrupt, and your language blunt and punctuated with expletives. No one enjoys the way a quarrel clears the air more than you do; you may even study approaches to "creative quarreling." Sex is another pleasurable subject of study and discussion, and its force could, if necessary, be sublimated in an orgy of writing. (Fast typing may be a therapeutic beginning, but the material typed should, ideally, be your own.) If you are angry, take extra safety precautions when you walk or drive; do not discuss sensitive subjects or pick fights, or even be so engrossed in angry thoughts that your present surroundings are tuned out—accidents or crimes are especially likely at such times. Also, do not drive when under the influence of alcohol or drugs, or ride with anyone else who is. At such times it's best to assert that Aquarian independence and say no to the lift.

Capricorn Rising or Fourth-House Sun (Home/Relationship with Father), 10 P.M.-Midnight: You probably have learned the meaning of *hassle* from an overly conservative, forceful, and vocal father. Domesticity is an especially sensitive subject with you; throughout your life you are continually embroiled in fights involving housework and who does it. When you *do* bother doing it—under protest—you go about your chores quickly and impatiently. However, in your haste, don't fail to take safety precautions against fires and accidents on the premises. The Capricorn-Aries combination also affects your internal struggle over how assertive or circumspect to be; the Aries energy wants to be released, while the Capricorn part of you acts as censor. You may frequently have to determine the extent to which your ambition and your family life can encroach upon each other.

Sagittarius Rising or Fifth-House Sun (Sex Life/Creativity/Attitude Toward Children), 8-10 P.M.: Your sex life is active. Hot-blooded and often the aggressor, you tend to have stormy elationships and frequent changes of partners. This results partly from Aries's roving eye and partly from Sagittarius's preoccupation with the joys of travel or education. Your partners may feel unappreciated, but not until after that first hot weekend! Your attitude toward your own pregnancy eventually becomes anger and if your pregnancy is carried to term, the birth experience is quick. Your relationships with children—anybody's—may be tumultuous, particularly if one of them interferes with your sex life. Struggles about children—the right not to have any, the right to abortion, the right to adopt, and the right to child-care facilities—may figure prominently in your creative work and in your feminist activities as well.

Scorpio Rising or Sixth-House Sun (Work and Co-Workers), 6-8 P.M.: You are capable of working with great enthusiasm and speed, but the work must be carefully selected with a view to the challenge offered. The Aries Sun craves change and the Scorpio ascendant craves mental challenge. Your curiosity and problem-solving talent must be engaged although your relations with co-workers may be difficult (your customary pace can make others look like idiots). You can help others channel their resentful feelings into efforts to improve working conditions and procedures. However enthusiastic or pressured you may be on the job, take better care of your health by eating more leisurely and nutritious meals; you are more susceptible than most to illnesses resulting from gulping down inferior food.

Libra Rising or Seventh-House Sun (Partnerships and Public Relations), 4-6 P.M.: Once under way, your partnerships develop a tone quite opposite from the one with which they began. If entered into in love, your partnerships become stormy and competitive. If begun antagonistically, the affection comes later. You may also have quarrels with clients, advisers, and the general public that you meet through your work. If you are married, you enjoy the give-and-take kind of relationship that Katharine Hepburn and Spencer Tracy developed so well in their movies; the frequent challenges stimulate you. Aries and Libra share a taste for a two-sided debate, although Libra conducts it with more sweetness than Aries.

Virgo Rising or Eighth-House Sun (Source of Money), 2-4 P.M.: You may earn your living as a doctor (surgeon, specifically), builder, welder, or athlete, to name just a few Mars-ruled occupations. Your attitude toward money is a sensitive point in your relations with your business partner or spouse. If he is spending too much from a joint fund, your fury will be remembered for years to come! You feel that you have to fight for every cent you get, and that everything you have was gotten by diligent effort. Probe more thoughtfully into financial disputes that threaten a partnership; arguments that begin about money are usually about at least one other thing as well. The Virgo energy gives you more patience to search for answers than Aries, who explodes first and asks questions later, if at all. The Virgo influence is also fortunate because it makes you question the necessity of expenditures you may otherwise go into heavy debt for.

Leo Rising or Ninth-House Sun (Public Expression), Noon-2 P.M.: Radio and television are just two of the means you utilize when fighting for your cause: you'd agitate to change legislation, appear in court, publish, teach, or even use the pulpit to make your stand known. Try not to let initial success at any of these make you too rash in your actions or premature in following the lure of excitement. Be careful, too, what you say in public; you need a lawsuit like a hole in the head! To give you credit where it's due, if Mars rules your ninth house you leave a scene when it isn't exciting *enough*, rather than when it's too much for you. Unlike the pacifistic Piscean, or Neptunian, personality, you are prepared to meet any confrontation more than halfway.

Cancer Rising or Tenth-House Sun (Ambition/Relationship with Mother), 10 A.M.-Noon: Whatever changes of status you gain are probably the result of a struggle. While the fight is going on you'd swear you were in the thick of problems, and are surprised by the let-down feeling when the fight is won and behind you. You may find yourself involved in a battle against an agency of the government, either for personal or collective reasons. If Mars or your Aries Sun is harmonious, the courage and eagerness with which you fight your battles is favorably noted by those in superior positions. Your mother's courage has probably been an early example of strength. If Mars or your Sun is discordant, your forcefulness impresses others as pugnaciousness and alienates them. Again, your mother taught you much of what you know about fighting, but in this instance she has been more antagonistic and bossy. If she succeeded in her professional life, you naturally have come to believe that fighting is the way to climb the ladder of success, without understanding that subtlety is important, too. Count to ten before exploding, and make the Cancer ascendant work *for* you instead of against you. Pay more attention to the needs and attitudes of others, instead of drawing the protective crab shell around you to desensitize yourself.

Gemini Rising or Eleventh-House Sun (Friendships), 8-10 A.M.: Your friendships may end suddenly and with arguments if Mars or your Aries Sun is discordant. When there is harmony you can strike up friendships like a house afire, and your fights are more likely to be in cooperation with and on behalf of friends. You will probably be attracted time and again to people who have displayed courage and daring in some form; they bring out a quality you would like to see more of in yourself. As you mature and your courage becomes stronger and more apparent, you attract younger people whom you guide as a mentor.

Taurus Rising or Twelfth-House Sun (Solitude and Privacy), 6-8 A.M.: You are capable of working actively and enthusiastically when alone. If Mars or your Aries Sun is discordant, your initiative, courage, or anger may earn you secret enemies working to thwart your aims and projects. When it comes to involuntary seclusion or solitude, you fidget and curse until you are freed or visited. A woman with Mars ruling the twelfth house hates lonely domesticity and is better off in a career which engages her enthusiasm. Use the Taurus patience afforded by your ascendant to see projects through to completion even after your enthusiasm flickers out. Your feelings about privacy run strong, and when Taurus's politeness fails you guard this right jealously, with Aries's blunt language.

Taurus
(April 22-May 20)

Taurus is ruled by Venus, which represents the qualities of physical beauty, graciousness, aesthetic sense, good taste (or flagrant lack of it) in personal adornment, friendliness, affection, kindness, and a desire to please.

Unless there are balancing factors favoring active work, a heavily discordant Venus or Taurus planet can produce an exaggerated desire to please or a demand to be taken care of as proof of love. When the chart shows indications of feminism, a discordant Venus or Taurus planet makes you sensitive to slights against womankind as well as to insults to yourself as an individual.

Since Taurus is a fixed sign, the presence of a Taurus planet in the chart gives stability of purpose and the patience to persist.

If you have a Taurus birthday and know your time of birth within approximately two hours you can see the ways in which you are *most* Taurean below:

Taurus Rising or First-House Sun (Personality), 4-6 A.M.: You are physically attractive, and your sense of style and color enhance this further. You tend to overeat, however, and the Taurean fondness for food can mean weight-gain unless you exercise caution. Your voice is one of your best features, possibly even the focal point of your career. Once you overcome stagefright you are able to win any audience's undivided attention. A favored tactic in interpersonal relations may well be to turn the other cheek, to take a lot of guff before you protest, and so you may experience recurrent psychosomatic sore throats—censoring yourself physically when the psychological pressure builds. Learn and practice assertive skills to prevent anger from building up within and threatening your well-being. Confront each situation as it comes.

Aries Rising or Second-House Sun (Money Managing), 2-4 A.M.: You are generous and enjoy shopping for gifts. You find the opportunity to combine the purchase of a beautiful thing with a favor for someone else irresistible. The special occasions and tastes of people you love figure significantly in your financial planning (as does sheer self-indulgence!). If you are an artist or a would-be artist, you delight in the sensual pleasure of buying your colorful supplies, and use this as a comfortable rationalization for postponing actual work. Avoid procrastination or failure to complete a project (a common Aries failing), and look for the pleasures as well as the profits in your work. Also, treat your time as the equivalent of money and don't be so forgiving when other people are wasteful of it. They may take advantage of your patience by keeping you waiting. Don't be afraid of the healthy temper and assertiveness conferred by your Aries ascendant and Mars. Speak up; your time is valuable.

Pisces Rising or Third-House Sun (Mind and Communications), Midnight-2 A.M.: You are attracted by the visual arts and are tempted to study at least one of them at length. Both Pisces and Taurus favor the more aesthetic lines of work. Your communications with people are warm and friendly, although Taurus is succinct and uses words only when absolutely necessary. If you are insulted you withdraw too readily, without realizing that the insult may not have been deliberate. You tend to shy away from confrontations for the sake of maintaining peace and avoiding embarrassment. Seeking relief in your work can be constructive, but you do owe it to yourself to make your attitudes known.

Aquarius Rising or Fourth-House Sun (Home/Relationship with Father), 10 P.M.-Midnight: Your father may have programmed you to be passive—either through example or through direct urgings. If he had, as Venus's rulership indicates, been a gentle, peaceful person who stayed home a great deal and whom many people loved, you would find it the most natural thing in the world to adopt his easy-going approach and win approval. Though you love a beautiful home, the Aquarius part of you can't help resenting assumptions that you have nothing better to do than keep it that way, especially if your home is your only base of operations. You may have found through painful experience that the only way to get your work done is to establish a rigid schedule and then force yourself to stick to it. Your kind nature makes it difficult to keep your door closed when a member of your family needs you, but you have to start someplace if you want to convince them that you, too, have serious work that merits respect. Taurus isn't inclined to give advance clues that trouble is brewing; you're quietly nice while concealing boiling rage—until pushed too far. Don't wait for the explosion; post your office hours *now*.

Capricorn Rising or Fifth-House Sun (Sex Life/Creativity/Attitude toward Children), 8-10 P.M.: Your love affairs may be genuinely loving (given harmonious aspects to Venus or your Taurus Sun), but under discordant aspects your lovers are likely to manipulate you through your excessive desire to please and to maintain peace. If the planets ruling this department of life make numerous aspects, your creativity favors the visual arts. Whether or not you ever have children of your own, you may be cajoled into teaching them, and at an age when you were just beginning to wonder what your talents might be. The lure of the money and the time off might be blinding. You may have genuine affection for children and be effective in teaching them, but your ambitious creative energies are bound to find additional channels nonetheless.

Sagittarius Rising or Sixth-House Sun (Work and Co-Workers), 6-8 P.M.: Your career may be in one of the arts or luxury occupations (hotel management, interior decoration, beauty advice, travel, fashion, gift items), and a nine-to-five schedule seems odious. If Venus or your

Taurus Sun is discordant, too many expense-account meals could have an adverse effect on your skin and circulatory system. Socializing with your co-workers may be a pleasant side benefit, but guard against oversensitivity. Allow the Sagittarius influence of your ascendant to strengthen your sense of humor.

Scorpio Rising or Seventh-House Sun (Partnerships and Public Relations), 4-6 P.M.: You are fortunate enough to experience partnerships that are kind, loving, and durable (thanks to the fixity of Taurus). Business partnerships or dealings with clients or advisers may begin with social contacts. When Venus or your Taurus Sun is discordant, you and your partner grapple with subtle questions of relationship— particularly your difficulty in asserting your rights—and the work at hand can be seriously disrupted. Show more of the self-reliance of which the Scorpio ascendant is capable. Try not to give full expression to your excessive need for approval or to your oversensitivity to slights that may never be consciously intended.

Libra Rising or Eighth-House Sun (Source of Money), 2-4 P.M.: You may succeed in profiting through any of the arts or through your diplomatic skill. You may also choose a career in managing other people's money. In times of discord you'll be tempted to run up excessive debts for the sake of luxury items (such as an art object you love). This is doubly likely when a relationship is on the rocks; consolation can be a very costly proposition. You'd be better off immersing yourself in demanding work.

Virgo Rising or Ninth-House Sun (Public Expression), Noon-2 P.M.: Consider a career in higher education or publishing, particularly in finance or one of the arts. When you appear as a speaker, you perform with enviable poise (although the Virgo part of you may come across as somewhat too didactic). When Venus influences this house of a career woman who also happens to be good-looking, she may be dismayed to find that she gets more attention for her looks than for her logic. Changing people's attitudes won't be immediate, but your steadiness proves highly effective in the last analysis.

Leo Rising or Tenth-House Sun (Ambition/Relationship with Mother), 10 A.M.-Noon: As with the ninth-house Sun, the Venus-Taurus influence on this department of life brings a disturbing awareness that you are getting attention for something other than your mental efforts. You will probably succeed in finding your way to the limelight, but you will be sensitive if your work is not appreciated in at least as much newspaper space as your physical appearance. You may benefit through your mother's influence, although under discordant aspects you think her too much of a pacifist. If you, too, have been inclined to hold back your real feelings, empathy with your mother could be painful. You may be tempted to become her opposite, but avoid extremes—you can learn a great deal from her subtlety and finesse. Devote considerable thought to what you want your public image to be, and why.

Cancer Rising or Eleventh-House Sun (Friendships), 8-10 A.M.: Your friends are kind, supportive, affectionate, and might even engineer a profitable break or two in your career; you are equally helpful when the opportunity arises. You find comfort in banding together with friends who share your sensitivity, but you should guard against wallowing in self-pity or permitting people to take unfair advantage of you. Self-imposed privacy for the sake of career progress should be your best therapy when the personalities and problems of others get you down.

Gemini Rising or Twelfth-House Sun (Solitude and Privacy), 6-8 A.M.: It is to your best advantage to use your solitude to work on creative projects; turn your artistic imagination loose. Teaching craft therapy to those in institutions may also be a gratifying outlet for you, but try to keep in check the sympathy you feel for those confined—it could impair your effectiveness. In your private life there may be a love affair that for one reason or another must be kept secret. It's not necessarily because your lover is married to someone else (although I wouldn't eliminate that possibility!); it may simply be your policy to keep your private life secret.

Gemini
(May 21-June 21)

Signs often have a certain distinctive physical feature—for example, the Aries eyebrow or the Taurus neck—and if there's one trademark of a Gemini, it's motion. Since Gemini seldom has just one of anything, however, you're going to see more than one kind of motion. Whether or not Gemini is physically traveling, it's a pretty safe bet that that incredibly nimble mind will be a few years ahead of itself and trying to juggle several different things at once. This suits Gemini just fine; it's very much in character for a Gemini to take pleasure in keeping you guessing! As a matter of fact, two or three of the Geminis I've known were fond of describing themselves as moving targets. If put upon, this is probably the closest this upbeat personality will get to expressing self-pity. Life is seldom—make that *never*—dull with a Gemini around.

The reason for Gemini's hyper pace is its rulership by Mercury. Mercury is the absolutely neutral (in sexual terms) planet of objective intelligence. It is never more than thirty degrees away from the Sun, and so it is in either the same sign as the Sun or the one just before or after. If your birthday is on or close to the cusp and you believe you think like both signs in question, this is because Mercury is in a sign other than the Sun's and not because the Sun is straddling the cusp.

Mercury rules mental work of all kinds: invention, analysis, writing, organization, classification, teaching, selling, and reporting, to name just a few. Where Mercury or a Gemini planet appears in your chart will indicate specifics about the particular kind of intelligence you have and the manner in which you express it.

When Mercury or your Gemini planet is harmonious, your mind is crystal-clear and your memory excellent. You are objective, articulate, especially able to grasp at least one other language, quick to comprehend technical subjects, able to trust your reflexes, logical, and witty.

When Mercury or your Gemini planet is discordant you may be equally quick, but experience difficulty concentrating. You may find more of a gap between a thought and finding the right words to express it. Avoid making flippant remarks at someone else's expense; they could backfire.

If you have a Gemini birthday and know your time of birth within approximately two hours, you can see the ways in which you are *most* Geminian below:

Gemini Rising or First-House Sun (Personality), 4-6 A.M.: Mental energy, curiosity, and mobility are your dominant traits. You are highly articulate, and a writing career seems a natural choice. Pursuits requiring strategy should also be considered. Quick and skilled with your hands as well as with your mind, your hobbies include crafts, games, or mechanical repairs. Since yours is a restless nature that hates eight enforced hours behind a desk, be careful whom you tell you can type.

Taurus Rising or Second-House Sun (Money Managing), 2-4 A.M.: You're quite adept at bookkeeping and checkbook-balancing, but are such an impulsive spender (a bibliomaniac, specifically!) that it wouldn't hurt to have an extra savings account in a bank you don't see every day. For your own protection, make it tough to get at some of your money. As your bank accounts increase—one for each budget item, with an extra for unspecified emergencies—along with the record books, your time may be consumed by penny-counting at the expense of your other interests. The motive for your bookkeeping is not stinginess, as it is with Saturn personalities, but a desire to know what your assets are. In budgeting, your fondness for books, gadgets, games, and other mental stimuli could get the upper hand. Mercury as ruler of your money can bring revenue from such occupations as writing.

Aries Rising or Third-House Sun (Mind and Communications), Midnight-2 A.M.: Writing, editing, contact with others, and study are your main interests. You are the person most likely to be the perennial student, postponing your career's actual beginning from sheer indecision. Your active mind finds a number of enterprises that tempt you equally. There is also the temptation of just one more advanced degree, which would inflate Aries's hungry ego. The first step in deciding on your career should be the logical elimination of anything that fails to give you the mobility you need. Studying the plans of your siblings and classmates can also prove helpful.

Pisces Rising or Fourth-House Sun (Home/Relationship with Father), 10 P.M.-Midnight: Your desire for learning was probably instilled early in life, in imaginative ways, by your father. As an adult, you feel that home is where your books are, and home may be your full-time office as well as living quarters. You probably prefer being self-employed, which permits you to come and go as you please. Housekeeping is something to breeze through as quickly as possible and nothing could bore you more.

Aquarius Rising or Fifth-House Sun (Sex Life/Creativity/Attitude Toward Children), 8-10 P.M.: Your natural ability for and interest in writing is probably best combined with your other absorbing interest: sex. This dynamic combination produces material that is detached and witty, and could be very popular. You may also be attracted to creating entertainment for a juvenile audience. When Mercury or your Gemini Sun is discordant, your mental work may be undermined by unreliable lovers. You favor the mental vitality of youth and enjoy the dialogue that younger lovers have to offer. You are ambivalent toward children: while nervous around inarticulate little ones who interrupt your train of thought when you're working, you enjoy the company of children several years older, especially as their conversational skills grow. Take special note of the plural: Geminians have an affinity for multiple births. It isn't the sign of the twins for nothing.

Capricorn Rising or Sixth-House Sun (Work and Co-Workers), 6-8 P.M.: Your occupation should include writing, editing, discussion, selling, or teaching—in any combination. The more autonomy you have, the better you like it. Mobility is another requirement of yours; sitting at the same spot all day is tantamount to suffocation (a favorite word of Air-sign personalities). Your working conditions are extremely important to you, and you blame faulty performances on less-than-optimum circumstances. Communicative with your co-workers (although the Capricorn influence makes you censor yourself somewhat), you enjoy exchanging all sorts of interesting information, which may or may not be relevant to the work at hand. It's best to avoid gossip and flippant remarks about the personalities at the office.

Sagittarius Rising or Seventh-House Sun (Partnerships and Public Relations), 4-6 P.M.: You have a natural talent for dealing directly with the public, clients, or consultants. If you marry, your partner will probably be egalitarian and intellectual, and will enjoy prolonged theorizing on relationship issues. It is very important to you that you and your partner share mutual interests, because a relationship based on either romantic attraction or economic convenience simply isn't enough for you. As a result, there may be more than one marriage in your life.

Scorpio Rising or Eighth-House Sun (Source of Money), 2-4 P.M.: Writing, teaching, editing, banking, insurance, or financial advising are all recommended occupations. If you have a partner—business or marriage—he may be erratic financially, so it's a good idea to clarify all financial arrangements and get the deal in writing—including a clause about not being responsible for the other's individual debts.

Libra Rising or Ninth-House Sun (Public Expression), Noon-2 P.M.: In the course of your education you may transfer more than once to schools in other cities because the promise of a new place is a mental stimulant. Teaching is a good career for you, specifically at the high school or college level. Aside from the joy you find in communication, opportunities for travel are extremely revitalizing. Your leisure should be used for writing for publication, too. When Mercury or your Gemini Sun is discordant, however, guard against plagiarism, censorship, editing that distorts your thesis, or defective translations. Any of these problems may necessitate a costly trip or lawsuit to straighten the matter out. In any event, your work will probably succeed in reaching an audience.

Virgo Rising or Tenth-House Sun (Ambition/Relationship with Mother),

10 A.M.-Noon: Your mother's attitude toward success and ambition may be ambivalent, but once you've decided to climb the ladder, she'll help you steady it and be your most loyal supporter. When you're planning to ask for a promotion, she'll help by adding a few pertinent remarks. You aren't inclined to hide your light under a bushel or to hold your tongue no matter *who's* out of line. If you can solve a problem, you'll make your solution known to anyone, up to and including the chairperson of the board. Leadership is as easy for you as breathing.

Leo Rising or Eleventh-House Sun (Friendships), 8-10 A.M.: You like your friends to be as cerebral as you are, thus jobs and classes are the most logical places at which to enlarge your social circle: at the same time that you're enjoying human contact, your mental growth is proceeding very nicely. In times of discord you may encounter difficulties in reaching the friend you especially need or in speaking freely.

Cancer Rising or Twelfth-House Sun (Solitude and Privacy), 6-8 A.M.: Involuntary solitude makes you restless and fidgety, but if you utilize the time doing work you can be proud of, you'll soon see solitude as a positive thing. Ambition to write may develop later in life; in youth you are attracted more to campus life and travel. You need to develop confidence in having a story to tell that others would want to read, and to develop your style of writing. Also, you may be shy about revealing thoughts and experiences you had always thought of as personal. Impersonal reporting, interviewing, or writing about the subject of privacy itself is gratifying for you. For your own well-being, don't crowd as much into a day as your restless mind would like; you hate enforced rest.

Cancer
(June 22-July 21)

Cancer's ruling planet is the Moon, whose domain is the subconscious mind, the senses, and emotional associations with the environment. It is the Moon's common rulership of all of the above that accounts for our ability to recall a past emotional climate, long believed forgotten, with the replaying of an old song, or the tasting of a food frequently eaten during a particular phase of life.

A luminary, the Moon affects both our physical sight and our psychic insight into human subtleties. A chart with a strong lunar influence, such as a Cancer Sun, shows qualities long associated with women but by no means monopolized by them: alertness to the reactions and needs of other people, sensitivity, sensuality, an interest in music or food, compassion for the disadvantaged or helpless, and some measure of domestic competence. (One man I knew, who had his Moon in Virgo, was frequently seen around his home with a dustrag in hand, happily tidying up without any urging from his wife.) Granted that the Moon is the most domestic of the ten planetary energies. And granted that the Moon is often said to be a good indication of the way one relates to females. And granted, also, that the Moon is the satellite of the Sun, which is said to indicate relations with the male sex—let's, nevertheless, stop short of the "obvious" conclusion: that women must resign themselves to satellite status. Unlike the Moon, women are endowed with enough free will to refuse to function as satellites. The "as above, so below" idea has its limitations.

Women are not astrologically—or in any other way—inferior to men. And the Moon's influence certainly does not make them subservient to men. Rather, it seems to me, that the reason the Moon is said to be important as the ruler of relations with women in a man's chart is that, for a man conditioned to be ambitious and self-absorbed, contact with a woman must of necessity make him aware that he exists among complex, feeling human beings (which women are urged to feel free to be) and not in a vacuum.

The Moon and Cancer rule water, nourishment, infants, music, adaptation to the environment or improvement of same, and the healing professions. If the sign of Cancer is strong in your chart, these elements figure significantly in your life and thinking. When the aspects to the Moon or to a Cancer planet are harmonious, your reactions to Moon-ruled things are pleasant and positive. When the aspects are discordant, ambivalence and emotional turmoil tend to prevail, especially at such turning points as pregnancy, illness, and a move to a new home.

If you have a Cancer birthday and know your time of birth within approximately two hours, you can see the ways in which you are *most* Cancerian below:

Cancer Rising or First-House Sun (Personality), 4-6 A.M.: Learning is easy and done by osmosis, although you have trouble regaining your concentration after an interruption. When aspects to the Moon, your ascendant, or your Cancer Sun are discordant, you may experience health problems involving sight, hearing, or digestion; restlessness; or emotional agitations. Base your career and other major decisions on rational premises (but don't be fanatic about suppressing your hunches about people); make your commitments at times when you are on an even emotional keel rather than during spells of upheaval and pressure. You are able to size up a situation instantly, which can be to your advantage if you bear in mind your immediate reactions as you gather additional facts. You are sensitive to the moods of others and solicitous when you sense pain or illness in others. Do not take rebuffs too much to heart; if people don't want to be fussed over, it has more to do with them than with you.

Gemini Rising or Second-House Sun (Money Managing), 2-4 A.M.: Frankly, there won't likely be much of it—managing, that is. You may bring in sizable sums of money, but the fluctuations seem too frequent to keep track of without a CPA. Once the security-giving basics of food and rent are taken care of, you indulge in impulse buying, most likely relating to members of your family. Keep a grip on your wallet when your sympathies are being appealed to—you may have a reputation as a soft touch. The Gemini influence gives you verbal skill and a thirst for constant learning, so ask for time to sleep on any request made of you, and dream of spending more of your money on self-improvement training to increase your earning power.

Taurus Rising or Third-House Sun (Mind and Communications), Midnight-2 A.M.: You may go through a great deal of experimenting and discarding before you commit yourself to a college or a departmental major. Social correspondence and telephoning—within the family circle *alone*—can interfere with your work. You owe it to yourself to be less accessible (and you probably daydream of ways to go about this), but you don't have the nerve to refuse a call until someone has taken advantage of you. When the Moon or your Cancer Sun is discordant, there is the danger of dilettantism and frequent distraction. Whatever discipline you eventually choose, the commitment should engage your emotions as well as your intellect.

Aries Rising or Fourth-House Sun (Home/Relationship with Father), 10 P.M.-Midnight: You may have frequent changes of home or dreams of moving. When you have a strong desire for a fresh start in life (the Aries influence), your dreams tend to involve relocation to a new city—and that's no simple matter because Cancer doesn't pull up roots lightly. When the Moon or your Cancer Sun is discordant, there may be floods, spills, or other physical difficulties. (When my own Moon-ruled fourth house was under stress, the ceiling fell on my head and I had to abandon that apartment the same day.) In addition, you may have conflicts with your father and his attitude toward domesticity. Take my word for it: he can get very emotional!

Pisces Rising or Fifth-House Sun (Sex Life/Creativity/Attitude toward Children), 8-10 P.M.: If a career in the arts is what you want, your first choice is probably music. In any event, your creative work is marked by memorable ups and downs. Your love life is also changeable to a dramatic extent. If you aren't fickle yourself, you will attract a partner who is. Fidelity is definitely an issue with you; even if you have two or more relationships going—which, of course, you would never admit—you would be hurt if you had to share a lover with someone else. You may find yourself wanting a child for reasons that have nothing to do with the child itself—to insure that your lover will stay, for example. Your relationships with children undergo frequent fluctuations of mood, as does your general attitude toward parenthood.

Aquarius Rising or Sixth-House Sun (Work and Co-Workers), 6-8 P.M.: You may experience considerable restlessness on the job and numerous changes of position or even occupation as you try on each role for size. Whatever your job, it should involve dealing with people, as the Moon's influence over this department of life makes solitude a waste of your knack for public relations. Your work may be with food, health care, plants, animals, music, welfare, packaging, consumer complaints, market research, or city planning. You should choose your occupation with a great deal of care, especially since a job that wastes your talents can also be the cause of psychosomatic illnesses—stomach troubles in particular tend to be linked with problematic job situations. For the sake of your health, try not to take your co-workers' personal problems home with you.

Capricorn Rising or Seventh-House Sun (Partnerships and Public Relations), 4-6 P.M.: You are strongly attracted to a career in which you would be in a position to give advice, and your genuine interest in problem situations and people makes you a compassionate counselor. Whether your training is in psychology, law, medicine, or astrology (though this last choice is more likely with Aquarius rising), you broaden your opportunities to help those in trouble. Speaking of trouble, your marriage can be a problem area—whether it's your first or your seventh—and you may well marry more than once. You may want to expand your world beyond your partner, and be frustrated when he reacts like a hurt child because his security seems threatened. Business partnerships may prove alternately nurturing or emotionally chaotic, and may parallel the prevailing mood of your marriage. Use the strength of Capricorn to keep your cool and establish more businesslike procedures. This isn't easy; insecure partners who are hungry for emotional reassurance from you will be quick to accuse you of indifference when you attempt to change ground rules. Explain that it isn't that your personal feeling for *them* has cooled—you just don't want the enterprise to go under.

Sagittarius Rising or Eighth-House Sun (Source of Money), 2-4 P.M.: Any of the occupations listed in the above paragraph for Aquarius rising will prove a rewarding career or sideline. You may work with another's funds as a broker or agent, and win your reputation through your ability to relate to each client's unique needs. If the Moon or your Cancer Sun is well-aspected, increases in salary may come through the favorable word-of-mouth publicity of sympathetic clients or bosses. Sagittarians have a gift for teaching; you may find additional profit by moonlighting and offering a course in your specialty.

Scorpio Rising or Ninth-House Sun (Public Expression), Noon-2 P.M.: You are keenly interested in long-distance travel and may relocate in a city or country that is very different from your home town, where you would feel more free to speak publicly. Your career may include speaking engagements requiring travel. Like one woman I know who has the Moon ruling the ninth house (she has written books and magazine articles, and has appeared on broadcasts and the lecture circuit), you might combine occupations. Your delivery is emotionally powerful and might even have an effect on legislation, depending on your cause.

Libra Rising or Tenth-House Sun (Ambition/Relationship with Mother), 10 A.M.-Noon: Word-of-mouth publicity brings memorable highs or lows, depending on the changing aspects to the rulers of the tenth house. If you've ever enjoyed some measure of fame, only to find people turning away from you, it is best explained by the tenth house, the house of the esteem in which you are held. When the Moon or your Cancer planet is under stress, you might be elected to an office or appointed to an advisory position. An ambivalent relationship with your mother is also a strong motivating force in your life. Whether you follow in her footsteps or blaze a trail in a totally different area for the sake of autonomy, there is considerable agony leading up to your choice. If your mother was unhappy in "woman's work," her energies could make her overprotective, and you will have to work all the harder to establish a different, autonomous personal and professional life. Beware of your tendency to capitulate.

Virgo Rising or Eleventh-House Sun (Friendships), 8-10 A.M.: You may experience repeated changes of attitude toward the prospect of increasingly close friendships. People are drawn to you because you are such a good listener; Cancer's influence makes you emotionally empathetic, while the Virgo ascendant makes you intellectually curious. Your questions draw people out with seemingly little effort. The examples provided by your friends and the situations you see them through color much of your thinking on the women's liberation question. Be more gentle than didactic when advising your friends, and try not to stew about their problems and conflicts to the extent that you lose sleep and can't eat. Your sensitivity is as apparent in your health as it is in your conversations.

Leo Rising or Twelfth-House Sun (Solitude and Privacy), 6-8 A.M.: Being alone with housework probably drives you nuts. Solitude *per se* has a positive value for you, but pressure to keep the floor spotless takes all the joy out of it. Your occupation may require you to work in an institution caring for the underprivileged or practicing medicine, and this solitude is preferable to listening to friends' or relatives' troubles on your own time. During your time off you need the restorative freedom to do what you're most in the mood for.

Leo
(July 22-August 22)

Leo's ruling planet is the Sun, the center of the universe, which accounts in part for the royalty syndrome so prevalent among Leos and those who have the Sun strongly aspected in their charts.

Leo, like the Sun, is a strong, self-sustaining, ambitious, purposeful sign. The Sun is the planet of the ego itself, the heart and the spine (of a person and, metaphorically, of that person's life). The department of life where the Sun appears in your chart shows what is most important to you, and the sign in which the Sun appears indicates the *manner* in which you pursue your goal. For example, given two political candidates who have the Sun in the tenth house, a Leo will surround herself with an entourage to pave the way for her and a Capricorn will depend primarily on herself to do as much work as possible.

The Sun rules the way we relate to authority figures—and thus, we are told, to the male sex. However, in reality it has more to do with our reactions to the wielding of power than to the sex of the person wielding it. The issue of power can well disrupt an otherwise amicable relationship. The harmony or discord of the Sun or a Leo planet shows both the extent of our need to be self-directing and the way we deal with power of our own once we have it.

In a woman's chart, the Sun is said to be doubly important: it is the key to her relationships with males. Traditionally, this is because the ego (often synonymous with the male sex!) must be dealt with (read "swept under the rug") if a man is to be attracted and held. Today a woman must confront her ego head on, not subvert it. It is not enough for a woman to want a man; she owes it to her own development, and to that of an honest relationship, to know exactly *why*. What exactly will you personally gain by a specific relationship? Might something at least as important be lost? Think about it. It matters.

If you have a Leo birthday and know your time of birth within approximately two hours, you can see the ways in which you are *most* a Leo below:

Leo Rising or First-House Sun (Personality), 4-6 A.M.: Your personality is strong—sometimes even overwhelming—as is your pride, and you impress upon those in your environment at a very early age that you are a person to be reckoned with. Take care that you do not appear conceited, as that could well bring out the worst in people and make them want to frustrate your goals. Although you are extremely ambitious, try not to overwork. The heart and spine are your most sensitive areas.

Cancer Rising or Second-House Sun (Money Managing), 2-4 A.M.: Whether your ego-gratification comes from generosity and showing off or from getting your luxuries cheaper than anyone else, your finances are definitely a matter of pride to you. And so, of course, is the amount at your disposal. You won't be satisfied with a title change or a move to a corner office if it isn't accompanied by an improvement in your paycheck.

Gemini Rising or Third-House Sun (Mind and Communications), Midnight-2 A.M.: Since you spend a good part of your spare time reading, you should consider writing and editing as viable roads to recognition. Relatives or neighbors may present stumbling blocks to success, so it's best not to publicize intentions but rather to present a *fait accompli*. An advanced degree or a published book would serve your purposes quite nicely.

Taurus Rising or Fourth-House Sun (Home/Relationship with Father), 10 P.M.-Midnight: Your father may be domineering and make it difficult, but not necessarily impossible, to break out of a domestic future. While your home is important to you, its appearance has value for you primarily as a showcase for your sometimes theatrical personality—not as all-consuming busywork. You like to be your own boss, preferably with a business of your own. Taurus's influence gives you the flair for making your setting the most effective and appropriate one possible.

Aries Rising or Fifth-House Sun (Sex Life/Creativity/Attitude toward Children), 8-10 P.M.: Love affairs that become problematic can crack under the pressure of ego-conflicts, especially since both partners are ambitious and play one-upmanship games in private relationships. Your partners might not be game-players at *first,* but if you proceed on the assumption that they are, they'll soon give in to the temptation to deal at the same level. Whether the recipient of your vitality is a lover or a creative art, you always make a wholehearted effort. Relationships with children—not necessarily your own offspring—may be a difficult contest of wills. Recognition may come through your talent for entertaining.

Pisces Rising or Sixth-House Sun (Work and Co-Workers), 6-8 P.M.: Your work may involve administration, but the job has to be one you can be truly proud of. Use the subtlety of the Pisces ascendant to find out how your subordinates feel about you, and treat them with sensitivity, compassion, and discretion as well as with the famous Leo authority. Try not to take personally the reluctance of male subordinates unaccustomed to working for a woman. As you gain recognition over the years, you'll find that work seems increasingly stimulating. Just the same, keep your hours moderate while you're still healthy.

Aquarius Rising or Seventh-House Sun (Partnerships and Public Relations), 4-6 P.M.: Whether or not you ever marry or enter into a business partnership, the implications of these relationships fascinate you. A discordant Sun aspect would manifest itself as a power-balance problem. The relationship might break up if you both refuse to budge even an inch. In your career, you may find that your most gratifying work involves either creative collaboration or counseling. You enjoy giving advice, and an audience of one is enough to unleash the drama of your presentation.

Capricorn Rising or Eighth-House Sun (Source of Money), 2-4 P.M.:
When something is owed to you, you are torn between going after it (you
would, if it's an organization that owes you) or writing off the debt but
stewing quietly about it (which is the case when a needy individual has
captured your sympathies). If a partner has a standard of living considerably less comfortable than your own, you might be tempted to give in
out of guilt. Leos are often said to marry beneath their station, and with
the Capricorn sense of duty you may find yourself giving more than you
would have liked in order to equalize the relationship. Your income
from a counseling or brokerage career, or from insurance, may be
considerable, but do not give in if it's guilt that's motivating you. It's
hard afterward not to feel used, particularly if your partner enjoys
ostentation.

*Sagittarius Rising or Ninth-House Sun (Public Expression), Noon-2
P.M.*: The prestige of the schools you attend matters a great deal to you;
to be a graduate of an Ivy League school or perhaps a foreign university
gives you extra confidence. Public life is irresistible to you; ever since
childhood you have thought about being famous. Once you have your
education, you feel confident to take your due place in any of the
following: broadcasting, the recording industry, publishing, the legal
profession, religion, legislation, teaching, or work involving foreign
countries or languages. The ninth house has more meanings than most,
and whichever occupation you may choose, the way you relate to an
audience and your complete poise and command are bound to be
noticed by someone in a position to help you and to yield feedback.

*Scorpio Rising or Tenth-House Sun (Ambition/Relationship with
Mother), 10 A.M.-Noon*: Your mother has taught you that nothing but
the best is good enough for you, although you and she may disagree as to
whether to pursue first the best career or the best husband. Don't be
surprised if your ambition gets you elected or appointed to a position of
leadership at least once during your career. Your drive is strong. So, too,
is your mother's influence—either as a well-known person in her own
right or as a depressing example of misdirected power drives, an example you would strive to differ from if you find her concentration on you
really suffocating. Once your efforts have given her something to brag
about, you'll be the best-known offspring wherever your mother goes.

Libra Rising or Eleventh-House Sun (Friendships), 8-10 A.M.: You are
unswervingly loyal to those who win your interest and flatter you. Leo
can be *too* susceptible to flattery and can waste energy on flatterers with

ulterior motives. But take heart: your social life is not all bad! The combined graciousness of Libra and Leo will win you the friendship of people who can help with career breaks. Try to differentiate which ego-issues are trivial and which are serious enough to drop a friend for.
Virgo Rising or Twelfth-House Sun (Solitude and Privacy), 6-8 A.M.: You may have difficulty in getting all the notice Leo is hungry for, and then in achieving privacy once fame has been gained. Glory comes through work done alone, such as any of the creative arts, or through an institution such as a university, a prison, or a hospital. Don't patronize those you work with behind the scenes; an offended boss or co-worker may undermine your efforts and influence.

Virgo
(August 23-September 22)

Virgo is ruled by Mercury, like Gemini. The two signs share Mercury's intellectual curiosity, and the similarity ends there. As a matter of fact, the two signs often can't stand each other—at least not in large doses.

By some strange quirk of nature, Virgo and Gemini tune in on entirely different facets of Mercury. Where Gemini tries to live at least two lifetimes at once because there are so many things that are stimulating and worthwhile, Virgo specializes, and, therefore, criticizes (and criticizes some more!) dilettantism. A favorite Virgo saying is, If it's worth doing, it's worth doing well. This may be amended to . . . worth doing *perfectly*. Having had a Virgo father, I was able to observe this sign in a wide variety of situations. Had he been alive when I began studying astrology, I would have taken him to school with me for show-and-tell.

If Virgos seem painfully critical of others, they are even more severe with themselves. Since they are thorough, painstaking, conscientious workers who drive themselves ruthlessly, it is just as well that they are health-conscious (to the point of hypochondria), and work just as hard giving themselves regular care. One day a cousin and I were comparing notes on the vitamins his Virgo mother and my Virgo father insisted we take (I was fifteen and he was ten at the time). His mother, overhearing us, said, "You sound like a couple of old hypochondriac *kvetches*!"

Because of Virgo's perfectionism and conscientious delivery of service, they are said to make excellent secretaries—which is usually a gross underestimation and waste of their talents. Almost certainly there is another calling that absorbs the Virgo intellect more compellingly. If you have a Virgo birthday and are tired of being a secretary, don't tell your birthday the next time you look for a job.

If you know your time of birth within approximately two hours, you can see the ways in wi ich you are *most* Virgoan below:

Virgo Rising or First-House Sun (Personality), 4-6 A.M.: Your vitality and mental energy are keen, and you are an excellent observer. Work involving interviewing, editing, or production proves satisfying, but whichever craft you decide to concentrate on, you earn your good references through your dedication to precision. You'd probably systematize the work methods of your whole department. For the sake of your health, take at least two coffee breaks daily or break the routine with a walk. Practice leaving your work problems behind at five o'clock, if it's at all possible. Your intestinal tract is especially sensitive, so try to relax, eat well and leisurely, and don't fret one second longer than it takes to solve the problem at hand.

Leo Rising or Second-House Sun (Money Managing), 2-4 A.M.: Money managing is definitely a major source of pride for you. It's not so much that you resist temptation—although you have a checklist of questions to ask yourself about the merchandise before you reach for your wallet—but that you often keep yourself too busy with your work to bother much with shopping. After all, there's got to be a more efficient use of your time.

Cancer Rising or Third-House Sun (Mind and Communications), Midnight-2 A.M.: Whether you're a student (probably all the way to a Ph.D. or M.D. degree), writer, or editor, you tend to agonize over your written work before you show it to anyone. Unlike the Fire-sign or Gemini personality, you don't show *anything* "hot off the typewriter." It's got to be polished—another favorite Virgo expression—and rewritten, and repolished, and retyped. And neatness counts. In spoken communications, control your desire to interrupt people to correct their grammar.

Gemini Rising or Fourth-House Sun (Home/Relationship with Father), 10 P.M.-Midnight: To say that you care about your surroundings is the understatement of the year. Neatness counts here, too, as well as scrupulous cleanliness. Your home has to be organized, especially since it's probably your office, too, and you don't want your family interrupting your work to find the Ajax. State your needs in the clearest terms possible. Get your family's active cooperation to keep every function going smoothly. (I continually stress this because I really don't think there's anybody who doesn't have to set the family straight at least once about good ol' Mom always being available.) Don't be afraid to say that your craft is as important to you as anyone else's, and that there will be regular times when you will concentrate on it. Period.

Taurus Rising or Fifth-House Sun (Sex Life/Creativity/Attitude toward Children), 8-10 P.M.: You may experience a pendulum-swing effect from old-maidishly particular and prudish to downright promiscuous— although in Virgo's case promiscuity is just a brief rebellion or quenching of curiosity. A pure Virgo (pure astrologically, if there *is* such an animal) isn't all that sensuous. The creator of *I Am Curious—Yellow* was probably a Virgo, considering the clinical attitude. The Mercury-ruled person may alienate lovers by emphasizing technique at the expense of a more personal and tender relationship, and may be overly fussy about getting up right away to shower! Try to show more of the patience afforded by the Taurus influence. Your creative efforts may center upon writing, or instruction in arts and crafts. Relationships with children may be difficult in the early years simply because little ones' creature comforts don't respect adult work schedules, and it's such a thankless task to keep a growing child clean! Guard against hurting sensitive childish feelings with a steady barrage of admonitions to "sit up straight and clean up your plate." It isn't until years later that children realize that's just another way of saying I love you.

Aries Rising or Sixth-House Sun (Work and Co-Workers), 6-8 P.M.: Virgos born at this time are intense about their work in a way equaled only by Virgos born in the morning or Capricorns born at *any* time. They are also extremely sensitive about their health; indeed, if they weren't working so hard, you might say they sat around all day with one finger on the pulse of the other hand. Although you get enormous ego-gratification from work well done, you owe it to your health to go out to lunch *some*time. It should be a refreshing change of pace to spend a lunch hour out, instead of sitting at your desk with a brown bag, checking your secretary's accuracy. Try not to brood over the comments and criticisms of co-workers, and be careful whom you confide in when you're finding fault with someone else (such as the laggard who gets promoted over you—thanks to your back-up work—without giving you due credit). Don't stand around the water cooler sounding off; simply

go to the appropriate person's office, and discreetly close the door.
Pisces Rising or Seventh-House Sun (Partnerships and Public Relations), 4-6 P.M.: If you work in public relations, you are probably the one teaching the craft of it to young hopefuls. In partnership, you—like the Gemini born at the same time of day—need a companion with similar mental interests, or someone who will teach you subjects you otherwise wouldn't take time to learn. When offering criticism, take care to word your comments in a face-saving way; your partner may be more sensitive than he lets on (especially true of a Water-sign personality). You, of course, wouldn't sit still for nagging. After you get through working yourself over, anybody else's put-downs are superfluous.

Aquarius Rising or Eighth-House Sun (Source of Money), 2-4 P.M.: If you go into journalism, try to get a column as a critic. Aside from the regular paycheck, think of what you'd save on books or theater tickets. You may also profit through one of the healing professions, such as veterinary medicine. If you sculpt, you can market your work successfully under harmonious Sun aspects. Better yet, design useful articles; Virgos seldom like anything that just lies there if they can instead devise something that blends utility with modern design.

Capricorn Rising or Ninth-House Sun (Public Expression), Noon-2 P.M.: Whether you teach, write, or edit, you are happy to help an author or would-be author by detailing her or his problems, down to the last exclamation point. It may seem merciless at the time, but after you've done your job they'll never forget "i before e except after c" again! Or what sloppy plotting *deus ex machina* devices can be. As a believer in the plot-grows-out-of-character dictum, you'd probably try on astrology for size, discussing it in your usual thorough style, and carefully explaining that you didn't go into it as a believer. Once you gain the attention of your audience, your approach is one of common sense and sanity and advocating your favorite health regimen. Critical of most things, you include the family religion in your scrutiny, and may convert to another faith sooner or later—*after* you've thoroughly researched it.

Sagittarius Rising or Tenth-House Sun (Ambition/Relationship with Mother), 10 A.M.-Noon: Unless your Sun is harmoniously aspected, this could be a difficult situation. With a mother who's not only alert and intelligent but highly critical—of *you*—you may come to feel (years before you accomplish something that gives you ego-strength in your own right) that you can't do anything right. But disadvantages and advantages are often flip sides of the same record: early criticism is, or should be, an incentive to prove you *can* do something right. Exercise that Sagittarius optimism that's dormant within you. Another plus to remember: your mother will probably come up with some common-sense methods for landing the job you want or for dealing with your subordinates, if you ask respectfully and show proper appreciation for her worldly know-how. The honors you win later will probably have a lot to do with the practical methods you learned at home.

Scorpio Rising or Eleventh-House Sun (Friendships), 8-10 A.M.: You are attracted to friends because they're "together," although the purist in you takes a while to analyze and assimilate a word as slangy as that. Your friends have to be people who know even more answers than you do, which is a pretty tall order! Relax your exclusive standards just a little: a lot of the best people don't have Phi Beta Kappa keys on their charm bracelets.

Libra Rising or Twelfth-House Sun (Solitude and Privacy), 6-8 A.M.: You probably aren't satisfied with just a bachelor's degree; if you haven't yet registered in a formal graduate program, you're at least using plenty of your private time studying what attracts your interest. (Notice I didn't say *spare* time; with all that you have to do, you never have any of that.) When reading or writing a book you like to proceed uninterrupted— even if it means you're educating yourself "out of a husband."

Libra
(September 23-October 22)

Because Libra and Taurus are ruled by Venus, you should consult the Taurus paragraph for your time of birth, after reading below (for comparison purposes, which is a very Libran thing to do).

Libra, being an Air sign, often seems more high-flown and ethereal than the earthy, sometimes earthbound Taurean. Your arguments are more elaborate and may completely disarm your opponent, as compared to the Taurean, who wins through sheer persistence and strategic silence.

Both Libra and Taurus like the good life, but Taurus is more likely to take the bull by the horns and go to work for it at a young age. Libra, on the other hand, would opt for a few extra years of school—both to qualify for a profession and, let's face it, to stall for a little extra time to make a choice.

Niceness is another important Libra feature. There is a strong Libran tendency to weigh and balance, and this sign is one of the most thoughtful of the zodiac. Speaking up isn't always nice; Libra, therefore, is benefited more than most by assertiveness guidance. Libra is most likely to speak up if everyone in the group is agreeing to the point of stultifying boredom. Then the Libran in the room will play devil's advocate for the sake of staying awake. Libra's peacefulness can be deceptive, however. True, the desire for harmonious relations is genuine enough—sometimes exaggerated to the point of a grotesque need to please—but if there isn't another person, preferably in a continuing partnership, to debate with, the Libran will argue both sides alone. One famous Libran, F. Scott Fitzgerald, described this perfectly: "The test of a first-rate intelligence is the ability to hold two opposed ideas in the mind at the same time, and still retain the ability to function."

If you have a Libra birthday, and know your time of birth within approximately two hours, you can see the ways in which you are *most* Libran below:

Libra Rising or First-House Sun (Personality), 4-6 A.M. : Your temperament is evenly balanced and you are often a calming influence on others. You delight in luxurious clothing and show the best of taste. Abstract logic, debate, and moral issues focusing on relationships have an enduring fascination for you. Encouraged in your youth to seek others' advice rather than forge ahead independently, you often listen very nicely, then go out and do precisely what you want. Since people are happy enough to be consulted and are often too busy to check on whether you actually took their advice, you can expect a growing reputation as a diplomat. Take care to avoid excesses of any kind so as not to jeopardize your sensitive constitution. The kidneys, complexion, stomach, and circulation are particularly sensitive areas for you, so choose a balanced menu, saving the rich food you adore for special celebrations.

Virgo Rising or Second-House Sun (Money Managing), 2-4 A.M. : The pleasure you take in gift-buying is equal to that of the Taurean, but the process is different. Where the Taurean would determinedly select a luxury item that would give full value for years to come, the Libran would be torn between two items at the very least, and would debate the merits of each with the store clerk, a friend, and anyone else who'll spare the time to discuss it. Remember that this house position for a Libra Sun often goes with a Virgo ascendant, which can make a person extremely finicky. If the calculation for the birthplace indicates a Leo ascendant instead, the recipient will get something that is big, beautiful, and expensive. The combination of Libra and money means fairness, generosity, and a great deal of thought devoted to taste. Unless there are balancing Capricorn planets, frequent temptations to spend money can bring trouble. A partner may provide a stabilizing influence—but don't bank on it.

Leo Rising or Third-House Sun (Mind and Communications), Midnight-2 A.M.: You are attracted to the arts, especially writing; the more elegant, the better. The Libran influence over the third house gives less certainty than Taurus and you invariably investigate several creative outlets before deciding which career you favor. After mulling over playwriting (a natural for a Leo ascendant), painting, graphic designing, and public relations, you may well decide to make all of them hobbies— to get to, someday—while you fight to get into law school or medical school (for psychiatry). Opportunities—or put-downs, depending on the harmony of the changing aspects—may come through relatives. Try not to waste your energy wondering what somebody really meant by a comment, a phone call, or a failure to get in touch. Keep your balance by putting such speculations out of your mind. And get back to work!

Cancer Rising or Fourth-House Sun (Home/Relationship with Father), 10 P.M.-Midnight: Lengthy discussions of ethical questions—including the allotment of housework—would have begun in your childhood. With aspects to Venus or your Libra Sun permitting, you would be blessed with a father who was relaxed and affectionate. If scrupulous fairness was the rule when you lived with your father (or if you still do), housework as an ego-issue fades into the background in adulthood. Under discordant aspects there is a subtle punishment for less-than-perfect neatness in the home: withholding of approval, for instance. Consequently, when you come of age you expend a great deal of energy trying for a balance that's more in your favor.

Gemini Rising or Fifth-House Sun (Sex Life/Creativity/Attitude toward Children), 8-10 P.M.: Libra's association with marriage is particularly relevant here. It's difficult for a Libra born at this time of day to have a love affair without testing the lover as a possible husband or wife; puritanism may be part of it, but mainly it's a need to continue the dialogue. You don't want to break up and start all over again with a new person just when you're beginning to figure out the first partner's peculiar logic. You may find yourself in unusual relationships, particularly after 1968; you could flip for people who soon prove wrong for you, people chosen primarily to prove you aren't uptight, bigoted, or incapable of loving—or all of the above. Your beautiful (aesthetic) taste could result in distinctive works of art, although the creative process is difficult for you owing to Libra's agonies of indecision. With children you can be genuinely loving and tender. Libra-as-peacemaker responds cheerfully to the challenge of mediating childish quarrels, but don't prolong the scene as an excuse to avoid creative discipline for *yourself*.

Taurus Rising or Sixth-House Sun (Work and Co-Workers), 6-8 P.M.: More gregarious than the Taurus born at the same time, you like to entertain your colleagues, and sometimes your subordinates, at elegant meals (the Taurus is more likely to keep affections for co-workers quiet but give gladly to the office collections). Personalities on the job are as important to you as the content of the work; if there are hassles that are so intense they make you physically ill, you would reluctantly move elsewhere despite the appreciation of your superiors for work well done. As with Librans born from 4 to 6 A.M., guard against overindulgence in rich foods.

Aries Rising or Seventh-House Sun (Partnerships and Public Relations), 4-6 P.M.: Pay special attention to the way you feel after giving in for the sake of peace and quiet. Peace isn't peace if you're seething inside. And if you're griping to everybody but the person responsible, you probably should investigate assertiveness therapy. The Aries influence gives you ideas of what to say, but your Libran fear of sounding aggressive holds you back. Your partner may also favor phony peacemaking, so you could achieve greater intimacy by investigating assertiveness therapy together. After a day of smoothing other people's ruffled feathers at work, you want a peaceful haven with the one person you consider your absolute ally. And peace you're determined to get, even if you die in the attempt! Ask yourself this: if I speak up, what's the worst that could happen? And is it really as bad as all that? You might be pleasantly surprised. . . .

Pisces Rising or Eighth-House Sun (Source of Money), 2-4 P.M.: Artistic talent or public relations ability can pay off handsomely for Librans born at this time of the afternoon. Your rich tastes require you to rule out all but the most glamorous jobs so that you can live in the style to which you'd like to become accustomed. This house placement for a Libra Sun suggests a partner who is kind and generous. I was not surprised to find Libra strong in the charts of antifeminist young women with grandiose dreams of the extent to which their men will take care of them. If you take the attitude that you have yourself, first and foremost, to credit or blame for your income, whatever extra comes in through the goodwill of others will be taken as a pleasant surprise, not as homage due you.

Aquarius Rising or Ninth-House Sun (Public Expression), Noon-2 P.M.: Your most likely choices of subject matter for teaching or publishing are art, philosophy, political science, jurisprudence, or the culture of a country that engages your imagination. You may actually go to that country, making the trip part of your work (with a professional convention or possibly as a diplomat). You would make an excellent moderator or spokesperson for a group's point of view; your calm manner of delivery will win you respectful listeners.

Capricorn Rising or Tenth-House Sun (Ambition/Relationship with Mother), 10 A.M.-Noon: You like glory and status improvements, but Capricorn rising can make you negative about your own potential. If what you've heard so far has been praise for your appearance and nice manners, you're probably ready for a more balanced diet of tributes to your talents as well. You and your mother may debate what your ambitions should be; if one of you says marriage, the other will bring up other interests to balance your life. You've probably already encountered the parental propaganda that your status comes from a man, and while you may be involved with someone in a powerful position, remain aware that you've got other things going for you. It's highly likely you can reach leadership status in your own right.

Sagittarius Rising or Eleventh-House Sun (Friendships), 8-10 A.M.: You often are called upon to give advice to your friends, especially if two of them are at odds with each other and need your even-mindedness to straighten out the mess. Libra can be unquestionably impartial, and Sagittarius is famous for being a just and good sport; ergo, a natural judge and mediator. At the same time you're weighing and balancing *their* points of view, you're weighing within yourself the issue of becoming involved at all. Yet it's so flattering to be needed, to be respected for your judgment, that it's no simple matter to say yes or no. There are so many fine points to consider. A grateful friend could act as agent in bringing you a career opportunity. On the other hand. . . .

Scorpio Rising or Twelfth-House Sun (Solitude and Privacy), 6-8 A.M.: When you want to be constructive, spend time alone working on a creative project or studying psychology. Take care that you don't waste your precious time nursing imagined insults or being exploited in a clandestine relationship. (A colleague of mine once commented that an informal study turned up an interesting—and, regrettably, unspecified —percentage of women with a 6 to 8 A.M. birth time involved in affairs with married men.) Use your twelfth-house energy positively by encouraging your more dependent friends to think of solitude as a potential asset.

Scorpio
(October 23-November 22)

Let's face it, Scorpios have what used to be referred to over the back fence as a "reputation." If you are a Scorpio, or have met a man who told you *he* was, the conversation probably got very direct and eventually led to the question, Your place or mine?

The sexual passion isn't overrated, but to dismiss a Scorpio as one who "scores" or "puts out" is to underestimate the passion at the core of this personality. Scorpio is ruled by *two* planets: Mars (to learn more about this planet, read the section on Aries) and Pluto. Both here and in the Aries section, find the paragraph for your approximate birth time and blend them, for the truth is a combination.

Pluto is the planet ruling investigation, research, radio, television, regeneration through will power, groups of all kinds, pressure tactics, coercion, persuasion, rebellion, cooperation, and telepathy (particularly, transmission of desires with an intensity someone else tunes in on and complies with). It is Pluto energy at work when people who feel helpless individually band together to further a common cause. Pluto's intensity in and toward sex is but a glimpse of the power associated with atomic energy.

If you have a Scorpio birthday, and know your time of birth within approximately two hours, you can see the ways in which you are *most* Scorpian below:

Scorpio Rising or First-House Sun (Personality), 4-6 A.M.: Your will and desire for self-determination are strong. Appeals for your cooperation must be directed toward your self-interest if you are to become involved. You are intensely curious about people and have uncanny luck in drawing personal secrets out of others with little or no effort, yet you remain closemouthed about your own private life. Under harmonious aspects to Pluto or your Scorpio Sun, you are cooperative and happy to work in groups and movements that arouse your sympathies. Your time is freely given, out of a position of strength rather than the obedience of weakness. Under discordant aspects you are more inclined to be a loner, feeling ill-at-ease in groups. If someone pressures you, your first reaction is defiance. Should the other person find some unavoidable reason why you must give in, you become passionately bitter and resentful. You are capable of great perseverance and courage, and should put your strength to constructive use in an occupation requiring investigation and problem-solving.

Libra Rising or Second-House Sun (Money Managing), 2-4 A.M.: Your attitude toward money is obsessive. When you want a specific thing you can't put it out of your mind until you have it. If Pluto or your Scorpio Sun is in opposition to a planet ruling the eighth house, you may have a battle of wills over money, perhaps one as dramatic as robbery. Pluto's intensity can turn a financial quarrel into a lasting grudge, with little inclination on the part of either to give an inch. Harmonious aspects to Pluto or the Sun indicate hope of an amicable solution.

Virgo Rising or Third-House Sun (Mind and Communications), Midnight-2 A.M.: Your mental tenacity is prodigious, as is your memory. You thrive doing any work involving research, whether it's in science or exposé journalism, and your talent for investigation should be utilized to the fullest. Under harmonious aspects you are cooperative in communications and may use your penetrating writing style to further a humanitarian cause, possibly through a series of books or articles on a single theme. Under discordant aspects you are rebellious when pressure is brought to bear, and you often feel cornered. A large family of brothers and sisters may be positive (as an early opportunity to practice cooperation for the sake of the whole group), or it may be your first cause for rebellion.

Leo Rising or Fourth-House Sun (Home/Relationship with Father), 10 P.M.-Midnight: When Pluto or your Scorpio planet is discordant, you rebel early in life against your father's exercise of authority. If he is overly coercive or inquisitive, you establish a pattern of rebellion and secrecy in self-defense which stays with you for the rest of your life. In your early years your father may have compelled you to get accustomed to domesticity. The less freedom you had in your parents' home, the more avidly and obsessively you would embrace women's liberation and investigate strategies to drastically improve your status in your family and in the world. Under harmonious aspects you feel secure as part of a close-knit group.

Cancer Rising or Fifth-House Sun (Sex Life/Creativity/Attitude toward Children), 8-10 P.M. : You tend to be a compulsive achiever and to direct your intensity toward several creative media simultaneously. Your fascination for obsessive sexual relationships despite your conscious awareness of the partner's unsuitability is also compulsive. If the attraction exists, so does an intense curiosity on your part to see how the story ends. Pluto is the most obsessive of the planetary energies, and is even more emotional in nature than the Moon. The partners you attract may provoke you to jealousy and suspicion and then delight in their power over you. Only when you show signs of breaking away would they do something kind to get you hooked again. Pluto is the planet of both sadism and masochism, and the most painful of relationships can prove to be the most difficult to escape. Even with therapy, the support of friends, and surging self-confidence in other areas of life, you have difficulty with the object of your sexual obsession. Tyrannical people don't let go of their victims willingly and the dominant feeling may be less love than addiction. If you get past such a "courtship" and marry, the landscape of the battlefield may change but the stormy climate remains. At best there's still the issue of ego-survival—yours *versus* your partner's—and very often there's another rebellion besides: against the coercion you feel to have children. You may even go so far as voluntary sterilization to prove your adherence to your convictions. Under harmonious aspects your policy with children—*any* children—is to dispense with patronizing baby talk and get straight to the business of helping them realize their potentials. For ego-survival, Scorpio, creative work is the key; writing suspense stories, doing medical research, or work in radio or television are the most likely Pluto-ruled possibilities.

Gemini Rising or Sixth-House Sun (Work and Co-Workers), 6-8 P.M. : Your compulsion to work is a life-long motivating force, especially if you are happily involved with investigative work (in medicine, science, law enforcement, statistical research, or journalism). You could also do well with a franchise of an established business and, under harmonious aspects, you can succeed in enlisting the cooperation of others. Under discordant aspects, however, cooperation is harder to come by. You may even encounter fanatic factionalism and union disputes. Also possible are overbearing behavior on either your part or a co-worker's, or a crime that takes place at your office. Whether your allegiance is with labor or management, when there's a showdown you'll never hear the end of it from those who feel you're against them. Perhaps a very different group—the first consciousness-raising group you join—would make an irrevocable change in your perception of your job.

Taurus Rising or Seventh-House Sun (Partnerships and Public Relations), 4-6 P.M.: Pressure from others plays a dominant role in your determination to marry at the time you do and can even prompt your refusal to conform by marrying. Under harmonious aspects you are capable of teamwork for a purpose larger than personal gratification, and are thrilled to have found your true soul mate. Dealings with advisers, clients, and the general public are also cooperative. Under discordant aspects you experience power struggles, and relations with advisers or those of the general public whom you counsel (perhaps in a rape crisis center) are difficult.

Aries Rising or Eighth-House Sun (Source of Money), 2-4 P.M.: Your income may be earned through work in such fields as labor organizing, fund raising for a cause, money management for someone else, tax or estate work, law enforcement, chemistry, or work involving the dead, such as embalming or murder investigation. Under harmonious aspects you and your partner agree about money—about whose income pays for what, taxes, wills, insurance, and so forth. Under discordant aspects you are locked in an uncompromising struggle on financial issues. Collecting on outstanding debts is an uphill battle.

Pisces Rising or Ninth-House Sun (Public Expression), Noon-2 P.M.: With Pluto linked to your ninth house, you are intensely attracted to higher education, including a possible medical or legal degree to give you added authority in your crusading activities. You may experience a genuine religious vocation that inspires you to work for drastic improvements in the quality of the lives you influence. Your work could include travel to foreign countries or to different parts of the country of your birth in the course of your humanitarian missions, possibly in cooperation with a church group. Radio, television, and publishing are additional forums for you. You could earn a widespread reputation publishing in such subjects as higher education, crime (rape, in particular), religion, or the occult. One book or article can lead to a series of related works and public appearances.

Aquarius Rising or Tenth-House Sun (Ambition/Relationship with Mother), 10 A.M.-Noon: Your need for recognition, beginning with your mother's approval, is obsessive, and you may win the desired fame through medicine, broadcasting, politics, crime detection, writing, or exposing government scandals. Your relationship with your mother is strongly ambivalent. Harmonious aspects enable you to see the reasoning behind her guidance and her need for your cooperation, and the bond between you could evolve into a strong one indeed. Under discordant aspects, however, she may impress you as being too arbitrary, and you would rebel. This rebellion, begun at an early age, may well affect your choice of a career. Your drive to succeed on your own terms is strong enough to sustain you in a career that requires years of training and still more time in apprenticeship jobs. If you felt misunderstood in your early years, part of your drive derives from a desire for revenge—a need to be envied and taken seriously by those who had made you feel inadequate. Worthwhile goals may be fulfilled successfully under discordant aspects, but the motivation is not necessarily related to the task at hand, and the process is not easy. Don't be surprised if publicity about you emphasizes your intense drive. Pluto's influence makes your drive, your libido, and your sex appeal readily perceptible, and this is applied more toward career advancement than to strictly personal passions. A note of warning: your obvious appeal is bound to inspire envy in others. Use your incredible energies to shrug off such trivialities and concentrate on more important things.

Capricorn Rising or Eleventh-House Sun (Friendships), 8-10 A.M.: You probably met the friends you feel you have the most in common with through a group devoted to your mutual causes. People who are intense and persuasive exert a strong influence on anyone who has Pluto as the ruler of the eleventh house. When there are discordant aspects and the individual is less evolved and less prepared to resist, the influence of friends could include antisocial, even criminal, behavior—and such friends would be coercive and difficult to escape. Under harmonious aspects there can be enormous spiritual satisfaction in working as a team toward a goal that is beneficial to future, as well as present, generations.

Sagittarius Rising or Twelfth-House Sun (Solitude and Privacy), 6-8 A.M.: You may at some time in your life work long hours in isolation on a research project or reform activity. Your work may be in—or working for the improvement of—a prison or hospital. Under discordant aspects you may be on the wrong side of prison bars; rebellious demonstration, with or without the assistance of a group or movement, may lead to your imprisonment. In any case, you tend to be a rugged individualist. When the aspects are harmonious you are relaxed about being alone, and use the time constructively to research a subject that deeply interests you, or for some other form of self-improvement (Sagittarius's influence may add sufficient religious vocation to participate in seminary or retreat training). When you grow accustomed to using solitude constructively, you will be able to function free of self-consciousness.

Sagittarius
(November 23-December 21)

Sagittarius is ruled by Jupiter, the happiest and luckiest planet in the entire chart. A *benefic* like Venus (only better), it indicates the sources of success, luck, joy, optimism, and help from others.

If you had the luck, as I did, to be brought up by a Sagittarian mother, you learned to prepare for the future with humor. Jupiter's influence brings faith in a higher being (remember Emmaline Pankhurst's motto: "Trust in God, She will provide"), a sense of humor, optimism yielding personal and professional growth, generosity, a desire for adventure, and a passion for honor and fairness. This is Jupiter at its best. Like the other planets, Jupiter has discordant aspects with problematic effects: fun can be overdone, and often pranks or jokes are at another's expense. Also, your sense of humor may be limited and your generosity taken advantage of, you may overindulge in food or drink, and your work drive may slacken. Your expectations of rewards may exceed the value of work done.

The Jupiter-Sagittarius personality often includes a genuine religious vocation, and its insights can be beneficial to others. Sagittarians have been chosen in some way and want to share the blessing. Sometimes this leads to affiliation with an established religion and sometimes to secular teaching, but it almost always leads to public speaking.

If you have a Sagittarius birthday and know your time of birth within approximately two hours, you can see the ways in which you are *most* Sagittarian below:

Sagittarius Rising or First-House Sun (Personality), 4-6 A.M.: You enjoy life greatly and your capacity for joy increases as you gain in confidence. You tend to be easygoing, resilient, forgiving, and fair, and would be a good choice for any profession requiring a genuine liking for people and a sense of humor. You have the capability to inspire others. Under discordant aspects you become lazy and take too much for granted, including your health. Refrain from overeating or drinking; liver trouble and fatty tumors may result.

Scorpio Rising or Second-House Sun (Money Managing), 2-4 A.M.: Money *mangling* might be more to the point! It's easy for you to be generous with material possessions. Preserving goodwill and being charitable mean more to you than counting pennies, and have more satisfying long-term effects. You may have found that playing a hunch has proved lucky, although under discordant aspects you could overdo the gambling.

Libra Rising or Third-House Sun (Mind and Communications), Midnight-2 A.M.: You set your goals high and read voraciously, whether to reach accredited professional status or for pleasure. As a diversion you would try your hand at writing, with more success and recognition than you had anticipated. Your spare-time reading matter and writing attempts tend to be strongly humorous. Communications and pleasure trips are abundant and fun, but they could cause your work to suffer. Your general outlook is cheerful and positive.

Virgo Rising or Fourth-House Sun (Home/Relationship with Father), 10 P.M.-Midnight: Your home has to be spacious, for you can't stand being fenced in. Your attitude toward domesticity is offhanded and indifferent; housework is done quickly and superficially, if at all. Too many other things, such as your professional work, offer happy distractions. If your father was a slob at home and got away with it, you'd probably rather be as happy as he was than follow the example of the wife who cleaned up after him. Your father's upbeat disposition would have been an inspiration to you.

Leo Rising or Fifth-House Sun (Sex Life/Creativity/Attitude toward Children), 8-10 P.M.: Whether or not you have ever married, love affairs are so enjoyable for you that you hesitate to jinx them by changing your status. In one love affair after another, you don't see the need for committing yourself to a single relationship (unless contraindications in the chart are much stronger than your Sun and Jupiter). Your creative work, which starts out as fun and becomes materially profitable, may be in show business or publishing, specifically humor. Sports are another good outlet for your abundant energy, and your confident attitude inspires others to bet on you. You enjoy entertaining children, but not necessarily on a full-time basis. You tend to get along better with other people's children than with your own; they see in you a glamor lacking in the adults they see every day at home. Your attitude toward parenthood can best be described as adventurous. At discordant times you see yourself as making the best of it, trying to salvage some fun.

Cancer Rising or Sixth-House Sun (Work and Co-Workers), 6-8 P.M.: You hate work of a menial and repetitious nature. Your aims are high and toward a profession, but if Jupiter or your Sagittarius Sun are discordant, your lofty aims are a rationalization for laziness. Your co-workers and employees are jovial and sincere supporters, and your liking for them is obvious. You have the gift of putting people at ease.

Gemini Rising or Seventh-House Sun (Partnerships and Public Relations), 4-6 P.M.: Your attitude toward marriage is genuinely indifferent. Those who have Jupiter ruling the seventh house tend to marry superior people, and they have the confidence to go it alone until somebody worthwhile comes on the scene. By the time of your marriage, both you and your partner have probably become established as professional successes. More important: regardless of either partner's profession, you are both generous, fair, and inclined to give the other breathing space. Your jovial, relaxed manner attracts the patronage of wealthy and influential people.

Taurus Rising or Eighth-House Sun (Source of Money), 2-4 P.M.: You could succeed financially as a manager of other people's funds, in the legal profession, or in medicine. Humor and appeals to the other person's sense of fair play help you collect outstanding debts. Unless your Jupiter or Sun is strongly discordant—or your prospective partner's is—a partnership arrangement in business could prove mutually advantageous. With discordant aspects, however, your partner or you would be extravagant with joint funds.

Aries Rising or Ninth-House Sun (Public Expression), Noon-2 P.M.: Publishing, the legal profession, religion, higher education, broadcasting, or travel are recommended careers for you if Jupiter rules your ninth house. Your first impulse as a child may have been to adopt one of these careers, but if you went in another direction entirely it's probably the result of adult intervention. Although you may feel you've been derailed, the Jupiter influence will still make its presence felt when you pursue your education, publish, are quoted publicly, or speak before an assembled audience. You may also find growth and pleasure in travel, the law as an avocation, religious affiliations, or the study of philosophy. Should you experience a religious conversion, the enthusiasm of both your Sun and your Aries ascendant will make you an inspiring and vocal advocate of your new faith.

Pisces Rising or Tenth-House Sun (Ambition/Relationship with Mother), 10 A.M.-Noon: The process of climbing toward a better status is as pleasurable to you as actually making it. You may be elected to an office, and would enjoy using your influence for humanitarian purposes. If, however, your Sun or Jupiter should form a discordant aspect with one another or with Saturn, you may experience conflicts with selfish interests. Fame is possible through professional work. Your mother's influence is a decided plus. Her example and outlook are positive and inspiring, and her promotion of you genuinely enthusiastic. Under discordant aspects her example or promoting may raise hopes difficult to fulfill, although her intentions, in any event, are the best.

Aquarius Rising or Eleventh-House Sun (Friendships), 8-10 A.M.: The people you come to know socially may be influential, wealthy, and good-natured enough to offer to help you in some way. Their financial standing aside, the important thing your friends have to offer is an optimistic approach to life. It's important to you that your friends have a sense of humor and appreciate forms of fun you can enjoy. Your friends are your most loyal supporters, sharing your progressive Aquarian attitudes. Most important of all, you can really relax with them.

Capricorn Rising or Twelfth-House Sun (Solitude and Privacy), 6-8 A.M.: You are among the truly fortunate, who derive genuine enjoyment from solitude. Being sent alone to your room was probably never one of your childhood punishments, and you view solitude as a starting-point toward growth. Your sense of fairness is often expressed on questions of privacy. Live and let live is your motto; you know what is and isn't your business so you never probe and make others uncomfortable. When on the receiving end of nosy questions you use humor to change the subject, and would indulge in a prank or in pointed jokes should subtlety fail. If for some reason a promised celebration or date does not materialize and you are unexpectedly alone, you accept the situation philosophically and use the extra time to do something else which you wholeheartedly enjoy. When you are alone, perhaps more than at any other time, you are most happily and completely yourself.

Capricorn
(December 22-January 20)

Capricorn's ruling planet is Saturn, which seems like a crash landing after the high of Jupiter (*down-to-earth* is praise for Capricorns, perhaps the highest a Capricorn will ever give). Saturn rules the need for security, and, as a result, the agonies of taking daring steps. Saturn is the planet of conformity, lack, limitation, self-pity, oppression, depression, and still *more* self-pity, and Saturn rules the most negative of fates. Though difficult, it is vital that Cap ,icorns be in control of their thoughts and strive consciously to combat Saturn's negative influence.

Saturn, when harmonious, can be a major force contributing to personal success. It makes us capable of logic, planning, organizing, budgeting, and structuring. It enables us to say no to ourselves and to others, protecting our resources for our own priorities. For this reason astrologers appreciate Saturn as the reality principle; it keeps us from going off the deep end in our well-intentioned enthusiasms. Capricorns, who seem to have an extra helping of Saturn, personify the assets as well as the liabilities of this planet.

If you have a Capricorn birthday and know your time of birth within approximately two hours, you can see the ways in which you are *most* Capricornian below:

Capricorn Rising or First-House Sun (Personality), 4-6 A.M. : You may remember your early years as lacking in warmth, joy, or affection; your childhood was a time when discipline prevailed. You remember best the parental no, which you may mentally confuse with coldness. The maturing process is seen as an obstacle course, and whether you feel adequate to meet the tests will depend on the aspects to your Saturn and your Sun. In adulthood you are probably so ambitious—to compensate for early frustration—that you overwork to the extent of physical fatigue and at the expense of your personal life. You have a businesslike manner, which is admired by some and deeply resented by others. With Saturn ruling your first house, you are the ideal person to call when organization, responsibility, and practicality are needed. There is a danger of the reliable old shoe syndrome, which can mean being passed over at promotion time. If you've seen this pattern in your life already, don't agree to a foot-in-the-door secretarial job unless you genuinely like the work and are desperate for money—your foot could get that door slammed on it.

Sagittarius Rising or Second-House Sun (Money Managing), 2-4 A.M. : You tend to be strongly materialistic and security oriented, and you may be miserly as well as a genius at budgeting. Under discordant aspects you may overdo cynicism and self-pity about how unappreciated you are (as documented by your paycheck) and suffer with every check you write. Under harmonious aspects your attitude is more positive and you are grateful for your small income's regularity.

Scorpio Rising or Third-House Sun (Mind and Communications), Midnight-2 A.M.: Your mind is logical and practical, and you speak succinctly. Under harmonious aspects to Saturn or your Capricorn Sun, you are capable of long hours of mental work. Under discordant aspects the long hours of work may still be managed, but are much harder to tolerate—especially when there's no advancement in sight. Conservatism, secretiveness, and a tendency to fixate on an emotion or idea are also characteristic of the person who has Saturn's influence in the third house. Although you sometimes feel you are in a rut, it is still difficult to break away from the familiar situation. Your fear of the unknown can cause you to sustain the most negative of conditions and associations for years. The people you communicate with tend to heap their complaints and pessimism on you. Not only does this take time away from the mental work required of you, it depresses you long after they had forgotten their grievances. However, fear of isolation and a good dose of guilt keep you continually accessible to these people.

Libra Rising or Fourth-House Sun (Home/Relationship with Father), 10 P.M.-Midnight: You feel that a woman's work is never done, and this guilt programming originates with an old-fashioned father. Discipline and schedule are endlessly included in your family life. If you had thought your work was done, your father would probably remind you of something you failed to do. Unless the aspects to your fourth-house rulers are strongly harmonious, you may have a lasting feeling of inadequacy resulting from the stereotype imposed years ago. To prove yourself you may work in real estate and even make shrewd investments of your own capital along the way. Your home may cost less than you can afford because you begrudge giving a large portion of your hard-earned money to a landlord. Or you may use economics, along with guilt, as an excuse for living with your parents long after you have come of age. You don't decorate lavishly; the basic functional pieces serve well enough for you, along with a few antiques that will yield a return on their investment as costs rise. The few things you do buy are good enough to last for years. You worked hard to be able to afford them, and besides, you have more important things to do than replace faulty furniture. There's all that office work you took home.

Virgo Rising or Fifth-House Sun (Sex Life/Creativity/Attitude toward Children), 8-10 P.M.: Love affairs, if any, are serious business with you (and *business* is a word you use often). They probably begin late in life and are constant reminders of the necessity for a responsible adult attitude. The person you become involved with may bring you responsibilities and anxieties, yet you tend to stick with him rather than start all over again with a stranger, or, worse, be alone. The conservative bent of Saturn impels you to internalize the old-fashioned programming about the only justifiable pairing for a girl being marriage. Since you want a secure, long-term relationship, you may be stiff and formal with the men you like most until you have the hoped-for ring on your finger. Relax. Make an effort to think of men as friends instead of as potential guardians or ravishers.

You find creative work frustrating and difficult. When experiencing a mental block you may indulge in an orgy of pencil sharpening or list-making to give yourself the virtuous feeling of having worked. One problem is that you tend to edit yourself before any inspiration can get a real chance to flow. You are your severest critic. Should you opt for parenthood, it would probably be out of a sense of duty rather than an innate enjoyment of children, and you are particularly susceptible to the guilt-inducing pleas of parents (or in-laws) who want grandchildren. Although conscientious about your parental duties, you secretly resent the sacrifices involved. Fear or coldness in sex, another Saturn problem, is often a mask for fear of childbirth, and homosexuality may be chosen as an alternative. Under harmonious aspects your relationships are reassuring and lasting. Under discordant aspects your situation is complicated by jealousy and paranoia. In general, Saturn as the ruler of the fifth house indicates the presence of the Puritan ethic; leisure-time activities, even the nonsexual ones, are seldom thoroughly enjoyed because of your nagging awareness of obligations and of work to be done.

Leo Rising or Sixth-House Sun (Work and Co-Workers), 6-8 P.M. : For the sake of your health, find work you enjoy, and then try not to think of it as work. If you don't think you can enjoy any kind of work, you either haven't thought long enough or you're suffering from malnutrition. What you're good at and would be appreciated for are strategy, budgeting, organization, and establishing and refining systems.

Whatever your occupation, you are conscientious to the point of endangering your health. You probably allow yourself insufficient sleep as well as insufficient nourishment—if you interrupt your work to get nourishment at all! When you do eat, put aside business problems. The more troublesome the problem, the more firmly you should keep mealtimes strictly for pleasure. Your relations with co-workers may be tense and alienated, especially because when others are more relaxed and sociable they resent your unrelenting all-business attitude. If you are really disturbed by the emotional climate at work, you may become physically ill. Consider it worth your while to pause for a few minutes every now and then to get to know the people at the office a little better. Saturn as ruler of the sixth house can mean alarming illnesses that accompany depression—running the gamut from the common cold to cancer. Harness this energy constructively through disciplined work with appropriate breaks for pleasure and nourishment, and don't allow resentment or hypochondria to control your thinking.

Cancer Rising or Seventh-House Sun (Partnerships and Public Relations), 4-6 P.M.: Your marriage occurs late in life, if ever. The delay linked with Saturn is very different in nature from the late marriage prompted by Jupiter; with Saturn, your attitude is more uptight and alienates prospective partners. Parental pressures and interferences, in addition to your own tense approach, can delay or prevent marriage. An obvious desperation for marriage, guilt manipulation tactics, and alienation characterize the Saturn-dominated relationship. When the need for anyone is stronger than the fondness for the person at hand, that person will probably sense it and retreat. An older person or someone unusually mature for his years would be best for you, and under harmonious aspects the relationship can be secure and reassuring for years. Business partnerships and associations may also be durable. You need, and find satisfaction in, continued association with another person. Under discordant aspects your partner may have an excessive need for security, and may make unfair demands that strain the relationship severely. I know several men having Saturn rulership of this house, and in each case the strong need (which could never be fully satisfied) for someone to be waiting at home took the form of punitive miserliness and tyranny. The reactions to this ranged from guilt to resentment to complete separation. If you regard a failed marriage as a learning experience and proceed to plan for the future instead of looking back and blaming your partner, you'll come out of it a lot healthier.

Gemini Rising or Eighth-House Sun (Source of Money), 2-4 P.M.: Your income is steady, although probably never large enough to satisfy you. A conscientious attitude and willingness to do time-consuming work will further your security goals more than any amount of complaining about poverty. If Saturn or your Capricorn Sun makes harmonious aspects in your natal chart, you're probably adept at managing not only your own money but your partner's and clients' funds as well. Your style leans more toward secure blue-chip investments rather than high-risk glamor speculations. Unless your partner's Saturn is more harmonious than yours, *you* should be the one keeping track of the finances. Under discordant aspects you experience either a loss through partnership (tax discrimination or responsibility for the other person's debts) or stinginess on the part of your partner. If the relationship terminates through legal action or death, you, as the remaining partner, may suffer financially and have your assets tied up in legal proceedings. Any tax refunds you receive will be smaller than you had hoped for.

Taurus Rising or Ninth-House Sun (Public Expression), Noon-2 P.M.: One of the worst problems in your life is the warping effect of orthodox religious dogma on the subject of the sexes and, in particular, divorce. Having to explain a breakup of your own to a conservative and religious family can magnify the trauma. You may well feel betrayed that their reaction is shame.

If, as a woman with a lifetime of programming for second-class citizenship, you find yourself with a first opportunity to express your convictions in public, it's probably more of an ordeal for you than anything else. Breaking with past teachings completely is difficult—if not impossible—unless you replace the old creed with a new ideology you've found on your own and wholeheartedly believe in. When you're really sure of yourself and your beliefs, you will want to help others benefit from your years of struggle and you may become interested in teaching or publishing.

Aries Rising or Tenth-House Sun (Ambition/Relationship with Mother), 10 A.M.-Noon: When formulating your career plans you may have to overcome conservatism on your mother's part or a relationship tangled with guilt. If your mother's work has made your education possible and you're really climbing in your profession, don't be surprised if she reacts with ambivalence; she's struggled to help you get where you are, and yet she may be jealous of your achievements. Under harmonious aspects your relationship with your mother is a reassuring haven, and your climb for status slow but sure. Under discordant aspects your relationship is problematic, but can be converted to a positive force if you let yourself benefit from her example. That example may be a reminder of what you *don't* want to put up with: a life as a martyr or a latter-day

Victorian. Her severity and "constructive criticism" may either spur
your ambition or increase your feelings of defeat and worthlessness. It's
up to you. If you give in to the latter, your employer may sense it and
exploit you or pass you by at promotion time. You should use the
frustration you feel as a motivation to show 'em, aborting depression at
the start. Use self-discipline. I know you've got it in you.

Pisces Rising or Eleventh-House Sun (Friendships), 8-10 A.M.: You may
relate better to friends who are older than you, and you find their
experience and influence a real comfort. You do not instantly call a
person *friend*; your respect for friendship is too serious to use the term
lightly. The people you do regard as friends have already proven their
loyalty and reliability. Under discordant aspects your friends may be
disappointingly uncommunicative, envious, disparaging, absent, or
selfishly demanding (testing friendship in general and you in particular
by asking for your professional services at no cost to them, or by taking
up too much of your time talking about their troubles). Even when your
work load requires that you make yourself inaccessible, you find yourself feeling guilty for refusing favors, withholding personal confidences,
and cutting phone conversations short. Also, work may be a pretext for
withdrawing from a friend with whom you have had a painful experience.

Aquarius Rising or Twelfth-House Sun (Solitude and Privacy), 6-8 A.M.:
Under harmonious aspects you are admirably constructive in your use of
the time you spend alone. When you put your mind to it, you can
accomplish wonders single-handedly, especially by devising strategies
to conserve time or money. You pride yourself on your efficiency—
justifiably—and are probably a list-maker. Under discordant aspects
you indulge in resentment and self-pity, and your insecurity makes
being alone a living hell. Negative thoughts and resentments can
become obsessions if no constructive diversion is begun. Your depression may also lead to the contemplation, or even attempt, of suicide to
make him (her, them) sorry. If this is the case with you, make the
difficult effort to come out of your shell. Accept invitations and keep the
talk light. The more you act as though nothing is wrong, the sooner you'll
gain perspective on your disappointment and begin to like yourself
again. If you feel you can't manage this alone, get professional help.
Your first attempts to relate to people with a cheerful approach may
seem shallow when you're depressed, but that's just the sort of approach
you need to learn. When Saturn rules your twelfth house, it is often a

severe strain to maintain an even emotional keel. But don't let that discourage you from taking one step at a time.

Aquarius
(January 21-February 19)

We live in the Age of Aquarius, and Aquarius is said to be the most modern, futuristic, progressive, and with-it—no, *ahead*-of-it—of the twelve signs. Aquarius is ruled by *two* planets: Saturn (to learn more about this planet, read the section on Capricorn) and Uranus. Both here and in the Capricorn section, find the paragraph for your approximate birth time and blend them, for the truth is a combination. It is this combination that explains why the friend you expect to be the most tolerant and modern surprises you sometimes with downright stodginess. Aquarians devote a great deal of thought to human nature in general and its complex possibilities, and a great deal more thought to their own personal prerogatives. Uranus is the planet of the individualistic urge, and it indicates the most likely sources of and obstacles to achieving autonomy. Uranus also shows human intervention and surprises from unexpected sources.

Famous for progressiveness, Uranus energy strives to change or destroy the old for the sake of the new, and is associated with such social concepts as the commune and the kibbutz. It emphasizes understanding of people and rules any profession based on the study of human nature; for example, psychology and astrology. The Uranian mentality sees tradition as far from sacred and likes to experiment with life-styles. Uranus rules electricity—both the mechanical and the interpersonal varieties.

When Uranus or an Aquarius planet is harmonious in your chart, you will find success and gain independence on your own terms. Your ability to influence others is strong, as is your intellect.

When the aspects are discordant you may be swayed by strongly charismatic personalities. You may be aware that something you are doing, at their bidding, is ill-advised, but this realization is accompanied by a peculiar sensation of moral paralysis. This is often called falling in love.

The combination of Saturn and Uranus, so very different in nature, makes Aquarians unique. Saturn's responses are negative and gloomy while Uranus's are upsetting and surprising. The two planets are in stark opposition in their approach to change, and Aquarians can feel a pendulum-swing effect between insecurity and independence, and an ambivalence toward the old and the new, toward orthodoxy and freethinking, and toward absolute moral codes and exciting existential options.

If you have an Aquarius birthday and know your time of birth within approximately two hours, you can see the ways in which you are *most* Aquarian below:

Aquarius Rising or First-House Sun (Personality), 4-6 A.M.: Your desire for autonomy is a, if not *the*, dominant motivation in your life. Under discordant aspects to Uranus or your Aquarian Sun, you may be so unreliable and abrupt that you alienate others and undermine the causes you are crusading for. People you regard as close to you upset you with unpredictable behavior, such as last-minute cancellations. Health difficulties may include psychomotor disorders—twitches or spasms, for instance. Under harmonious aspects you enjoy living spontaneously, your intelligence is keen, and you have the ability to assess people quickly and to influence them.

Capricorn Rising or Second-House Sun (Money Managing), 2-4 A.M.: Your approach toward money is erratic, alternating between impulse buying and elaborate, even brilliant, bookkeeping schemes. Money represents a prerequisite to independence for you and to asserting same. Your accounts are in your own name and you are definite about your veto power over your own finances. Others may advise, and you, asserting your independence, may do just the opposite for the sheer pleasure of it.

Sagittarius Rising or Third-House Sun (Mind and Communications), Midnight-2 A.M.: Your mind is quick, perceptive, scientific, inventive, independent, and possibly of genius caliber. You are attracted to any discipline that promises greater insight into people. If you choose astrology your interest is primarily scientific and lies in the potential of the computer and in statistical correlations, as contrasted with the Piscean's more mystical attraction to reincarnation and nirvana. You might study astrology as a buffer against future shock. Your mental interests change drastically, as does your style of expression. Under discordant aspects your telephone manner is abrupt, and some of the calls you receive may be highly upsetting to you. Mental work is an important means to liberation, and you do not suffer interruptions gladly.

Scorpio Rising or Fourth-House Sun (Home/Relationship with Father), 10 P.M.-Midnight: You probably can't get out of your home fast enough. Ever since you first ran away from home as a child, whenever you are nervous or restless your immediate plan is to move out. Your preferences tend to be out of the ordinary: a camper truck, a houseboat, or perhaps even the White House. The reason for the move—whether pleasant or negative—is indicated by the harmony or discord of the aspects. Your home life is progressive, and chores are allotted by time and talent rather than by sex-role stereotypes. Under harmonious aspects your father's influence builds independence through example. Under discordant aspects his erratic behavior builds your independence as an alternative to relying on somebody like him.

Libra Rising or Fifth-House Sun (Sex Life/Creativity/Attitude toward Children), 8-10 P.M.: Your relations with lovers are memorably abrupt in their beginnings, developments, and endings. New loves enter your life in unusual ways; your relationships progress at a dizzying pace; and just when you start getting optimistic about the future, your partners drop out without giving an understandable reason. But they are soon replaced. Even though you realize that a person is wrong for you, you find yourself stifling vestiges of common sense as they threaten to surface. This is partly out of morbid curiosity and partly because the excitement of the affair is so stimulating. Unusual relationships (incest, adultery, or miscegenation, specifically) may start because you want to make a negligent lover attentive again; or perhaps just for the sake of experiment, to see how you react in a new situation. Rebellion could well be another incentive, and just being different seems to be its own reward. Whatever art form you choose for your creative energies, your inspiration is distinctive. You may become an inventor or an author of science fiction. If you decide to have children of your own, the prevailing feeling is one of curiosity. You find that combining abstract theories of progressive child-rearing with the reality of a specific child is a mental challenge and you encourage your children to be independent, to question traditions, and to wipe the cobwebs off antique assumptions. You especially enjoy older children who can be mentally stimulating.

Virgo Rising or Sixth-House Sun (Work and Co-Workers), 6-8 P.M.:

Your mental restlessness directs you toward work of a temporary nature, possibly a free-lancer's career. Unexpected changes may occur in your duties, co-workers, or work environment—changes so upsetting that you may want to quit. Your interest in your co-workers is abstract, idealistic, and statistical rather than sentimental. You are curious about what makes people tick, but would rather stay independent of office intrigues. You excel at work that involves psychology, market research, science, engineering, computer technology, or mechanics.

Leo Rising or Seventh-House Sun (Partnerships and Public Relations), 4-6 P.M.: It is in marriage or the avoidance of it that you best express your independence. You may experiment with new ways to relate in marriage or new living arrangements with your partner. You may also refuse to take your husband's name. Divorce is likely, and your partner will initiate proceedings when least expected. A shock like this can precipitate either a nervous crisis or personal growth, depending on how you choose to deal with the unexpected opportunity for independence. If your occupation involves clients or dealings with the general public, you may have to deal with very unusual or erratic people and frequent emergency situations.

Cancer Rising or Eighth-House Sun (Source of Money), 2-4 P.M.: You may earn your income through erratic temporary or free-lance work; through work of an intellectual, scientific or mechanical nature; through computers; through damage payments from an insurance company after an accident; through psychology or astrology; or through work of a controversial or revolutionary nature. Under discordant aspects there may be unpredicted losses: repair costs for machinery, friends' foisting the dinner check on you, or tax audits. Computer foul-ups may cause billing errors that try your nervous system still further. On the positive side there may be a tax refund, a reversal of tax regulations in your favor, or a legacy from someone you wouldn't have supposed remembered you.

Gemini Rising or Ninth-House Sun (Public Expression), Noon-2 P.M.: You are attracted to teaching, especially of controversial scientific or revolutionary subject matter. Any public medium would appeal to you in your promotion of your farsighted ideals. Established religion's attempts at modernization are not fast enough for you, and your religious thinking may involve a drastic break with your family's traditional religion. You have a questioning mind and are drawn toward changing life-styles. Thanks to the rulership of Uranus, opportunities to speak your mind in public crop up in unusual ways.

Taurus Rising or Tenth-House Sun (Ambition/Relationship with Mother), 10 A.M.-Noon: Fame may come through unexpected channels. A friend or acquaintance may mistakenly assume a hobby is a full-time profession (or is about to be) and spread the word until the hobby gathers momentum and becomes a full-time enterprise after all. Or you may gain recognition through an invention or through publicizing progressive attitudes about social change. To you, fame and independence are synonymous. Celebrity status gives you assurance, and you enjoy building a reputation for your individualism as you indulge your idiosyncrasies. Your restless nature impels you to change careers from time to time; you have a good chance of climbing if your approach is original and daring. Your mother's influence takes the form of urging you to think for yourself. Under harmonious aspects you appreciate her more and are grateful for the example of self-reliance she offers. Under discordant aspects you may feel she is rushing you to jump ahead faster than you are ready, and you feel insecure and nervous. Unexpected job developments also aggravate your nervousness. Whatever the course of events, hear your mother out. She's probably smarter than you think.

Aries Rising or Eleventh-House Sun (Friendships), 8-10 A.M.: Your friends and acquaintances are probably out of the ordinary: inventive and charismatic, progressive and independent, they tend to be leaders in social reform. Under harmonious aspects you, too, have charisma enough to attract such people as friends, and enjoy sharing the mental interests that brought you together. Under discordant aspects you are upset and irritable as a result of unexpected cancellations from friends, drop-in visitors, or bad temper on anyone's part. You should select your friends carefully, as their influence on your mind is powerful.

Pisces Rising or Twelfth-House Sun (Solitude and Privacy), 6-8 A.M.: You prefer working with a great deal of freedom in an isolated place, without the stares of others as you go about your business. So intent are you on working alone on intellectual problems that you may convey a "mad scientist" impression. Scientific research or inventions may be your life-work, but a discordant aspect can mean another person will claim credit for your discoveries. You tend to be a loner and emphatically self-sufficient. Eager to discover your capacities and to further your autonomy, you rush to learn from experience.

Pisces
(February 20-March 21)

The Piscean is said to be an enigma, so you can imagine the hyperbole a *female* Piscean gets! One reason is that Pisces, the last sign, is supposed to be the ultimate experience in reincarnation. It is also said that Pisces combines the traits of all the signs. Maybe. But then, we *all* do; every sign is on at least one house's cusp in the chart of each and every one of us. So why is Pisces such a puzzle?

The enigma has more to do with Neptune's rulership than with inconclusive conjectures about reincarnation. But then Pisces is also ruled by Jupiter, and can be deceptively gregarious. This raises the complexity to another power entirely! (To learn more about Jupiter's effect on the personality, read the section on Sagittarius.) Both here and in the Sagittarius section, find the paragraph for your approximate birth time and blend them, for the truth is a combination.

Neptune is the planet of the utopian urge, the creative and poetic imagination, and the longing for better conditions. Your fondness for the ideal makes you quick to idealize the objects of your affections, and as a consequence you tend to suffer intensely when you discover your heroes have feet of clay. Neptune also rules role-playing, artifice, intuition, glamor, manipulation, deception, efforts to get publicity, narcotics, alcoholism, and escapism. Under harmonious aspects this energy produces fiction, drama, poetry, photography, and movies.

If you have not been encouraged to develop your creative talents, the alternative will probably be to follow a convenient cultural myth. Young people are, in all too many cases, brought up with distorted notions of the "ideal woman" and the "ideal man." If painful reality threatens, escape may take the form of a comforting delusion, a clandestine affair, or a chemical anesthetic such as alcohol. If Saturn or Uranus energy is strong and you face reality, cold turkey, a new frame of reference or ideology may develop, such as feminism.

Under discordant aspects to Neptune or a Pisces planet, your creative imagination may run riot and yield very imaginative work in at least one art form. What's so bad about that? The process. False starts, restarts, and changes sap your vitality and require isolation from the comforting social life you desire. Under harmonious aspects your artistic ideas develop with more ease and speed, and your imagination functions through more rewarding channels.

If you have a Pisces birthday, and know your time of birth within approximately two hours, you can see the ways in which you are *most* Piscean below:

Pisces Rising or First-House Sun (Personality), 4-6 A.M.: Your imagination, dramatic ability, and personal style are distinctive. In everyday life you have a sense of theater and a flair that make your personality memorable. Under discordant aspects there are dangers of food poisoning, schizophrenia, paranoia, alcoholism, frequent exhaustion, drug addiction, side effects from medication, illnesses that cannot be readily diagnosed, and hypochondria. Other Neptune problems are pathological lying, gullibility, absentmindedness, frequent drowsiness, infidelity for the sake of intrigue, and depression resulting from the problems you sympathetically listen to when your friends need consolation.

Aquarius Rising or Second-House Sun (Money Managing), 2-4 A.M.: Although you find the subject of money dreary and mundane, you should still make an effort to protect what's rightfully yours. The losses you experience are primarily the results of your own negligence, whether through pickpocketing, con artistry (stifle your receptivity to get-rich-quick schemes and hard-luck stories), or absentmindedness. A typical incident could well be that you daydream when paying a cashier and walk away without getting your change. Although the comforts money can buy are welcome, you may think it's petty and demeaning to keep track of where your money is spent. Time-wasting emotional upsets about lost money can be avoided if you'd only bother to make note of a cab fare here and a tax-deductible doctor bill there.

Capricorn Rising or Third-House Sun (Mind and Communications), Midnight-2 A.M.: Neptune as ruler of the third house can really be an asset if you have ambitions to write, and apply Capricorn's potential for self-discipline. The fiction, poetry, or drama you produce is unique. Consider, too, writing for or about film. Under discordant aspects you are difficult to communicate with, as your thoughts are far away and engrossed in a private dream. Speech impediments are also likely. You are probably forgetful about letter-writing or returning calls, and your excuses to the people you've neglected are very creative. For maximum benefit from this energy, channel your imagination into marketable writing.

Sagittarius Rising or Fourth-House Sun (Home/Relationship with Father), 10 P.M.-Midnight: Your home life may be different from that of your contemporaries—a difference which is magnified in your own mind—owing to the literal or psychic absence of your father. Whether death, divorce, or indifference removes him from an active role in your everyday life in childhood, his absence heightens his importance in your eyes. Your father is the most probable perpetrator of the home-is-fulfillment myth in your life. (A *male* with Neptune ruling the fourth house is more likely to be told by his father that a man's home is his castle, and someone is sure to wait on him.) Your attitude toward the home may at first be reverential. But when reality becomes unavoidable a pattern of escapism begins, and whether or not you experiment with drugs, you tend to become increasingly unreachable. When this energy is used constructively, your home can become an effective showcase and studio where distinctive works of art are produced.

Scorpio Rising or Fifth-House Sun (Sex Life/Creativity/Attitude toward Children), 8-10 P.M.: Love and, later, parenthood, often occupy your imagination, although you have intermittent periods of disillusionment. The lovers you're attracted to may be appealing mainly because of their extreme cultural differences and your need to have intrigue in your life. You have difficulty perceiving lovers as they really are. It's partly your desire to idealize them, and partly their misrepresentation of themselves to you. You have to steel yourself against susceptibility to the kinds of detours (such as drugs) they introduce into your life. If you are a mother, it was probably to no small extent due to cultural programming and your family's idealization of babies; you are a mother with a capital *M*. As the reality of baby care becomes increasingly overwhelming, you seek relief in daydreams of the career you could have had. You look at other families, and as you see other mothers adding interests to their lives that are wholly their own and earning money from them, you feel envious and think wistfully that if it weren't for your children. . . . But parenthood needn't be an insurmountable obstacle if you're serious about your work. Establish a schedule of hours during which you'll be inaccessible to your family, and post a notice of them where they can't miss it, increasing these hours as your family gradually adjusts.

Libra Rising or Sixth-House Sun (Work and Co-Workers), 6-8 P.M.: A routine job with routine hours is not your cup of poison. You want to do your own inspired thing and have that work coincide with the hours when you are naturally at your best, which may not necessarily be between 9 A.M. and 5 P.M. You tend to be a night person, engrossed in your ideas while those around you sleep. When the ideas are really flowing, you are capable of working yourself to exhaustion—but don't fail to take care of your health; your illnesses are difficult to diagnose, and it is *very* important for you to take preventive measures. In a businesslike compromise with the Puritan ethic, work for artistic survival and self-respect by establishing a minimum number of working hours each day; do your own thing, but this time keep a contract with yourself.

Virgo Rising or Seventh-House Sun (Partnerships and Public Relations), 4-6 P.M.: If anyone has ever told you to begin your relationships with caution and common sense, you probably thought they were jealous or wet blankets. You may by now have learned from painful experience that relationships entered into too quickly tend to go from blind adoration to bitter disillusionment. The fault may not necessarily lie with a deceitful partner but, rather, with your own unreal expectations about him and about such relationships in general. You are inclined to be so engrossed in the abstract concepts of partnership that few real human beings, despite their good intentions, can measure up. Disillusionment seems inevitable unless you seriously rethink your approach. In dealing with the general public, you prefer to put up a smoke screen to preserve your privacy, while presenting the image of honesty and intimacy.

Leo Rising or Eighth-House Sun (Source of Money), 2-4 P.M.: You may gain through any of the creative arts, stock investments, legacies, gifts, unemployment or welfare payments, pensions, trust funds, or profit-sharing plans. Guard against get-rich-quick schemes and any promise of money that seems too good to be true. Don't give in to the temptation of a con artist or jump into a deal with a stranger. Make it a general rule to investigate promises and the people who make them. Ask pointed questions, insist on taking time to consider each deal, and read every clause in any document *before* signing. Better yet, show all unsigned contracts to a reliable attorney. When Neptune or a Pisces planet is discordant, promises and schemes fall through.

Cancer Rising or Ninth-House Sun (Public Expression), Noon-2 P.M.: Religion and education affect you as the transmitters of cultural myths, and if you explore these ideas in your creative works you may find considerable satisfaction in publishing or films. Under discordant aspects your work may be interrupted by appearances in court (unless you protect your copyrights early). You might be a receptive follower of a popular guru and happily spread your newfound ideals. Stirred by your ideals to create a better world for yourself elsewhere, you may go so far as to dissolve your marriage, abandon the entire household (children, too), and move to a new city with a new name. Whether or not you disappear, you would feel an intense desire for a complete break with a life that has ceased to be real and meaningful for you. The more vividly you feel this, the more powerful your emotional impact on others will be.

Gemini Rising or Tenth-House Sun (Ambition/Relationship with Mother), 10 A.M.-Noon: Your mother has a strong hold on your imagination, and under discordant aspects she may have channeled her energies into any of the Neptune-ruled subversions: martyrdom, deception, hypochondria, alcoholism, adultery, or "charming" irresponsibility. In any case, she is a compelling example—positively or negatively. If she is in a creative profession herself, she may dramatize her accomplishments and glories, thus intimidating her offspring and at the same time encouraging them to follow suit. As a result, you would soon propel yourself toward fulfillment.

Taurus Rising or Eleventh-House Sun (Friendships), 8-10 A.M.: Under harmonious aspects your friends share their dramatic ideals and experiences with you. Under discordant aspects your friends can be harmfully deceptive influences—too escapist and inclined to blame others for their disappointments. Promises from them are not to be believed, especially if money or a professional break is involved.

Aries Rising or Twelfth-House Sun (Solitude and Privacy), 6-8 A.M.: You can put your imagination, Aries enthusiasm, and solitary time to good use by working energetically at your chosen art form to create something extraordinary. Under harmonious aspects the likelihood of this is greater; you might even lie to prolong your solitude. Under discordant aspects you may be on the receiving end of lies that result in unexpected and involuntary solitude, and you may overdramatize your problems. If you permit such waste to begin, depleting illnesses or self-defeating pastimes may result, eventually undermining your creative work.

Planets and Signs: A Summary

The zodiac is complicated by the fact that five planets—Mercury, Venus, Mars, Jupiter, and Saturn—rule two signs each; and three signs—Scorpio, Aquarius, and Pisces—are ruled by two planets each.

To make matters worse, astrologers suffer from the constant threat of new planets being discovered. As things stand now, in 1977, the planets' workload may be clarified as follows:

Mercury's rulership of *Gemini* stresses the quickness and versatility of the planet, while its rulership of *Virgo* stresses the didactic and detail-minded facet.

Venus's rulership of *Taurus* stresses the fondness for physical comforts, while its rulership of *Libra* stresses diplomatic skill.

Mars's rulership of *Aries* stresses the eagerness to put concepts into action, while its rulership of *Scorpio* stresses the ability to get to the crux of a problem.

Jupiter's rulership of *Sagittarius* stresses the ethical basis of religion and of justice, while its rulership of *Pisces* stresses the tendency to indulge others to the point of martyrdom and to make excuses for people who may not deserve it.

Saturn's rulership of *Capricorn* stresses the ambition that motivates years of perseverance, while its rulership of *Aquarius* contributes to ambivalence toward change and security and to persistence in scientific study.

The combination of Mars and Pluto as rulers of Scorpio tends to operate like a bullet and the intelligence directing the gun: Mars is the violent force and Pluto carefully surveys the environment, finds the places that need to be blasted open, then aims and fires.

The combination of Saturn and Uranus as rulers of Aquarius has been discussed more fully in the Aquarius section, so I won't say more here except that it is the discordant or harmonious *aspect* between these two planets that specifies how the person's nervous system reacts to unexpected change and progressive thinking.

The combination of Jupiter and Neptune as rulers of Pisces can manifest itself as an extraordinary gift for imaginative productivity—finding work that is pleasurable as well as profitable—or as overindulgence in escapist pastimes and bluffing. Again, it is the aspects that will indicate the benefit or harm this combination can bestow.

Houses

The houses are determined by a series of mathematical steps relating the birth date to the moment and to the longitude and latitude of birth.

Not only are the sizes of the houses thus determined, but also the signs on the lines beginning the houses—the cusps. These signs indicate the nature of our reactions to and treatment of the given department of life, and sometimes may be the *only* clue. In a house where there are no planets, the planet(s) ruling the cusp sign will acquire extra significance.

Fortunately, there are several constants in astrology which act as reassuring rocks among all the variables:

1. Every chart has twelve houses—never more nor less.
2. The astrological order is always Aries, Taurus, Gemini, Cancer, Leo, Virgo, Libra, Scorpio, Sagittarius, Capricorn, Aquarius, and Pisces, beginning with the rising sign (found on the zodiac wheel in the nine o'clock position) and following counterclockwise.
3. The meanings of the houses are the same from chart to chart.
4. No house is ever without a cusp sign—every department of life has at least one planetary ruler (but the more planets there are ruling a given house, the stronger that house is said to be).

As you have seen in reading about the Sun's effect on the house it occupies, certain themes are associated with each of the houses, regardless of the particular planets therein. The strongest of the houses in the chart often bring conflict, even without obstacles from other departments of life.

For our purposes, the *dominant* house(s) shall be defined as the one(s) with more planets than any of the others. A planet represents energy to burn, both physical and mental. Therefore, the more planets you have ruling a given house, the more concentrated energy you have. To simplify matters, let us establish an arbitrary three-planet minimum for a house to be considered dominant. Those of you who don't know your birth time but do know yourselves well can recognize what applies to you.

A colleague of mine facetiously calls a cluster of planets in conjunction in the same house a "clutter," a term I'll use in the following paragraphs for clarity's sake.

If the clutter is in the first house (personality), you have a powerful personality and ego, which is an asset, but can be a liability, too, depending on the harmony of the first-house planets' aspects. Your career may develop from personal associations and interests, and may require frequent in-person appearances. Your interests center upon questions of self-expression, identity, self-understanding, and self-improvement. Emotional problems may be disguised as physical ailments or accidents—especially if Mars rules the first house. You usually know what you want and how to get it, and you like to control your environment as much as possible. Unless there is a balancing strength on the opposite half of the wheel, your self-analysis may be excessive.

If the clutter is in the second house (money managing), your career may involve capitalizing your own business, a risk you prefer to take for the sake of being able to call the shots. Your most frequent question is What will this cost me? whether the currency be money, time, or personal freedom.

If the clutter is in the third house (mind and communications), your career may involve neighbors (such as door-to-door selling), communications (from installing telephone equipment to professional writing), or transportation. Relatives may be strongly influential in your professional life and your mental outlook—or interruptions when you're trying to write or study.

If the clutter is in the fourth house (home/relationship with father), your career may involve land, the home, any base of operations, and the uses to which any of these may be put. Fourth-house dominance may manifest itself in housekeeping and the departure from it to the development of an art career or a business based in the home. Related occupations include real estate, architecture, interior design, and city planning.

If the clutter is in the fifth house (sex life/creativity/attitude toward children), your life is more complicated than most, owing to the conflicts between highly personal demands (sex, miscellaneous pleasures, children) and possible professions and sublimations (art, drama, poetry). Typical fifth-house professions are entertainment, teaching young children, or anything involving speculation—from sports to the stock market. Any combination of these meanings may be important to you throughout the years. You probably have several creative outlets and wish you could really perfect *one*. Creative efforts combined with an active and intricate sex life make your existence a colorful one indeed.

If the clutter is in the sixth house (work and co-workers), you may choose a medical career, work involving food or animals, or a job in an office or factory. The problems faced—mainly centering on working conditions, efficiency, and relations with co-workers—can be causes of psychosomatic illnesses. When sixth-house aspects are harmonious your abilities are recognized and rewarded with greater ease than when there is discord, and the hours spent at work are gratifying.

If the clutter is in the seventh house (partnerships and public relations), your career may include any of the advisory professions, such as medicine, the law, psychiatry, marriage counseling, or astrology. Your most constant concern is the way people relate, starting with yourself, and you are fascinated by any study of human nature. The seventh house deals with marriage as well as advisory relationships. If the seventh house is full *and the first is empty*, you may be too aware of your partner's changing moods and interests at the expense of your own.

If the clutter is in the eighth house (source of money), you may have numerous responsibilities involving the money of others, such as in tax-return preparation, investment counseling, insurance, estate law, trusts, banking, or bookkeeping. Work relating to death—another meaning of the eighth house—is another career possibility: care for the terminally ill, mortuary management, cemetery work, or murder investigation.

If the clutter is in the ninth house (public expression), long-distance travel, publishing, radio, television, teaching, lecturing, religious work, or the law yield professional opportunities. Any of these choices involve traveling long distances for either job transfers or professional training. Legal activities of all kinds, such as testifying at a trial or suing for equal opportunities, require a ninth-house aspect.

If the clutter is in the tenth house (ambition/relationship with mother), your relationship with your mother (or your lack of relationship) is the prime motivating factor in your climb toward success. Your ambition is powerful, and fame and leadership are within your reach. The planets forming the most favorable aspects to or from the tenth house indicate the smoothest means of achieving recognition, and the best ways to deal with it once you've gotten where you want to be. If you are in a hierarchy (government, for example) you may be elected or appointed to a prestigious post and may even be blamed for something you haven't done. In general, you prefer the responsibilities of recognition to the freedoms of anonymity.

If the clutter is in the eleventh house (friendships), you are most strongly interested in social issues. Whether you focus your energies on personal friendships and clubs or on broader humanitarian concerns, dealing with people is enormously important to you. Jobs and professional opportunities may come through a friend or acquaintance, and you have an impressive network of social contacts. When the eleventh house is discordant, the influence of friends and acquaintances may prove to be against your best interests.

If the clutter is in the twelfth house (solitude and privacy), solitude is an important factor in the shaping of your personality. The more harmonious your twelfth-house aspects, the more constructively you regard and utilize your time alone. When the twelfth house is discordant, your attitude toward solitude is negative and your disappointments are overdramatized and overemphasized. A severe inability to cope with the outside world may result in hospitalization. Paradoxically, you prefer a career that requires solitary work, despite the fact that enforced solitude when you were growing up may have been a problem. Twelfth-house energy can be put to good use in research (whether in the library or the laboratory); investigation; behind-the-scenes activities such as writing, designing, astrology, statistics, strategy development, or theater production; or work in a cloistered environment (hospital, university, prison, or religious order).

Aspects

Traditional astrology has three kinds of aspects: neutral, harmonious, and discordant. The neutral aspects are the parallel (the only aspect *not* determined by zodiac signs), the conjunct, and the inconjunct (zero and five signs apart, respectively). The harmonious aspects are the semi-sextile (one sign apart), the sextile (two signs apart), and the trine (four signs apart). The discordant aspects are the semi-square (one and a half signs, or approximately $45°$ apart), the square (three signs apart), the sesqui-square (four and a half signs, or approximately $135°$ apart), and the opposition (six signs apart).

Traditional astrological concepts of harmonious ("good") and discordant ("bad") aspects are being held in abeyance as astrologers debate among themselves just how lucky trines really are. "Good" aspects—good in that events occur with few, if any, problems—tend to sour as we confront actual personalities whose charts are well endowed with these blessings. An abundance of advantages and sheltering early in life, unbalanced by "bad" aspects which establish limits and the need for strength, can develop a nature that's permissive and dependent on the generosity of others to an unhealthy extent. Later reactions to relatively trivial inconveniences—not to mention real tragedies—are out of proportion to the event. Those who have been conditioned to expect a steady stream of goodies with little if any effort have difficulty coping with setbacks, and suffer more than most the awareness of being disliked.

The "bad" aspects bring feelings of irritation, frustration, and agitation, and the need to make a decision. Discordant aspects test our strength; without problems we wouldn't begin to know the extent of our power to solve them and survive. It was Truman Capote who said, "The philosopher is grateful for every rotten thing that happens to him."

If there's one phenomenon that merits special attention in an astrological guide for women, it's the opposition—as it involves the *either/or* premise—so frequently encountered in women's lives. Following are the most familiar instances of this aspect:

If you have an opposition between planets ruling the first and seventh houses, your conflict is between the self and the other—whether that other is a marriage partner, business partner, or any stranger dealt with as an equal. With *any* opposition the alternatives are equally compelling and one of them must give way. In the case of the first and seventh houses, either self-interest or the partner's needs will be suppressed, and this could result in a break. Until that break becomes a fact, there will probably be great physical tension. Fundamental issues of self-hood are the order of the day.

If you have an opposition between planets ruling the second and eighth houses, your conflict is a financial one. Who pays for what? Whose earning power makes for dominance in the relationship? Money quarrels usually camouflage more emotional issues, which the natal chart can clarify. Astrologers check the other departments of life ruled by the planets in question, as well as the drives represented by the warring energies. If the Sun is in the aspect, it's essentially an ego-question argued in terms of dollars and cents; if the Moon, the question concerns caring; if Mercury, communication; and so on.*

---

*Venus: love and tenderness. Mars: sex and anger. Jupiter: humor, being taken for granted, or religious or philosophical differences. Saturn: oppression, selfishness, stinginess, insecurity. Uranus: independence. Neptune: cheating, misrepresentation, difference in ideals or goals, one partner's dubious—or simply naive—perception of reality. Pluto: obsession, jealousy, rebellion, dispute about group affiliations.

If you have an opposition between planets ruling the third and ninth houses, your conflict involves mental activity and the extent to which it is publicly expressed. In the chart of a writer, this can mean decisions about ghost writing, pseudonyms, how fiercely to fight for a by-line, and lawsuits to protect copyrights. This aspect also indicates family trouble between married partners, specifically the problem of division of time between one's own family and one's in-laws.

If you have an opposition between planets ruling the fourth and tenth houses, your conflict may be between your parents. Whether or not they actually separate or divorce, you may be put in a position where you must take the side of one parent and feel guilty about deserting the other. Although your parents may remain married, the tension between them produces a triangle effect on your consciousness, and ensuing anxiety. In adult life this opposition has the additional effect of conflict between the recognition for professional accomplishment and family life.

If you have an opposition between planets ruling the fifth and eleventh houses, your conflict is somewhat more complicated than a full fifth house: creative work *versus* social life, children *versus* friends, and a love life that may cost friendship and social approval. This is the opposition which seems to tear people apart the most.

If you have an opposition between planets ruling the sixth and twelfth houses, your conflicts center upon your work circumstances (to be with a company or to free-lance? to what extent to mix with colleagues?) and health (to stick with a profitable job that's ruining your health, or to quit and take a professional step down? to return to work after an illness, or to continue convalescing in a cloistered environment?).

If your aspects are predominantly squares and oppositions, don't feel sorry for yourself. The more awareness, vitality, and strength you have, the more barriers you can overcome.

PART TWO

3

Family Relations:
Woman as Parent, Daughter,
and Sibling

Despite liberation, most of us continue to be involved with our families, caring emotionally despite (at times) political conflicts. I have organized this chapter by *rising signs*, presuming that you have at least an estimate of yours with the help of the previous chapter. (If you do not have any idea of your birth time and have read the section devoted to your *Sun* sign, remember that the odds are eleven to one against the rising sign being the same as the Sun sign. *Caveat emptor*.)

The distinctions you may find between relations with one's mother and father are based entirely on the *houses*. The fourth house describes the father and the relationship with him, the tenth house the mother. Were I to talk about the Sun and the Moon in this context, I'd be skating dangerously close indeed to thin sexist ice. There is some disagreement among astrology students as to which house rules which parent: shouldn't the tenth house be the father, because the father is the more ambitious traditionally, and usually has an uninterrupted career? And shouldn't the fourth house be the mother, because the mother stays home? I doubt it. At any rate, I've found the reverse (as I will show) descriptions to be the ones that work. Ambition and mother are not strangers. Our earliest ambitions are first heard by our mothers, women whose own ambitions may have been deferred in order to bear children. Is what we want to become what *we* really want? Or do we feel forced to become what our mothers would have been themselves? Are we working hard because we have the energy or because we're proving something to our first boss and judge? When we win honors, who is it really all for? Hence, it is not farfetched to combine our career ambitions and the maternal relationship in the same house rulership. Similarly, the fourth-house dominion over both our domestic feelings and our paternal relationship has its logic: it is usually our father's dictates that determine where we live, and our fathers who show the most interest in maintaining sex-role stereotypes in the next generation. I know from personal experience that it was my father who interrupted play periods—mine, not my brother's—to teach me cooking and dishwashing (my mother didn't have the patience to explain chores to any of us). So, regardless of whether the sign is appropriately masculine or feminine, the fourth house will delineate the father, and the tenth the mother.

Aries Rising

As Parent: Leo, hence the Sun, rules your relationship to children and the question of parenthood itself. Paradoxically, this youthful, child-loving sign has long been linked to problems in conception, pregnancy, and delivery. From the day you first hold your child in your arms, you are determined that the best is none too good for it. You might overwhelm the child with pressure to be a credit to you—particularly in the case of an only child. Although it won't be easy, try hovering less and listening more to your child's wishes and choices.

As Daughter: Your first rebellions were probably against your own overprotective parents. With strict Saturn ruling the mother and tenaciously solicitous Moon energy impelling the father, it's a draw as to which of them allowed less personal latitude. If they urged you into a career that offered more tangible security than personal freedom—which can be said of some marriages!—your frustrated vitality and authority may vent itself on your child. You may rebel another way, by limiting the size of your family or by becoming involved with an art form such as the theater, which has a way of setting conservative parents' teeth on edge. Whether or not your parents' fears about your choice of lovers materialize, try not to add fuel to the emotional fire. Hear them out until they calm down; then discuss your rights in a detached, rational manner. Show more confidence in your own stability than you may feel, and gain strength by dealing calmly with the situation.

As Sibling: Early relations with siblings were probably highly ambivalent and turbulent, marred by hassles over pranks and tattling. This is due to the influence of your Aries ascendant. As you grow older you feel more of the effects of the reasonable Gemini third house, the house associated with sibling relationships. It is in adolescence that amicable relations between siblings stabilize, with the increasing likelihood of shared mental interests. Correspondence becomes frequent as soon as the oldest goes away to school and the age difference becomes progressively less important.

Taurus Rising

As Parent: Virgo on the fifth cusp gives Mercury rulership of your attitude toward children and parenthood. Before becoming a parent you devote a great deal of care and forethought to the practical measures you have to take and to the effects on your work. Once you decide to see a pregnancy through, you follow a sensible regimen carefully. The child's infancy may prove nerve-racking, but you enjoy parenthood more during the school years. You are extremely conscientious in your function as your child's teacher, but sometimes—such as when the child's friends are around—it might be best to refrain from offering corrections. Relax and allow more unselfconscious play activity.

As Daughter: Aquarius on the tenth cusp promises an unusual relationship with your mother, while Leo on the fourth cusp indicates a profound impact from your father. At times it may seem that there's as much of a generation gap between your mother and father as between your mother and yourself. On occasions when your father acts the autocrat, your mother intercedes on your behalf. Set in your ways, you're shocked when your mother thinks *you* antiquated. When you and she are at odds, it is over issues of habit *versus* spontaneity. During adolescence you may have retreated into a shell of monotony and routine, feeling threatened by maternal pushes toward independence. Independence was something you had to warm up to gradually, but once you were of age to leave home and your parents supported your move, you incorporated more progressive attitudes into your thinking. While you may rebel against paternal authority and feel threatened by your progressive mother, you share with them a certain fixity of purpose.

As Sibling: With Cancer on the third cusp, the Moon rules your relationships with siblings. Regardless of your position in the family, somehow you act more like a parent than a contemporary. The Moon's speedy motion can make for some turbulent scenes—particularly when parental relations are at issue—but you are fiercely protective of any sibling in times of trouble with outsiders. You may find yourself playing a major role in the the rearing of nieces and nephews.

Gemini Rising

As Parent: Libra on the fifth cusp gives Venus rulership to this department of life. Both Libra and Gemini undergo enormous difficulties in decision-making, and the issue of parenthood is no exception. In relating to children you are capable of childlike spontaneity, and you enjoy children's games and riddles. If you have to referee the little ones' quarrels, the due solemnity you give to the matter makes them feel important. Parenthood is not an impediment to your much-loved mobility: Gemini rising is the most likely person to pack the little one up papoose-fashion and conduct business as usual.

As Daughter: Virgo rules the paternal relationship, hence your father encourages your appreciation for books and learning. If your father actually *is* a Virgo, there may be a clash in your approaches to life. Eager to turn to a change-of-pace activity, you may disappoint him with your lack of perfectionism. Pisces rules your relationship with your mother, and her encouragement to dream about your own future is a good start in planning your career education. At times communication between you may be difficult: her memories of her own girlhood may get in the way of current dialogue, and your rhetorical jumps from one subject to another may be confusing to her. You may well feel confused yourself, caught between your father's advocacy of more work and your mother's feeling that you don't play enough.

As Sibling: Since Leo is on the cusp of the third house, the Sun rules your relationships to sisters and brothers. You make a great effort to keep in close touch with sisters and brothers, which is not always easy when one moves around as much as you do. You have a heightened appreciation for those blood relatives who have mental interests in common, although if you are the first-born you tend to be bossy and slightly autocratic. Otherwise you are more egalitarian.

Cancer Rising

As Parent: Cancer often gets sentimental about babies, and the smaller they are, the better you like them. With Scorpio on the fifth cusp, you may fixate on the issue of whether to actually go through with a pregnancy of your own. A strong believer in security for the child, you may have to defer childbearing until you can find a suitably responsible father for your baby. Once you have a child, you're tempted to hover more than may be good for it. A parent with Scorpio on the fifth house is likely to tell a child, "I know you inside and out. There's nothing you can hide from me." This is a mistake because it defies a child to test the parent's remark about his or her transparency. Although the child may pick some highly inconvenient moments to rebel and break away from the family unit, it could ultimately improve your relationship to permit the desired solitude.

As Daughter: Libra and Aries rule your relationships with your father and mother, respectively. The sometimes shy, often peace-loving Cancer may feel more affinity for the calm approach used by the father, but sometimes his detachment can be maddening. He may suggest that the other person in your youthful arguments might have been right—or at least had good cause—just to have the fun of watching you justify yourself. When this bewilders you, you may align yourself with your mother, often comparatively late in life. While before, her impatience and abruptness may have bruised your sensitive feelings, you *do* have a taste for excitement, and her style is blatantly partisan.

As Sibling: Mercury's rulership of this department of life makes you the logical choice as tutor to your siblings in their school difficulties. This situation may carry over into later life if you allow yourself to maintain a didactic attitude in your transactions with them. They can appreciate your common sense more if it is offered in a casual, offhanded way; the alternative you would wish for them must be presented as one of several choices, giving them the freedom to veto. Try not to make an issue of a rebuff.

Leo Rising

As Parent: Sagittarius on the cusp of the fifth house gives Jupiter rulership of this relationship. While you have an adventurous and enthusiastic attitude toward children, there may be physical difficulties interfering with childbirth that require your abstention from parent-hood altogether. If you should become a parent, whether through pregnancy or adoption, you have high ideals for your children's upbring-ing as ethical individuals (although your concern is more with the spirit of their standards than with religious rituals). Freedom-loving yourself, you don't want to tyrannize the fun out of them, just to make sure they're fair and square in all their dealings. Fond as you are of indulging them, if they step out of line you'd let them know where you stand. A little of that Leo authority can go a long way.

As Daughter: Taurus, hence Venus, indicates the progress of mother-daughter relations, while Scorpio rules relations with the father. Your mother's patience in dealing with you is soothing, although you are irritated at what she tolerates from other people and feel frustrated if she doesn't show enough pride and self-respect. When it is necessary for her to refuse a request, you would rather she said no directly (but not to *you*, of course) than that she evade the issue. Relations with your father may prove difficult for a different reason: he refuses too arbitrarily and, especially when you become old enough to have dates come to your home, expresses his concern for you by subjecting your friends to the third degree. What both parents have in common—with one another as well as with you—is fixity. You feel it's nigh unto impossible to change either one of them, but then you have an increasingly stubborn grip on self-sovereignty yourself.

As Sibling: Venus rules sibling relationships, owing to Libra's presence on the third cusp. Siblings are at best a source of genuine affection and moral support for you. Any problems that arise stem from slights (often imagined), or the necessity on your part to be a referee between a sister or brother and somebody else. If you are in such a difficult bind, take courage from the fact that it's because the others have such high regard for your reasoning.

Virgo Rising

As Parent: Anxiety about your own health as well as about your work makes your decision to have a child a long and trying one. Once you have a child, you begin its obedience training early. Whether or not you are juggling a career along with motherhood, you want everything to run as systematically as possible, and this means engaging the cooperation of every family member in one capacity or another. If you teach by example, even a preschool child can learn to relieve you of a simple task or two. No shirkers allowed!

As Daughter: Gemini and Sagittarius rule your maternal and paternal relationships, respectively. As has been explained in the previous chapter, Gemini and Virgo's joint rulership by Mercury creates such sufficiently different outlooks that they might as well have different ruling planets. If your mother is a Gemini herself, your differences are even more pronounced. She will try to change your procedures and make them more flexible and casual, whereas you would just as soon work doggedly at improving your efficiency. What you share is a fondness for intellectualizing problems; if the problem can be identified and articulated, it's half-solved already. Both of you may get so involved with details that you really need the Jupiterian approach your father is likely to introduce: the reminder, the *permission* to relax. A compulsive worker, you may be confused by urgings on the part of those you most want to please—your parents—to have a little fun once in a while. Do not interpret this as their failure to appreciate all that you're trying to do. They are simply looking out for your overall well-being.

As Sibling: Scorpio on the third cusp means Mars and Pluto share rulership of sibling relationships. This can be volatile, since Pluto tends to think in extremes: if you aren't one hundred percent *for* me, you're *against* me. Siblings whose charts show a fondness for moderation may not be in total agreement about a particular issue, but they are not against you. Meet them halfway; you could be pleasantly surprised to learn they are not diametrically opposed to your causes and principles.

Libra Rising

As Parent: Accustomed to dealing with people as equals, you may find the hardest part of parenthood is the daytime shortage of adult company. Aquarius is on the fifth house, making you desire time away from the little one, time to talk to your contemporaries. You are a firm believer in teaching children self-sufficiency and a healthy respect for consultation and permission. You bring up the issue of independence very early on because of your own need for breathing space, but as your children mature you'll enjoy them more. The workings of their minds will fascinate—even shock—you.

As Daughter: The Moon and Saturn rule relations with your mother and father, respectively, and these planets are as opposed in temperament as the signs they rule are in their positions on the wheel. The Moon undergoes frequent changes of mood and idea, while Saturn stays put, preferring to limit changes to improved career developments. In view of this contrast, it is just as well that you have that moderate, balanced sign,

Libra, on the ascendant. You may frequently find yourself caught
between your parents in their disagreements with one another, and you
intercede with your father on your mother's behalf more than she does
for you. As you mature, you may feel that you are more of a mother to
your mother than she is to you. Your father's conservatism may madden
you at times—he never sees the other person's viewpoint; you always
do—and you learn early to appeal to his tastes for practicality, economy,
and safety. If your father is a Capricorn, he'll be more likely to treat you
as an adult if you keep your presentation calm and matter-of-fact. For
special campaigns of yours, make an appointment for his undivided
attention—and use the time in between to prepare your case. Whatever
the outcome, his respect for you will increase as you show due respect
for his time.

As Sibling: Jupiter is the key here, owing to Sagittarius's presence on the
third cusp. You are fair, generous, and light-hearted in your dealings
with siblings. Shared ideas of fun and memories of trips taken bind you
together. Under discordant aspects there may be practical jokes that
upset the family, or humor at somebody's expense. Major business
breaks or expenses can come through a sibling's intervention or need.

Scorpio Rising

As Parent: The presence of Pisces on the fifth cusp produces the shared
rulership of Jupiter and Neptune over this sector of your life. Jupiter's
influence makes you enthusiastic about the possibility of having a child,
and you see children as natural expansions of the feeling you have for
your partner. If discordant aspects to the ascendant bring physical
problems during pregnancy and childbirth, you are doubly appreciative
of the child, treating her or him as a miraculous arrival. In fact, Neptune
and Jupiter's combined rulership gives you a tendency to idealize your
child; your first impulse is to spoil the child rotten. The fierce loyalty
that you feel will cement the bond between you, but be alert to a
possible blind spot where your child's faults are concerned. Take preventive measures by introducing structure, organization, and discipline
into the child's life in a gentle but firm manner.

As Daughter: With Leo and Aquarius on the tenth and fourth cusps,
respectively, you have the Sun indicating relations with your mother
and Saturn and Uranus to describe relations with your father. Fixed

signs on these angular houses combined with a fixed sign on the ascendant can mean deadlocks and stubbornness all around. Your reaction to what you perceive as excessive interference on your mother's part is to dig your heels in and repeat what you were doing or saying before—as often as necessary until she gets the message. Although what she wants for you is the best, you don't always agree on what the best *is*. Your father may play the detached, innocent bystander, secretly rooting for your independence—until you show a desire to be independent of *him*. You may demonstrate this independence by perversely doing the opposite of what you anticipate he'd want, a likelihood that increases if his approach strikes you as maddeningly know-it-all. You have a strong need for privacy, and don't want any parent telling you they know what you're going to do. Remember, though, that automatic opposition is as predictable as automatic obedience. As you mature, you'll find (if you haven't already) that you'll win more respectful treatment if you deal with each situation as it arises on its own merits—sometimes agreeing, sometimes refusing, but always giving the matter due consideration.

As Sibling: Saturn rules this department of life, since Capricorn is on the cusp. Whatever your place in the family, you take your sibling relationships seriously indeed. If you are the first-born, you feel as responsible as a parent for those who are younger, and suffer unduly any unfairness to which outsiders may subject a sister or brother. You adopt their trouble as your own. You may be alienated for a time by surprisingly conservative attitudes from at least one sibling. If you are not the first-born, you may feel cramped and oppressed by the parental strictness affected by those older than you. When you're very young, the first thing you comprehend is behavior that oppresses you—people who say no to you and who pry into your secrets. It takes a while before you realize that their motive is love, but by then you're set in defensive, secretive ways. In any event, you loyally stand by family in times of trouble.

Sagittarius Rising

As Parent: Jupiter rules your first house, the self, and Mars rules the fifth, your children. With two Fire signs associated with childbearing, it's very likely that your children were conceived in the throes of passion. (Fire signs, after all, seem most alive in the heat of the action!)

If you do have a child, whether accidentally or on purpose, you are most exuberant when the baby is first born, then with each of baby's progressive firsts. Although you are often cheerful and upbeat—unless your Sun sign and other chart factors indicate a gloomy, negative nature— you won't have a child run roughshod over you. When the noise gets to be too much for you, you believe in an eloquent smack on the seat.

As Daughter: Mercury, Jupiter, and Neptune give the clues to your relationships with your parents. With Jupiter and Neptune coruling your attitude toward your father, you tend to prefer his indulgence over your mother's more critical nature. You enjoy your relationship with your father, and he is largely responsible for much of your growing courage and self-esteem. (If your mother seems painfully critical of you at times, it may simply be her desire to balance the indulgence and flattery your father offers, to keep you from getting a swelled head. In relating to your mother, it helps to have a mental interest in common.) Neptune's influence makes you idealize your father to such an extent that you may never know the fallible human being he really is. It is also likely that he may be removed from your life fairly early in your development—either through divorce or death—and you will fantasize about the better life you could have had if only you had had a full-time father. Try not to give in to the temptation to blame problems on your father or lack of one. Use your abilities to improve conditions on your own behalf.

As Sibling: Saturn and Uranus corule your sibling relationships, hence there is a great deal of ambivalence. (For details on Saturn's influence on this department of life, read the preceding section on Scorpio rising.) The influence of Uranus adds insight into your siblings' motivations and makes you want to know them better as friends. Under harmonious aspects you think of your siblings as best friends who incidentally happen to be related to you, and you may increase your friendships as a result of introductions they provide. When Uranus aspects are discordant you become nervous and agitated by siblings' unreliable behavior or by news you receive of or from one of them by mail or phone. The nonconformist attitudes shared by your family, whatever the harmony of the aspects, give you a common bond with your siblings.

Capricorn Rising

As Parent: Capricorn on the ascendant suggests that personal choices such as parenthood may be deferred until later in life for the sake of the career. Venus rules parenthood, however, and once parenthood is undertaken you are as loving as you are conscientious. The earth influence impels you to plan in advance in as great detail as is humanly possible so that your professional interests do not suffer from the time taken out for parenthood. You firmly believe that the quality of time spent is more important than the quantity, and you back this up with matter-of-fact, reasoned explanations to your children. They probably enjoy seeing where you go to work each day as much as you enjoy showing them off to your co-workers.

As Daughter: Libra and Aries describe your mother and father, respectively. As with Cancer rising, the pacifism of the Libran parent is soothing, although you still wish for a more committed show of loyalty to you. Yet, unlike the Cancerian personality, you bottle up this frustration inside you. You may well feel, especially in adolescence, that neither parent understands you. Your mother's grace and poise with people is difficult to imitate—awkward politeness is more your style, especially with blind dates—and you may exaggerate in your own mind what her social ambitions for you must be. Your father's vitality and advocacy of achievement may also be intimidating for one who thinks of herself as a conscientious plodder. Don't knock yourself out anticipating paternal demands on you that don't necessarily exist. Even if they *do* exist, explain calmly that you have to make your own way at your own pace. You may impress them with your logic and maturity beyond your years.

As Sibling: Pisces on the third cusp gives two planetary rulers for your sibling relationships: Jupiter and Neptune. The Capricorn-ascendant personality tends to hold back on personal problems, particularly with younger siblings; you don't want to burden the others if you can help it. Your strong sense of responsibility and need to be heroic combine to make you strive for self-sufficiency and to shoulder your problems alone. This limitation may be therapeutic, but if you allow Saturnine gloom to set in it can lead to psychosomatic illness. Although you may think of your siblings as sheltered babies—babies you have to *continue* to shelter—they are probably more mature and resilient than you give them credit for, and would not be grateful to learn the extent to which you had shut them out.

Aquarius Rising

As Parent: The combination of Saturn and Uranus, which rule the self, and Mercury, the ruler of your attitude toward parenthood and children, makes you edgy about a major step that could limit your personal freedom. In the time prior to deciding on pregnancy, as well as in the months of pregnancy, there is an increased likelihood of erratic behavior. It is probably truer of you than of anyone else that a conservative is a liberal with children; this is merely the Saturn energy coming to the fore as you face the responsibilities of parenthood. Gemini on the fifth cusp makes for undisguised ambivalence about the entire experience. On the one hand, your personal freedom must undergo revisions, and yet you look forward to the adventure of teaching a young mind. You may make the mistake of arguing logically with the child before she or he can understand you—after all, your own voice may be the only adult voice you get to hear all day—but you'd still prefer to err on the side of bewildering the child than to embarrass both the child and yourself with baby talk.

As Daughter: Mars and Pluto rule relations with your mother, and Venus rules your dealings with your father. The maternal relationship is the more volatile one. Your mother's forceful personality, firmness, and insistence on your obedience (all the more true if she is a Scorpio) give you your lifelong taste for rebellion and independence. If your mother frequently hovers close to you, supervising the various labors you perform, you are probably going to react with a sharp, "Mother, please, I'd rather do it *myself*!" It is mainly in later life, when you gain perspective through experience, that you feel gratitude for your mother's strength. As a basically strong (stubborn, even) personality yourself, you would not have as much confidence in your own strength had you not had parental resistance. In your relationship with your father, you develop the friendliness for which Aquarius is famous (although sometimes getting words out of him is like milking a stone, particularly if he is a Tau,us). The signs ruling your relations with both parents indicate fixity, conservatism, and sometimes downright mulishness. When faced with arbitrary refusals to your pleas for independence, the temptation to do something drastic is enormous. Under a strong Uranus progression you would act first and think later, if at all. With Saturn energy dominant you would instead discuss in advance the solutions you might try, and give your family the choice of several alternatives attractive to you. Deliberate and strategic tactics will win their support more than a drastic uprooting for the sake of drama.

As Sibling: Mars as the ruler of this department of life indicates turbulence unless there are strong contraindications in the natal chart. If you are the first-born child, and a prodigy at that, you do not suffer gladly sharing the spotlight with a little sister or brother. Juvenile wrestling matches and competition in games quicken your wits and reflexes. A positive consequence of this may well be that you feel gratitude for whatever childhood occasions motivated you to compete and excel, hence warmth for your first opponents. Arguments and debates just for the sake of stirring up excitement—to keep the dust from settling—can be an enjoyable change of pace; especially after the twelfth consecutive chess game you've just won.

Pisces Rising

As Parent: With Jupiter and Neptune ruling the self and the personality, you have the greatest expectations for your personal life. With the sign of Cancer on the fifth cusp, your attitude about parenthood may undergo countless daily reversals; the Moon moves so quickly that your attitudes change quickly. On the one hand, you enjoy babies, while on the other hand, the business of caring, feeding, and diapering seems overwhelming. Visiting other people's babies doesn't really prepare you for the full impact, and when you make the commitment you may be overprotective. Cancer's inclination is to hover over the little ones. Combine this with the strong imagination of Pisces (visualizing as it will all the dangers a child can meet with) and the result boggles the mind. The kindergarten revolutionary you save may be your own!

As Daughter: Sagittarius and Gemini on the tenth and fourth cusps mean Jupiter's rulership of the mother and Mercury's rulership of the father. Partly Jupiter-ruled yourself, you tend to share with your mother ideas of fun and a conspiratorial laugh or two at the foibles of the male sex. If there is a problem in this relationship, it is most likely to be a sensitivity on your part to jokes at your expense. If you are self-conscious about a defect, you tend to build this up unreasonably in your imagination. Your relationship with your father represents both fun and confusion in your life. If he is a Gemini this duality is doubly true. Eager for a companion on his frequent spontaneous trips around the neighborhood, he would have started teaching you to walk, talk, and read before you felt ready. His tendency to vacillate may prove confusing as you try to sustain a coherent conversation, but at least you can never say your home life is boring. Chaotic, maybe. But never boring.

As Sibling: Taurus on the third cusp gives the assurance of the Earth's stability and Venus's genuine affection. Sibling relationships are highly gratifying to you, and any problems that arise most likely stem from your imagination's readiness to assume a slight or insult, regardless of conscious intent.

4

On Women and Men, For the Woman Who Hasn't Given Up Yet

Liberated women are still falling in love. With men, even. I couldn't tell you how many per day, but my practice confirms that love is still a going concern.

Earlier I merely hinted at the heterosexual goings-on. Now I'm really warming up to my subject. But this isn't going to be what Erica Jong would call a "whoreoscope," a how-to-get-him guide. You won't hear shave-your-armpits-and-agree-with-him from *me*! Nor will you get the "inside dope" on the male of each sign. No; what interests me is the interaction of all the possible combinations. (I think I've lived all the *im*possible ones!) I'm not going to tell you how to get him—just what it's like being with him—because it's entirely up to you whether he's worth the effort. This is only a book, not a butterfly net.

Aries

You're Both Aries: Aries is nothing if not fast. You begin relationships fast, break up faster, and make up again at lightning speed. You're also both assertive, unless a Pisces planet or ascendant clouds the issue. The Aries assertiveness may win your man many of the worldly benefits you'd like in your own name. If, however, he feels defeated at work or, worse, ignored, he's apt to overcompensate at home for this frustration.

You can get pretty audible yourself. If a brilliant creation of yours is slapped down on the pretext that your presentation is too "ballsy" for a woman, you won't be a cooing lovebird either! For two fiercely competitive people, nobody else seems quite as exciting, fast, dynamic, enthusiastic, or sexy as one of your own kind. Should you ever sincerely want a rest, you'd better consider separate vacations. Being together means being active, and being with someone else may seem a hassle, a bore, or a strain by comparison. If only you weren't so jealous. . . .

You're Aries, He's Taurus: As you are no doubt aware, little girls are trained to ask and work for the male's approval, to defer to his greater authority. It's when little girls grow up to become thinking women that the trouble starts. An Aries female will never ask permission; if you mention your plans or desires to a Taurus lover, it is only to keep him informed. If he understands your intent for what it is, fine. Taurus can be the best of listeners and most loyal of fans. It's when he makes the mistake of assuming you have just asked for permission that the fireworks start. He can come on like a broken record and you can expect at least one hassle in memorably earthy terms. Remember, Taurus is an Earth sign.

You're Aries, He's Gemini: It's a plus that you can both pack up and go as far as you can afford on just a moment's notice. A change of scene may be exactly what you need to rev up a routine sex life, and he's willing enough to let you lead him to the places of your choice. (While his favorite places may be bookstores, don't automatically assume that a bookish-looking man has got to be a Gemini.) Emotionally, there could be trouble when the decisiveness he loves you for starts to impress him as insensitivity, and his willingness to let you call the shots begins to strike you as monumental indifference. But, whatever else happens, your shared mental interests will prolong the relationship as a friendship.

You're Aries, He's Cancer: This relationship stands a better chance of continuing if you first meet when you feel less than your best—in a doctor's waiting room, say—and he's not so apt to be overwhelmed by your vitality. If he's receptive to your influence, it's because your enthusiasm is probably the most he's seen (outside of Yankee Stadium with the bases loaded) concentrated in one person. He needs encouragement to show his own enthusiasms—encouragement he probably didn't get from his mother. In fact, comparisons with his mother are bound to crop up, and they could damage this relationship irreparably. Aside from the fact that you hate unflattering comparisons, you feel very strongly about living in the here-and-now, a feeling that doesn't allow much room for his mooning about his mother and his childhood. He's sensitive, though, so be as kind and considerate as he is on his good days. Don't tell him his childhood is still going on.

You're Aries, He's Leo: This relationship can be a pleasure because you share a sense of adventure and drama. You probably outdo each other creating all kinds of memorable scenes: happily romantic trysts, bitter ego-hassles, teary farewells, and passionate reunions. Aries can usually forget unpleasantness once the storm clears, but Leo can be bitter. For you, Aries, once you've loved a Fire sign it's difficult, if not impossible, to switch to a "civilian." (Whoever wrote "I'd rather fight than switch" must have had Fire-sign emphasis!) The pleasure? Drama. The Problem? Perhaps too much of a good thing. His imperial delusions on the home scene may infuriate you, but his vanity cracks you up. Laughing, I mean.

You're Aries, He's Virgo: Unless he's got a planet in Leo, or perhaps you have Taurus rising, I'd be very much surprised if this combination turned into a love affair. An intellectual friendship? Maybe—if you have a mutual interest in a profession or a hobby. You might confuse respect with passion; his admiration for your ideas could be intoxicating, especially if someone else recently put you down; and your ingenuity could spark creative ideas in him which he might confuse with sexual chemistry. Even if he analyzes your relationship the way he analyzes everything else, he'd be tactful with you while he still thrills to the affair's novelty. Once he starts feeling irritated by your daring words and actions he'll be more frank. This combination is better as a working partnership than anything else.

You're Aries, He's Libra: These signs are opposites, and opposites attract. Which means, of course, that each of you has a quality the other lacks and could use. Aries eagerly plunges ahead, propelled by the force of the moment's excitement, while Libra stops and thinks and rethinks. True, Aries could do well to be more thoughtful before rushing into action, and Libra may seem definitely in need of the red-blooded Aries decisiveness. But to live in close proximity with someone who constantly finds you wanting can drive you absolutely nuts! It can drive you to glaring opposition, which is where we came in.

You're Aries, He's Scorpio: Spontaneous combustion is what it is. If there's any interest at all, it starts at the sexual level—in competition. The relationship may end over sex, too, since jealousy tends to be an issue between you. Neither of you wants to give the other any leeway, and the fighting can get pretty nasty. Aries explodes in a monologue, then forgets the cause, while Scorpio takes everything in, broods, tries cross-examination, then some more brooding. For an Aries woman just beginning to discover freedom, the Scorpio's fondness for strategy and exploration can be fascinating. It can even be helpful if directed toward career issues. Personal matters fare less well, as you'll agree if you've encountered a Scorpio who has used his grueling tactics to question you.

You're Aries, He's Sagittarius: You're both exuberant, adventurous dynamos who seem to make things happen effortlessly—anything from a practical joke for two to a bash for three hundred. Word-play and good-natured insults keep you laughing much of the time, although the Aries personality takes on a cutting edge at times. Innocence personified, the Sagittarius doesn't acknowledge any faults unless he's cornered. If you stay together it's probably because you haven't found anyone more adventurous and you're now ready to relax and settle down.

You're Aries, He's Capricorn: When you first get to like each other, you may find his quiet nature calming and steadying, and he would find you exciting. After a while, it's more like a case of an immovable object meeting an irresistible force. This is a better professional collaboration than a private one. If, for instance, you were writing a book together, you would offer much of the inspiration and enthusiasm and he would contribute the project's structure and background information. On an intimate basis your forcefulness would grate on him, and his coolness would frustrate you. Don't be surprised if his ego is hurt when you don't ask his advice before you act, or if he retaliates by withholding honest communication—or *any* communication. This strong, silent type would have appreciated the opportunity to stop you before you went off half-cocked and did something dramatic that might embarrass him. While you might benefit at times from a more deliberate approach, he still could learn a few things about openness and honesty from you. Unless he takes a more realistic attitude about women and their abilities, you may give him some rude awakenings.

You're Aries, He's Aquarius: On the positive side, you're both quick-minded, extroverted, and inclined to live at a hectic pace. Since you are both independent and tend to express yourselves abruptly (out of eagerness to get on with the action), neither one of you would be likely to make an issue out of the other's alleged indifference. Like two Ariens, you can drive each other to progressively more intense states of mania until exhaustion intervenes. The excitement and the genuine companionship add pleasure to your life, but the constant fever pitch and occasional flash-fire fights can make you both nervous wrecks. Aquarius will probably express feminist sympathies. You'll want to show him off to your consciousness-raising group.

You're Aries, He's Pisces: You're both idealistic, and probably work best together when intensely involved with a cause benefiting an underdog. You also have a love for excitement and for unusual situations in common, but your different approaches may create difficulties. Your approaches to intimacy are drastically different. The Piscean man is subtle, indirect, poetic at best, and manipulative at worst. As an Aries woman your style favors direct, blunt confrontation. You're apt to look him squarely in the eye and say, "Okay, cut the crap! What's eating you?" He'll raise an eyebrow, look at you as though you're supposed to know without asking, and quietly tear up the sonnet he was writing. You still may not know what's eating him. But then, it's even money he doesn't know either.

Taurus

You're Taurus, He's Aries: This can be a good, if brief, fling, but it could be difficult as a long-term setup. If you've been stuck in a rut, the exciting, whirlwind Aries may be just what the doctor ordered. If you think of the affair as an adventure and don't build castles in Spain, the experience is more likely to be positive. Taurus tends to fixate, while Aries has a roving eye, so don't kid yourself.

You're Both Taurus: Your mutual fondness for material comforts and luxury makes you respect each other's chosen living arrangements, and your need for emotional continuity gives the relationship hope for a long stretch. Both of you are inclined to economy—of words as well as money—and you may settle prematurely into a rut. Although you might marry young and happily, you could later feel discontented because you had missed worthwhile experiences. Don't look critically at your partner as the source of your limited existence; it was what you both wanted and needed at the time.

You're Taurus, He's Gemini: You and he share a fondness for exploring the pros and cons of the most pragmatic of problems; indeed, Gemini looks into all kinds of problems sooner or later, if not for long. It's an intellectual deep knee-bend of his. He may think your needle is stuck in a monetary groove much of the time, and you may well be annoyed at his scattering of his energies. If only he would concentrate some of that brilliance, his career would really be something to write home about. Although it makes sense to hate waste of any kind, including human, if you talk in those terms don't be surprised if he says you're materialistic and *thing*-oriented. He's hurt that you imply he's a thing that's being wasted. And you're hurt that he thinks you're a stick-in-the-mud. Have you thought of taking a course together? Gemini is a perpetual student, and you might find a course that's beneficial for you both, personally or professionally.

You're Taurus, He's Cancer: You both enjoy good music, food, the tangible comforts of home, and family life. Continuity with a select few people can make or break your health—you both know this very well—so you both make active efforts to keep your private world an emotional haven. You're both so practical that you may forego travel for the sake of economy. But there's a difference: you merely like to make sure of value received, while he's downright stingy.

You're Taurus, He's Leo: Both fixed signs, you pride yourselves on your talent for sustaining love and, in fact, hanging in there for the long haul is your greatest strength. You can also be stubborn; neither of you is willing to budge an inch. This can be stormy.

You're Taurus, He's Virgo: Both Earth signs, you share tastes for sensual pleasures and enjoy similar attitudes toward economy and hard work. The Venus influence of Taurus makes you gravitate toward aesthetic interests and at the same time makes you highly sensitive to criticism of your artistic efforts. Mercury's influence on Virgo, however, makes for a severe and relentless critic. Brace yourself for wounded feelings—and never show him unfinished work.

Your're Taurus, He's Libra: Both Venus-ruled signs, you value gracious living highly and treat each other with courtesy and respect. Both eager to please, you may overdo your avoidance of the realistic confrontations that adjustment entails. This is the household where one partner eats a vegetable he can't stand night after night but would rather suffer in silence than hint at less-than-perfect harmony and pleasure. A little more assertiveness can only help you.

You're Taurus, He's Scorpio: You are both exhaustingly self-critical and exhaustingly stubborn. This is another example of opposites attracting, and the most probable arenas of head-on opposition are jealousy and sex. The Taurus personality is romantic and fond of tender foreplay, while the Scorpio's ability to disregard the frills sometimes alarms his more sensitive partner. The Scorpio may also give in to the temptation to arouse jealousy, to preserve his defenses by permitting the nearest woman to love him while seemingly feeling nothing in return. This can bring out your stubborn determination to stick with him, rationalizing, "After all I've suffered, after all the time I've devoted to you, I'm not about to step aside and let some other woman get you now." The Scorpio man may well brag, "No woman is going to tame me," but no doubt he certainly enjoys watching someone try.

You're Taurus, He's Sagittarius: You both like the material things in life. For you, a designer label represents status, while he says that quality means comfort—and why not have the best? Of the two, you are the more practical; you like beauty but you hate waste. He, on the other hand, is an impulse buyer and he doesn't share your patience for comparison shopping. In love you may experience jealousy—the Sagittarian is notorious for his roving eye—and may escalate an incident into a breakup. It doesn't have to be hopeless, though; he prides himself on being fair and may actually have a take-it-or-leave-it attitude about other women.

You're Taurus, He's Capricorn: You're both clear-thinking realists and hard workers; frivolity is seldom a problem he'd threaten you with. If anything, you'll probably find yourself wishing he would devote slightly less time to business and more to you and your social life. This combination makes a particularly good working team.

You're Taurus, He's Aquarius: You respect one another's fixity, but you respect your own steadfastness even more. He seems more dedicated to his causes and group concerns than he is to his private life, leaving you to shake your head in bewilderment at his last-minute cancellations. Paradoxically, he is deeply wounded in the face of accusations of negligence. The most hopeful feature of this combination is a shared liking for people.

You're Taurus, He's Pisces: You both enjoy aesthetic pastimes, but he may be quietly hurt if you aren't more enthusiastic about him or more obvious in your show of affection. On the whole, the value you both attach to serenity, peace, and the emotional continuity from one person's sustained caring makes you work hard to keep this relationship alive.

Gemini

You're Gemini, He's Aries: As with the Aries woman-Gemini man pair, you're both restless and recognize this trait instantly in the other. When the Aries personality becomes especially bossy, the Gemini may retaliate by playing the moving-target game. On the whole, a quick and lively partner such as Aries could spoil you for a quieter but steadier man.

You're Gemini, He's Taurus: You're both sociable and like to take advantage of all the cultural events your city has to offer, no matter how much running around you've done all day in pursuit of your careers. Of the two, the Taurus is the more likely to opt for an occasional quiet evening at home. Unless you have quieting Taurus planets in your own chart, you chafe at what will seem like a leash around your neck. You may rebel, too, if this partner tries to convince you of the wisdom of concentrating your energies.

You're Both Gemini: You're most likely to meet through your work (mental and verbal work, of course) and to enjoy a continuation of light-hearted banter in person or over many pleasurable telephone conversations. Probably nobody anywhere has a higher phone bill than a couple of Geminis pooling resources. Nervous tensions that arise every now and then can be overcome when both are willing to listen and adapt a little.

You're Gemini, He's Cancer: Whether for business or pleasure, you're more likely to be on the road than he is. This may be the ultimate cause of the breakup when, typically, you walk out despite his emotional protests. This is a strange combination and, unless you're willing to have your wings clipped, an ill-fated one.

You're Gemini, He's Leo: You both enjoy moving about town, and he appreciates your spontaneous humor, but watch it: no jokes at his expense. That Leo ego is very sensitive! Your standards of fun may diverge slightly: to him, it's taking you somewhere to be seen, a place with snob appeal; to you, it's being with people you can talk to—which may or may not be the same place. Tread cautiously. He means well.

You're Gemini, He's Virgo: Both Mercury-ruled signs, you enjoy mental work, conversation, puzzles, and games of strategy; but on the whole, you probably make a better team as co-workers than you do as lovers. This stems from the fact that Gemini tends to skip from one project or interest to the next as soon as boredom arises, while Virgo tends to do things methodically and meticulously, to the point of perfection. In love Gemini would opt for spontaneity and would be turned off by Virgo's emphasis on technique and hygiene.

You're Gemini, He's Libra: Both are Air signs, and this is traditionally a good combination. Both signs are sociable and crave human exchange; if there's any drawback, it's that Gemini may have more than one lover while Libra favors the more orthodox monogamous partnership.

You're Gemini, He's Scorpio: Definitely an unlikely and peculiar combination! If such a couple has lasted together for five years or more, I'd like to hear how you managed it! As a Gemini you are much too restless to want to work at taming the untamable Scorpio man and much too intelligent to arouse his jealousy and thereby tempt irreversible wrath. This mating of the most fickle of the signs with the most jealous takes a very special nervous system or generosity of heart to sustain.

You're Gemini, He's Sagittarius: These two opposite signs will probably find a great deal of fun together. Both are adaptable, spontaneous, and enjoy the humor inherent in everyday life. Problems may arise because Gemini tends to fuss too much over details and Sagittarius tends not to fuss enough. As a matter of fact, it's only in comparison to the Sagittarius that a Gemini can seem fussy at *all*. As a rule, the Gemini personality shares the Sagittarian's flexibility.

You're Gemini, He's Capricorn: Unless you met at a time when you were confused about your career and he was in a position to offer some crucial advice, it's unlikely you would have had any spark of interest in each other. Your pacing is different and so are your interests. You may think him difficult in a conversation—too economical with words, as with money—and he may think you a scatterbrain because of your overwhelming diversification. For him, focus and concentration mean security as surely as money in the bank.

You're Gemini, He's Aquarius: You're both quick-witted and spontaneous, but he exceeds you in inventive genius. You both value friendship and tend to enjoy the friendships you formed as individuals in addition to those you sustain as a couple. This is a happy combination, particularly since you are both genuinely capable of giving one another breathing room.

You're Gemini, He's Pisces: You share a fondness for travel, cultural events, and spontaneous forms of fun and games. If you are both free to travel, either locally or on major trips, the bond between you is likely to be an especially strong one. The Piscean personality is highly sensitive. Don't wound him with flippant words if you want to keep his friendship.

Cancer

You're Cancer, He's Aries: His take-charge attitude can easily knock you off-balance—an event that wouldn't disturb him too much. It may not be fashionable to admit it these days, but he *does* take pride in his machismo. For a woman new to the strengths of feminism, you may soon feel he sets your cause back by a few years. His enthusiasm and flair for excitement make him a tempting companion, but his unwavering self-confidence can make it difficult to assert yourself as an individual. This is a better combination for a short, exciting whirl than for a sustained, intimate relationship. You'll probably be more comfortable with an egalitarian Air sign or with Taurus, Leo, or Scorpio.

You're Cancer, He's Taurus: This is one combination of Sun signs I'd recommend sight unseen. Both signs are ruled by planets associated with kindness and consideration, and are therefore likely to meet each other halfway. Also, both signs like people—but in small, quiet, intimate doses; a small dinner party for six or eight people is infinitely preferable to a noisy blast of wall-to-wall strangers. Both signs are noted for steadfast affection and a deep love of emotional continuity. If one or both of you has natal Mercury in the adjacent sign Gemini, it's an added blessing for keeping mental interests and communication alive. Of course, a contented silence every now and then is a pleasure you can both appreciate.

You're Cancer, He's Gemini: You both enjoy travel, particularly to places where you can swim or sail. Frequent changes of scene delight both of you as long as there are plenty of other people around for spontaneous parties and you can get some decent meals. Should problems arise between you, it is most likely because you feel hurt by his limited attention span and he feels crowded by your possessiveness.

You're Both Cancer: Probably no one but another Cancer can give the extensive reassurance a Cancer is inclined to crave. If anything suggests inbreeding, it's this blend; this is the sign most likely to marry a cousin and keep the family circle a closed one. Whether or not you ever have children, you ought to think about expanding your social circle. In this particular combination it is a good idea to have your charts compared and progressed. To security-loving Cancerians, settling down can often mean settling down to stifling quiet and to mediocre incomes.

You're Cancer, He's Leo: If you've ever mooned over romantie fairy tales or watched soap operas by the hour, here's a chance to live those scripts! Leo is nothing if not theatrical, and he'll take great pride in introducing you to scenery and supporting characters you'll always remember. Your relationship itself may seem like a soap opera at times, with dramatic separations and reunions. A Leo man may take as his royal due the affection and cooperation of those—especially women—who orbit around him. That's how *he'd* put it. You may find that it takes all the courage you can muster to set him straight about that satellite business. He's going to believe what he wants to! If you're hooked on the drama and the noble ambitions of this man, and you want to keep the excitement he offers in your life, you'd probably be better off with a separate-residence arrangement.

You're Cancer, He's Virgo: He brings out the efficiency expert in you, while you make a humanist out of him. This may prove a more satisfying work relationship than love affair; you share high standards and know good work when you see it—but he wouldn't let up on the home front. He's the one most likely to check the beds for hospital corners! Unless you're exceptionally thick-skinned, as a Cancer you may find his criticisms difficult to endure.

You're Cancer, He's Libra: Aesthetic interests make a good beginning for a bond here, but emotional questions can upset the balance that Librans—that *both* of you—deeply need. The Cancer personality is capable of and expects total emotional commitment and loyalty, while the Libran tries to be fair and impartial at all costs. Blind devotion is not in the Libran's vocabulary, and as you dry your tears over some unintentional slight, the Libran will probably look at you, all injured innocence, and say, "I was just trying to be *fair*."

You're Cancer, He's Scorpio: If you don't come on like the jealous female the Scorpio male expects, you'll bewilder him and have him wondering what you're up to. To live harmoniously with this mate you have to be mercilessly analytical and honest with yourself. Instead of saying "He wants me! Full speed ahead!" allow a little extra time to ask yourself, "But what do *I* want? What am I or am I not willing to invest of myself?" On the positive side, you can probably learn more with a Scorpio about self-improvement and overcoming one's own drawbacks than with any other sign but Virgo.

You're Cancer, He's Sagittarius: You both have an offbeat sense of humor, and Sagittarius enjoys making you laugh because 1) his ego gets a benign thrill that he's got the power to do so and 2) he likes the sound of your laugh and wants to hear it often. You both like good living—particularly rich, well-made food. If there are any problems, they're due to logistics (he likes to wander spontaneously, you like to stay home) or that humor again: jokes he makes at your expense. You might be anxious about other women, too, although he's probably too lazy and casual to cultivate a serious extracurricular relationship.

You're Cancer, He's Capricorn: This is a fortunate combination in that both signs value security—material and emotional—and habitually consider the other person first. Each finds reassurance in the steadiness of the other, in the regularity of daily schedules and the other's dependable presence, but your emotional thermostats are diametrically opposed. The Cancer is demonstrative, particularly when unable to get a perceptible reaction from the other person, while Capricorn can be self-contained and stoic. As with Virgo, you will probably make an ongoing attempt to humanize the pragmatic Capricorn. If you don't mind Machiavellian politics and constant talk of strategy, structure, order, hierarchy, system, management, compartmentalization, and power in the running of your private life, you'll probably never lose sleep wondering where he is at night.

You're Cancer, He's Aquarius: You probably enjoy his sense of humor; he makes you laugh when you least expect to. Introducing him to your friends at parties is a pleasure because he's such a good listener. Brace yourself for last-minute cancellations or disappearances, but don't throw anything until you've heard him out. He's usually telling the truth about 1) forgetting (no, he doesn't often think up white lies to soften the impact), or 2) some mechanical gadget, like his car, that thwarted him. Another frequent reason for inattention is his absorption in a cause, particularly some humanitarian movement like civil rights. As a woman with a cause of your own, would you want someone without a social conscience?

You're Cancer, He's Pisces: You both have vivid imaginations and a reluctance to make waves (a frequent expression, by the way, of Water-sign people). You enjoy sharing cultural pleasures, and each adores the other's finesse with other people's sensibilities. Both of you are idealistic; you might have dreams of having or adopting children together. A snag in the relationship, however, is the inclination of each to fantasize about the other's infidelities and assorted other sins—without ever asking a direct question.

Leo

You're Leo, He's Aries: Volatile Fire-sign people both, Leo-Aries could be a dramatic pairing that spoils you for more serene men. His initial enthusiasm bowls you over, leaving a permanent impression on your memory, but his equally quick shift to the next attractive prospect could seriously wound your vulnerable Leo ego.

You're Leo, He's Taurus: His reliability makes you feel secure, but you can't help wishing he'd speak more romantically. Or even use more words. I won't say it can't work—your own Hollywood concept of romance is probably the major stumbling block—but you have more than your share of communication difficulties. Even if you didn't have Leo's need for flattery and deference, you'd still need some soul-satisfying discussions. If you can't play out the scene that's nagging at you, you'll have difficulty devoting much thought to anything else until the problem is resolved.

You're Leo, He's Gemini: With Gemini you won't, of course, have to worry that he isn't talking enough. If anything, he'll talk your ear off and make it tough for you to keep up your end of the conversation. You'll probably think him good company—he has an intriguing intellectual curiosity about the places and people you want to show him—and problems might arise should you 1) find you're not the only woman in his life and/or 2) notice he tends to be satirical and tongue-in-cheek about the romantic adventures you regard seriously. Leo, a Fire sign, is passionate; Gemini, an Air sign, is cerebral. You can, though, find a common ground in your enthusiasm over shared interests.

You're Leo, He's Cancer: You both need a partner to brag about; if one—preferably both—of you enjoys a prestigious position in your career, the relationship stands a better chance. Cancer's domestic streak makes him the perfect house-husband for the woman on the rise. You may disagree about the frequency of your parties (for you, the more the merrier) or the size of the guest lists, but as long as you confine your bickering to trivia you'll enjoy emotional security for years.

You're Both Leo: If this pair ever gets together, it's because of the harmony of different-sign ascendants and other parts of the chart, for the Leo usually prefers to "marry down" to improve the fortunes of someone with fewer attributes—someone who will be duly grateful for and improved by the association. In short, Leo has a little difficulty with equal relationships, owing to the Sun's rulership, which manifests itself as a royalty complex. If there isn't any real equal, Leo might as well share the wealth with someone who needs it. There really *is* nobility in the Leo spirit, and it shines best when there's no would-be boss or usurper hovering around.

You're Leo, He's Virgo: You have a healthy regard for yourself, physically and psychologically, and have reason to believe from all those compliments you get that you're conducting your life just fine; perfectly, even. So it may well come as a shock when that Virgo man you know looks you in the eye and tells you your hair color is brassy or your blouse is all wrong for your suit. Virgo's brutal honesty would be a lot easier to take if he limited his "constructive" comments to occasions when the two of you were alone and if you learned to take it less personally. If you could share a common interest, such as an art or a craft, it would go a long way toward cementing your relationship.

You're Leo, He's Libra: You both love an overly romantic courtship, and you both want the best of everything life has to offer. Devotees of elegance and style, neither will knowingly offend the other's aesthetic sense. Difficulties that may arise are most likely to stem from your differences in steadiness: Leo is the more faithful of the two and would long retain the hurtful memory of being other than number one in her lover's priorities.

You're Leo, He's Scorpio: While Scorpio would be proud that a magnetic and sexy Leo woman has chosen him, he may at the same time be jealous if you are a more attractive physical specimen than he is. As you both have incredibly fierce pride, it may take days for one of you to muster up the nerve to apologize after a fight. You both respect privacy and can trust the other with your secrets. The desire for *someone* and the need not to be left alone can keep you together long after desire for this particular other person has gone. It's perfectly respectable for a woman to go it alone, so be honest with yourself and with him. Whether you marry or not, you may yet salvage a durable friendship.

You're Leo, He's Sagittarius: It's highly likely you would meet on vacation, since you both love travel a great deal; he even more than you. Sagittarius arouses you like an adrenalin shot, and with him you soon feel that your outlook is younger. If you've ever adapted to a man by subduing your natural high spirits, you'll celebrate vigorously not having to with him. Should you separate—temporarily or permanently—it would most likely be because he feels taken for granted, or a flippant remark of his has hurt you. The hearty humor you both enjoy can help ease the tension.

You're Leo, He's Capricorn: You both have respect for power and authority; sometimes it seems more like reverence. Leo, however, is more of the royalist in temperament, while Capricorn suffers chronic self-doubt and works harder than most to conceal and overcome it. With Capricorn any height can be attained—regardless of natural advantages or disadvantages—as long as he's willing to put in hard work. He tends to see costs in terms of man-hours spent working to earn the money, and he won't be too keen about slaving away so that a woman can sit at home in luxury. He is essentially a traditionalist, although he hopes that his wife will be willing to work by his side. Leo's hunger for recognition should be motivation enough to build a distinctive career. An emotional snag that may arise is the gap between the affection Leo desires and the notoriously undemonstrative style of the Capricorn. This combination is better for a business alliance, with Leo as the promoter and Capricorn shaping the organization and budget.

You're Leo, He's Aquarius: Both signs are fond of socializing, but their individual styles are diametrically opposed (they are, remember, opposite each other on the zodiac wheel). Leo is interested in individuals and evaluates each new acquaintance on her or his own merits. Leo likes to use theatrical effects when entertaining at home, such as themes or games, and enjoys listening to the romantic adventures other people may discuss. Aquarius, however, is more of a sociologist at heart, listening to others with a view to how they are typical of their socioeconomic, racial, occupational, or astrological peer group. He can listen to strangers for so long that his intimates often complain of neglect. Leo-Aquarius can level off to a platonic friendship after the romantic experiment—which is what *he'd* call it—is out of the way.

You're Leo, He's Pisces: A love for drama and poetry can bind you together intellectually and romantically, and your mutual talent for histrionics would probably result in a lulu of a love affair! He may become difficult to communicate with if he feels you've been neglecting him or have been less than honest. Only then would he succumb to the temptation to enjoy a secret affair to restore his eroded ego. When that happens, don't wallow in self-pity. Feel sorry for the *other* woman: remember, she doesn't know the half of it!

Virgo

You're Virgo, He's Aries: This is a very odd couple indeed, a blend of temperaments like oil and water. The Aries approach is damn the torpedoes, full speed ahead, and he's not likely to express himself calmly and gently when his Virgo companion lingers behind to examine details. However necessary such details may be, you have to stretch your good intentions to the fullest for tactful ways to tell him he neglected to think about some very important preliminaries. He's likely to accuse you of nagging—accusations which can freeze a woman and stifle further exchange. If your life has been sheltered and uneventful before meeting him, you might well mistake your latent fondness for mental stimulation for attraction to *him*. As with the Aries woman-Virgo man combination, this relationship is better as a business team.

You're Virgo, He's Taurus: This can be a solid and comfortable association, since businesslike Virgo isn't likely to demand words of love and monosyllabic Taurus is satisfied to leave it at that. What he says voluntarily is fine, of course, but Virgo isn't about to ask leading questions. There are too many more constructive things to do with time! Between these two thrifty signs there is less than perfect agreement about what constitutes luxury and what should be bought with the occasional tax refund or bonus. Taurus would opt for a piece of sculpture—art can appreciate in value—while Virgo would rather invest in equipment for the work area. As you thrash out this conflict, he'll find he's more than met his match in you. The famous Taurus silent treatment doesn't faze you. Mercury's rulership of Virgo makes you articulate and inclined to feel contempt for the nonverbal person who won't enter into reasonable discussions.

You're Virgo, He's Gemini: You have Mercury's rulership in common and you're both avid readers and travelers. Virgo is more stable, however, and is pained by Gemini's tendency to fritter away time and talents on dilettantism, while Gemini deplores your lack of spontaneity. Difficult communications are better than none, for both of you.

You're Virgo, He's Cancer: This promises to be a comfortable combination, as you both like peace and quiet (especially Cancer) and an orderly home life (especially Virgo). Both signs are famous for a keen love of food, but their approaches are somewhat different. Cancer loves to keep refilling the family's plates and puts a high value on homemade food. Virgo would just as soon say no to seconds (cholesterol, you know) and quote newspaper accounts of the latest food-poisoning episode. Virgo is more methodical about diet, nutrition, and health care; Cancer is more emotional, hating to see anyone leave the table hungry. Arguments may start with questions of domesticity, cooking, or who does what around the house, and end up anywhere!

You're Virgo, He's Leo: Any home you occupy jointly would be an impressive stage set to show off the talents of both. Leo is a firm believer in entertaining business associates, and in his own home, among his prized possessions, he shines most brightly. Virgo likes to have people in if they are good conversationalists—and if they admire Virgo's crafts experiments, so much the better. As with the Leo woman-Virgo man pair, criticism of the Leo by the Virgo can be a constant source of problems. Complaining in general does not sit too well with the Leo personality, as he prides himself on being above pettiness.

You're Both Virgo: You have a great deal in common, in both positive and negative ways. Observant to the nth degree, you notice problems, errors, and deviations from specific standards more than any other sign of the zodiac. Knowing that the other can be as upset as you by a safety pin on a hem or a lump in the mashed potatoes, you can anticipate problems and eliminate them before they occur, freeing your time and your minds for more important—intellectual—discussions. You are both duly appreciative of the other's attempts to minimize your trivial problems, and enjoy articulate conversations. Come the day one of you feels humiliated by one correction too many in front of others, suddenly nothing that the other does, says, wears, or eats is right; no grounds for divorce can be too small!

You're Virgo, He's Libra: Your shared fondness for elegance and clarity in your environment is your happiest common ground. You can discuss questions of form and symmetry for hours! Virgo should be the keeper of the checkbook; without restraint, the Libran is likely to spend frivolously on clothes and personal trinkets. To slow his extravagance down, you should use humor rather than stern criticism, which he'd soon tune out. While staving off the specter of debtors' prison, show him by example that you don't have to be extravagant to be decorative—with ingenuity, taste, and sensible, healthy habits you can qualify as a suitable companion for a Beau Brummel! He's not stupid. He'll get the message.

You're Virgo, He's Scorpio: You're both self-improvement mainliners, demanding the most of yourselves to ward off painful criticism from anyone else. You each respect the other's knowledge, hunger for learn-ing, and analytical capabilities; you just don't want excessive analysis by the other—it makes you feel threatened, naked. Your attitudes toward sex often separate you, as Virgo can do without more easily than Scorpio can. During sex the Virgo can be insultingly aware of technique, putting a damper on Scorpio's more emotional passion. This combination stands a better chance as a platonic friendship or a business partnership.

You're Virgo, He's Sagittarius: With the exception of a mutual interest in education, this relationship is difficult to comprehend. Temperamen-tally, these two signs are poles apart: Virgo is a finicky planner while Sagittarius enthusiastically (and sometimes sloppily!) plunges ahead on a gamble. Virgo can get so bogged down in details, though, that a relaxed Sagittarian may be a godsend. Sagittarius, for his part, can benefit from Virgo's wisdom in advance scouting and starting a project fully pre-pared. Combining work solidifies the foundation of this marriage.

You're Virgo, He's Capricorn: Stable and reality-oriented, you can both become workaholics for the sheer pleasure that professional attainment gives you. Capricorn gets his kicks from the climb up the ladder; single-mindedly, he keeps his eye on his destination and remains bliss-fully obsessed by all that he has to overcome to get there. Virgo, also interested in office politics, studies each step of the way as if it were a chess game. Unless the Virgo chart has some Libra energy favoring social life, you're in danger of a highly lopsided life together. A happy side effect of this seemingly grim work obsession is that neither is likely to pout because the other spends too much time at the office. Ambition is the most understandable thing in the world—for you both.

You're Virgo, He's Aquarius: You'd probably meet in a night-school class you took to advance in your job. That is, *you'd* be after advance-ment, while he'd be there to study the people who'd take such a course, and besides, it gets him out of the house once a week. All goes well at the restaurant afterward—talk is a strength for both of you—but somehow you find yourself confusing friendship and intellectual stimulation with something else. Which is odd, because your self-analysis is usually so clear and *right*. In his company you can be sure your brain is getting a healthy workout, but your nervous system is getting mysteriously fraz-zled. You're an orderly, regular, reliable, punctual person; and he's erratic, chaotic, often late, or even absent altogether. Trying to figure out how much of it to take personally can drive a systematic person like you up a tree!

You're Virgo, He's Pisces: He probably appeals to the stifled streak of poetry and laziness in you, and you feel ambivalent as to whether to get involved with him. His creative work, possibly free-lance life-style, and unusual way of seeing things and of goofing off send you right back to your analyst. Should your Pisces man drink heavily, take drugs, or be hiding a wife from you, you may need *twice* as many fifty-minute hours a week. If those unhealthy habits of his make you want to hang up on him, yet at the same time you're irresistibly attracted to him, it will probably be an on-again-off-again relationship. You want him to bring some romance into your life without dragging you under. At the same time, you want to bring some system and order into *his* life without being rejected as a nag. This relationship is better as a vacation fling than as a full-time romance.

Libra

You're Libra, He's Aries: This combination of zodiac opposites can be a strong attraction initially. With each having a quality the other needs for balance, you can learn an important lesson during the brief time you have together. I say *brief* because of the theory I have about opposition relationships: once the attraction of opposites is established, and you have succeeded in internalizing some of the partner's unique strengths which you don't have, the need to stay together diminishes. Besides, it's rare that a person would want a long-term reminder of past inadequacies. The specific dynamics of the Aries-Libra combination can be found in the Aries section.

You're Libra, He's Taurus: Both Venus-ruled, you value the amenities and beauties you can add to everyday life. You are both eager to please, often overdoing pacifism at the expense of your peace of mind. In times of conflict you are the more likely to clear the air, while he inclines toward silence of epic duration. Most of the time you maintain a veneer of poise or lightheartedness, and this is probably a major reason why he chose you in the first place. He takes things too much to heart at times, and is so afraid he might do lasting damage that he hates to open his mouth at all (and is therefore prone to constriction ailments—laryngitis, constipation—that symbolize the censorship he has imposed upon himself). To a diplomatic Libran whose favorite sport is negotiation, refusal to talk to you is an offense that wounds deeply. Lessons in assertiveness could be the best thing that ever happened to the two of you.

You're Libra, He's Gemini: Both Air signs, you enjoy and are very good at talking for fun and profit. I once knew such a pair who could stay up all night playing bridge or psychoanalyzing their friends. Probably any other man would throw a pillow at you by 3 A.M.! If there's a separation it's because Libra is more romantic and Gemini more cerebral. If you come to feel that his heart just isn't in the candy-flowers-poetry approach, you might impulsively pull away from him. If you stop and think it over (as usual) you'll probably see it a bit differently: he may not take to classical courtship forms naturally, but if he does it's because he doesn't want to lose you. And there's nothing wrong with that!

You're Libra, He's Cancer: You both enjoy cultural events, especially music. You like to eat well and you will with him, solidifying many worthwhile friendships over a good table. As with the Cancer woman-Libra man pair, the problem comes in the different ways of evaluating interpersonal situations: Libra thinks more abstractly and can be maddeningly ambivalent. Cancer's wholehearted support or censure is based on a gut-level emotional response.

You're Libra, He's Leo: Your shared fondness for high-style living and all forms of luxury would cement your friendship whether romance lasts or not (unless, of course, one of you spends the other's money till bankruptcy). You may disagree about the companions you socialize with, and this issue can become intense if you feel that he's misplacing his precious loyalty on an undeserving flatterer with ulterior motives.

You're Libra, He's Virgo: Libra, like Virgo, can be a perfectionist, and would never stint on self-care. The Virgo, who has a severely critical way of seeing things, may say a deflating word or two about the new garments you bring home, and because he is also economical you may dismiss his comment as stinginess. On the positive side, he likes your taste. When he's critical he's disappointed because he believes you're capable of better; and although his idealized mental picture of you is flattering, it may be hard work to live up to it. Through it all, you both respect each other's intellect and frequently ask for objective advice. You know you'll get it.

You're Both Libra: Sophisticated works of art, especially symmetrical ones, would be abundant in any home you shared, as would projects you had done yourselves. You both enjoy talking, particularly about hypothetical moral dilemmas, and may even suffer severe depressions if separated for any length of time. It isn't so much a passionate love affair (unless you have Scorpio planets between you forming a conjunction) as a continuing dialogue. To have to do without the second voice is like doing without air!

You're Libra, He's Scorpio: That balancing scale keeps dipping back and forth as you silently deliberate if this is a situation you want to get into. He certainly fascinates you; you've probably never before met anyone who makes a decision as fast as he does—and then won't budge an inch from it. You can't help admiring that. *But*—and Libra never makes a decision without two or three *buts*—you're a little put off by the speed with which he's moving in. Literally! He's the one most likely to bring in his clothes and tennis racket before you can finish saying your first "Why don't we"! You're nervous, too, because he asks all those questions about your past men, about where you were last Tuesday when you said you were working late, and don't you agree your secretary has the hots for him. . . .

You're Libra, He's Sagittarius: You enjoy him, but sometimes you get the spooky feeling you were his mother in a previous life. You often watch him with his buddies, and as they become engrossed in their sometimes sophomoric locker-room jokes and pranks, you lovingly shake your head and say, "Boys will be boys." He loves you for being such a good audience, but his humor may go to extremes if he thinks you're not relaxed enough. When his jokes are at another's expense, you turn cool instead of laughing, and he just tries harder to get you to crack a smile.

You're Libra, He's Capricorn: If, to paraphrase Antoine de St.-Exupéry, instead of facing each other you face the outside world together, you stand a good, fighting chance to make it. You both like the good things that money can buy. And if you're both career-minded and are earning full-time salaries, the odds get better every day. I've seen one instance where this wasn't the case; the Libran wife wanted both the "family's" jobs to be her husband's so she could live a life of leisure by the pool, and the marriage died a slow, agonizing death. Capricorn has too much respect for the sweat of his brow to want to slave his way to a solitary stroke. Another such combination, where the wife worked in a gratifying occupation, fared considerably better.

You're Libra, He's Aquarius: Both signs are sociable and hunger for stimulating intellectual contact. To a large extent Libra and Aquarius provide this for one another, but neither is satisfied with just one person to talk to. Libra is a receptive listener who can bring out Aquarius's wit, but suffers more keenly than most when the whimsical Aquarius disappears.

You're Libra, He's Pisces: Here's another type who can upset your hard-won balance: the poetry in his soul is reminiscent of a romantic Fanny Hurst novel, but when he's remiss with his promises you want to drown him! He can become increasingly difficult to get through to—he tunes out easily—when he feels you're emotionally detached; he wants someone whose passion is at least as intense as he thinks his is. (I say *thinks* because he's not above a little role-playing when he's bored. Pisces can be the con man of the zodiac when he wants to be.)

Scorpio

You're Scorpio, He's Aries: Did you blink? Then you missed it! The Scorpio-Aries effect is like a flash fire. These signs, because they are Mars-ruled, are especially highly sexed, and when they lock eyes across a crowded room everybody in between can sense something has happened. As both try to be dominant and to overwhelm, and both would stand their ground (if they're standing at all), they'll soon deadlock, get bored, and split. Scorpio, especially an emancipated female Scorpio, isn't about to be tamed by a macho Aries, no matter *how* sexy he is; and the Aries attention span is minimal. In any event, there are so many other women out there he hasn't met yet. Easy come, easy go.

You're Scorpio, He's Taurus: The main stumbling block here is stubbornness, but other than that Scorpio-Taurus could be the peaceful relationship Scorpio goes through life thinking she craves. The Scorpio-Taurus relationship is probably better for the Scorpio than for the Taurus. Scorpio needs the Venus-influence of the Taurus partner, but while Taurus could benefit from learning assertiveness, Taurus is probably far better off without the brooding, the self-reproach, the sexual jealousy (or arousing of same), or the sometimes scathing sarcasm of the Scorpio. Taurus isn't a total masochist, though! Scorpio can offer him an unswerving loyalty, a prolonged sex life, and faith in personal talents for overcoming adversity. It's a strength that's contagious.

You're Scorpio, He's Gemini: Both are theater-lovers and bookworms, frequently sharing favorite mystery stories to see who names the culprit first! Geminis are understandably proud of their problem-solving abilities and feel perfectly secure in praising their mates for the same talent. It's an attraction that sustains them through separations that may become frequent. A courtship between these two signs is nothing if not literate (I know of one such couple who regularly celebrates Dorothy Parker's birthday) and they enjoy putting other people on with prearranged dialogue. Problems occur when Scorpio expresses dissatisfaction with Gemini's vacillation over crucial decisions, and Gemini retaliates by saying that Scorpio's instant decision is a gross oversimplification and serious problems rate respectfully long deliberation processes. Even with such a problem standing between you, you have a good chance of staying friends for life. Each is probably the best audience for subtle wit that the other has ever known, and a joke-loving Gemini would probably define hell as a place where the only one laughing at your jokes is yourself.

You're Scorpio, He's Cancer: Both are Water signs, and therefore feel emotions very intensely. You also share the awareness that some sublimation of emotions must occur if major work is to be accomplished; otherwise this combination could well drown in a pool of tears. Scorpio is the more objective—particularly with any Libra emphasis in the chart—and your probing questions can keep this relationship afloat. Cancer, on hearing anyone cry, can offer sympathy, shelter, and even louder crying. With this kind of tenderness you find yourself wanting to protect him from other people's troubles.

You're Scorpio, He's Leo: You have in common an intense feeling for drama and occasion. On birthdays, anniversaries, and holidays, you both delight in devoting full pomp and ceremony to the occasion. Pride is the dominant motivation throughout this relationship—a feeling that no doubt attracted each to the other in the first place. You can both be stubborn mules when you disagree. You deeply want a long-term love, but neither wants to give in and apologize. The fixity of both your natures keeps you working at the relationship; breaking up is the *easy* way out and you share contempt for cowards.

You're Scorpio, He's Virgo: If there's one thing a Scorpio knows perfectly well, it's herself. Shamelessly and unflinchingly. You can be very self-critical and can go so far as to tear your self-esteem to shreds. You also have some specific ideas about how to improve yourself and what to do when; therefore, when someone infuriates you by giving unsolicited criticism, you can really lash out! As with the Virgo woman-Scorpio man pair, there's a difference in the passion each musters. Scorpio values Virgo's know-how and skill, but wishes he wouldn't be such a clock-watching efficiency expert about it—especially in the bedroom. (I've heard it said that if there's one thing a Virgo never takes off—except to protect it when he washes himself—it's his watch.) If you enjoy talking in bed, Virgo is a good choice; he's one man who won't roll over immediately afterward to go to sleep.

You're Scorpio, He's Libra: He prides himself on being a charmer, so you'll probably know many a jealous moment. Even when your fears are groundless, he'll probably be flattered that you thought he scored. If you meet him when you're both quite young, when his success as a Don Juan is running high, you may often have that walking-on-eggshells sensation: you want him to know he isn't putting anything over on you, yet you don't want to sound like a nag, either. When he's behaving himself he can be irresistible, and he'd be a great companion at cultural events.

You're Both Scorpio: Unless you're equally educated and, more important, equally interested in giving to the other the best you have to offer, you're in for rocky going. Whichever has the more discordant Sun, or, in other words, the more problems with self-esteem, will initiate jealousy games to test the other's feelings. Unless the partner is extremely mature, the retaliation and rec.iminations can go on indefinitely until one of you does something drastic. Scorpio is highly sexed, and it is sexual addiction that may cement this relationship longer than it deserves. If, however, you are equally devoted to each other and to making the relationship a lasting one, it can be the best thing that ever happened to you. Love means never having to say you're sorry— because he can read your mind.

You're Scorpio, He's Sagittarius: His casual approach to just about everything may exasperate you at times. Who, after all, wants to agonize *alone* over real or imagined problems? He's good company, though, and you can learn about relaxation from his example. If you're intently pursuing a profession, he may complain of neglect, but on the other hand, during the football season you could stand stark naked in front of him and he'll tell you to get out of his line of vision. You know. You've tried that already.

You're Scorpio, He's Capricorn: You're both fiercely ambitious— Machiavellian, even—in your careers. This doesn't leave much time for romantic activity, and Scorpio, being a Water sign, feels the lack more keenly. Capricorn, the pragmatic Earth sign, can work twenty-four hours a day and then some. While he needs a little more balance, he'll strenuously resist any attempts to interfere with him and the office. It's difficult for him to express emotion, so he'll probably keep to himself his appreciation that you care enough to try. Take one step at a time, and ask him to pencil you in one day for lunch.

You're Scorpio, He's Aquarius: Maybe there are such couples, but I haven't seen any. The fixity both signs share can make you lifelong friends; however, your widely different boiling points make intimacy very difficult. Scorpio has considerable trouble comprehending Aquarius's cool and his inclination to befriend all kinds of people indiscriminately. Aquarius, for his part, has little patience with Scorpio's tempests in a teapot. Mentally, though, each has a strong appeal for the other.

You're Scorpio, He's Pisces: Traditionally and theoretically, this is a perfect blend. Both are Water signs. Both, however, must be equally interested in preserving the relationship—as with the Scorpio-Scorpio pair—or Scorpio will fantasize about Pisces's affairs while Pisces's ego laps it up and enjoys it. Whether or not affairs occur, Scorpio has an insecure jealous streak and can brood over the matter endlessly. On the other hand, Pisces's love of drama and intrigue could propel him into a clandestine relationship Scorpio neglected to conceive of! When this pair is together, though, the emotional intensity and the poetry of it keep both partners trying to work problems out.

Sagittarius

You're Sagittarius, He's Aries: Your shared sense of humor and sportsmanship can make your fondness last for years. This can also be a good platonic relationship, although not initially. Aries is highly sexed and can come on ridiculously strong at times. If anyone can laugh at him without alienating him completely, it's you.

You're Sagittarius, He's Taurus: He's intrigued by the travel that's possible through your job, but may sulk when you have to go away without him. You both like high living, and you chafe at some of the economies he suggests for your own good. With him you have to think before speaking; something you blurt out may offend him and you'll never know it. He'll just be silent for a day or two.

You're Sagittarius, He's Gemini: This travel-loving pair may have frequent job-related separations. On the occasions you're together you enjoy puzzles and games, playing tourist in your own or any other city, and light-hearted banter comprehensible only to you. As with the Gemini woman-Sagittarius man pair, you disagree on how to go about preparing something: thoughtful planning (Gemini) *versus* spontaneous doing (Sagittarius). It's a better combination for friendship or collaboration in work than it is for sustained romantic passion. Both signs enjoy humor and satire so much that conventional forms of courtship would probably break you up laughing!

You're Sagittarius, He's Cancer: As with the Cancer woman-Sagittarius man pair, you're united by humor but divided by logistics. Travel is Sagittarius's lifeblood, but Cancer craves the reassuring roots of home. Cancer is highly sensitive, so don't blurt out jests unthinkingly. Free-speech addict that you are, you may be climbing the walls from all this self-censorship—which, of course, creates a dilemma. The Cancer can be great to come home to, but you might feel more comfortable with a thicker-skinned man you can speak freely to. Someone you met on your travels.

You're Sagittarius, He's Leo: His sense of drama can make your life exciting, though your sense of humor and your sense of proportion may cause you to stick a few pins in his delicate balloons. It's hard to stop yourself; he's so funny when he's pompous! As a couple you arouse much admiration—you're both gregarious—but if he made just one remark about "the obedient little woman" that roaring laugh they'd all hear would be yours. He may take quite a while to forgive the humiliation. Even though you couldn't help it.

You're Sagittarius, He's Virgo: You may often see him checking the dishes for grease spots and the window sills for dust. It irritates him that you'd sooner throw the rag at him than do it again "the right way." Or that you don't pause long enough to think up something more diplomatic than that joke you just told about his hypochondria. He doesn't understand that you're merely letting off steam, a defense against the rising heap of medical journals and the growing collection of pill bottles. You have in common a strong reverence for health, but you approach it differently: Virgo fusses about physical threats while Sagittarius believes that a good laugh can clear you up just as surely as a high colonic. At least *you* feel better; he's not convinced.

You're Sagittarius, He's Libra: You share an attraction for comfortable living and the extrovert's love of a good party. Sagittarius likes the challenge of a large group, while Libra shines best in small, intimate gatherings—a noisy blast is disconcerting to him. Libra is somewhat more refined than Sagittarius, whose direct and rowdy humor can upset Libra's balance. As both signs are drawn toward the legal profession, the two of you probably enjoy debating ethical questions and can spend hours analyzing a hypothetical problem. Libra enjoys playing the devil's advocate, while Sagittarius's humor at strategic moments keeps the discussion interesting and lively.

You're Sagittarius, He's Scorpio: Humor keeps the wheels of this relationship oiled and rolling—but only if used in the proper places. Scorpio wants the only jokes at his expense to be his *own*, so limit your targets to outsiders if you want to stay together. He has a habit of mistaking your business trips without him for sexual adventures and he needs a great deal of reassurance. Despite these drawbacks, Scorpio is exciting when he wants to be, he understands your humor, and he does let you know where you stand with him—in no uncertain terms.

You're Both Sagittarius: You're equally ambitious, and you like the freedom to travel and to use your many talents. You like to be off at the races one day and in the mountains skiing the next, and you both value fun as a vital ingredient in a complete life. You can be excessively extravagant, though, and unless one of you has a strongly aspected Capricorn planet to protect your mutual resources, financial chaos can interfere with the pleasurable companionship you've been enjoying. A Sagittarius (or two) who can't give in to a generous impulse feels only half alive.

You're Sagittarius, He's Capricorn: Capricorn's example of seriousness and diligent application to work would probably do you a great deal of good, but you often find yourself trying to balance him a little bit by "jollying the stiff out of it." However much he may seem like a stuffed shirt, go easy in your humor; while he may not risk his dignity by saying so, he does *not* enjoy jokes at his expense. You would make good business partners: Capricorn is good with budgets, organizational charts, and negotiating bargains, while Sagittarius is a good promoter and salesperson.

You're Sagittarius, He's Aquarius: This is another combination with a great potential for good. Not only do you both enjoy people on the everyday level of socializing, but you share bigger, humanitarian ideals for improving social conditions. Both believe that by educating the individual to improve—on a mass scale—you can improve the quality of the species. Sagittarius's approach to this is somewhat more religious, while Aquarius tends to be a freethinker. You probably would have met in the course of furthering your idealistic goals, and enjoyed each other's company so much you stayed together.

You're Sagittarius, He's Pisces: Humor, vacations, theater, and noble causes are interests that bring you together. Jupiter rules both signs, and you're both flexible and tolerant. The Neptune rulership of Pisces, though, can undermine a potentially good thing; Pisces' creative imagination can go haywire when Sagittarius shows an innocent interest in another man. Pisces may not give voice to his suspicions, but his silent suffering may cause him to withdraw gradually, leaving Sagittarius bewildered.

Capricorn

You're Capricorn, He's Aries: You're both ambitious, but you put in longer hours at the office than he does. Capricorn often feels underrated, and as a consequence you work doubly hard at whatever you do. Brace yourself for his complaint that he has to make an appointment to see you. You're so businesslike and organized, and he's so impulsive, that you probably make considerable efforts to reform one another in your own image. You complain he's too slipshod. He might not talk much—just knock that to-do list out of your hands and sweep you off your feet!

You're Capricorn, He's Taurus: This combination is easier than the above to live with on a day-to-day basis. He may feel your devotion to your work is a threat to his ego just as keenly as the Aries man, but he would be less likely to try to do something about it. For one thing, he respects your ambition and realistic bent. For another, he's not inclined to pick a fight. He's a realist, too, and can welcome time to be alone. This combination is good for a relaxed friendship, but it's difficult to maintain romantic intimacy if you're hardly ever together. Of course, that wouldn't bother you for long; friendship is more durable than passion, anyway.

You're Capricorn, He's Gemini: You would go after an education that's especially relevant to you and would concentrate on that one major area at the expense of a diversified liberal education—and he'd have trouble understanding this. You would have trouble watching in silence while he lived like a dilettante; it hurts you to see him fritter away his intelligence. You would differ, too, about spontaneity: if he suggests a trip, he'd soon get impatient and lose enthusiasm for it, while you would still be agonizing over what to pack. Spur-of-the-moment is his approach; be prepared, yours. But you might still keep in touch for an occasional game of chess.

You're Capricorn, He's Cancer: You have in common a love of security; but for you it's financial, while for Cancer it's emotional. Family first. As with the Cancer woman-Capricorn man pair, Cancer may experience hurt and frustration in the face of Capricorn's undemonstrative style, and Capricorn-the-frugal may wince as the emotional Cancer compensates for emotional pain with an occasional extravagance. This is a pair of opposites that may stay together much longer than is healthy, out of fear of the unknown.

You're Capricorn, He's Leo: If you reinforce each other's egos after a grueling business day you stand a better chance of lasting as a couple than if you compensate by trying to boss each other. Capricorn believes that logic, system, and economy should prevail, while Leo might argue a man's divine right to be king of his own castle. (Remember, I *told* you Leo has a royalty complex.)

You're Capricorn, He's Virgo: You're both strong pragmatists and are as economical with words as you are with money (actually, Capricorn is the more economical of the two—with both). You take great pride in the smoothness with which you run your own life, but if the Sun in your chart is discordant, you may have a major ego-problem when Virgo contributes common-sense methods that may be even more efficient than your own.

You're Capricorn, He's Libra: You both admire high position and the luxuries money can buy—or, rather, you like to have the money as recognition for your hard work, but actually hate frittering it away. Libra craves leisure more than you do; you think it's laziness and goofing off. It's a difficult relationship, particularly since Libra wants more constant companionship than you may feel free to offer.

You're Capricorn, He's Scorpio: Self-reproach and brooding is nothing new to you, but when you see the Scorpio withdraw and go into one of his blue-funk numbers, you're quick to blame yourself for the problem and punish yourself more than even the most vindictive Scorpio would have dreamed of! Ambition and talk of strategies for success and power keep you together longer than any other common interest. Sex, however (and I do mean sex *however*!), could prove a dividing wedge; Scorpio prefers frequent experimentation, while Capricorn likes the same old trusty ways and on the usual day of the week.

You're Capricorn, He's Sagittarius: As with the Sagittarius woman-Capricorn man pair, this relationship's greatest hope for survival is a shared business venture, as each provides a talent the other needs in order to make the business thrive. You may differ on religious questions: Sagittarius favors a generous, positive spiritual attitude without making denominational distinctions, while the Capricorn clings steadfastly to the religious traditions her family has always held. This difference is, typically, less important to the Sagittarius.

You're Both Capricorn: Your initial meetings were probably difficult, as you tend to be uncomfortable in purely social settings. Were you to meet in business, however, you would have a natural beginning for conversation and would soon be at ease. It would take you two longer than most people to assert a personal interest, and, to others, your courtship seems peculiarly old-fashioned. If you are of the same religion, your chances of staying together are considerably improved; converting "out" is not something you would agree to lightly.

You're Capricorn, He's Aquarius: You are extremely ambitious and enjoy the climb to success for its own sake. The more intent you are on business, business, and more business, the more likely your Aquarian man might be to try shock tactics to get you to relax and let go. Questions of independence arise frequently between you, since Capricorn may need to lean heavily on that "someone" at home—even if it's only knowing where he is at what time. Aquarius may do unpredictable things just to assert his independence, unless he, too, has Capricorn planets and strong security needs.

You're Capricorn, He's Pisces: In one sense, this combination is good because each provides something the other needs: Capricorn could use some whimsy, imagination, and leisure; Pisces needs system and order. As often happens with any couple, the divergent needs that brought them together can threaten to split them apart. Capricorn the compulsive worker has trouble coping with a mate's leisure (sloth, you'd call it), and Pisces grumbles that Capricorn is a slavedriver. Also, Capricorn often has puritannical sexual morals and Pisces can be an indiscriminate flower child.

Aquarius

You're Aquarius, He's Aries: Unless you have a strong Mars in your chart, you're not as highly sexed as he is, and his impulsiveness could turn you off entirely. You're probably better as friends and would enjoy cohosting a party every now and then.

You're Aquarius, He's Taurus: With any of the Earth or Water signs, who like reliability, you may be upsetting with your spur-of-the-moment style and frequent lateness (your car is especially consistent in its perversity). You have trouble with advance planning despite your best intentions; things just seem to happen that make your promised prompt appearance impossible. Socializing in small groups can be a pleasure for both of you, but you'll have to go to your large shindigs alone. The steadiness that makes him reassuring also makes him frustratingly unbudgeable at times.

You're Aquarius, He's Gemini: Both of you being Air signs, you share a fondness for books and stimulating talk. Incredibly, you have somebody even more spontaneous than you are. You enjoy having a Gemini around; he has so many different interests you'll never be bored. And he has no hangups about your striking out on your own.

You're Aquarius, He's Cancer: You love to take off at a moment's notice, and Cancer might take off with you more speedily than he really wants to; he just doesn't like the alternative of being left alone. He's a good listener and good at bringing out your natural inventiveness. He takes intimate relationships more seriously than you do; don't be surprised if he takes you to meet his mother on the second date. You may naively think you're just being friendly, and then find yourself in over your head.

You're Aquarius, He's Leo: That king-of-the-castle complex could assert itself in direct proportion to your own tuggings at the leash as you delve deeper and deeper into women's liberation. Your chances as a couple are better if you met when you were young and grew together. Another hope is if you both genuinely believe in the right of each individual to grow independently. You appreciate one another's intelligence and miss the stimulation of debate when separated. Aquarius can be outrageous on occasion, just to break up the monotony.

You're Aquarius, He's Virgo: You both value intellect and are well endowed with it. Your approaches are out of sync, though, and this can make you grate on each other's nerves. Virgo's attention to efficiency and detail irritates Aquarius, who feels more interest in human motivation and social trends. Virgo's habit of asking questions may threaten Aquarius's independence.

You're Aquarius, He's Libra: You are attracted to this poised, attractive Air-sign type, whose conversation puts you at ease in a crowd. Ambivalent as Librans often are, though, he may misconstrue your independent attitude as a hard-to-get tactic, then treat you as a buddy. You want him to treat you as a friend—but you *don't* want to hear about the other women! Whether or not you want a serious affair at the time you meet him, you can be direct with him with perfect confidence. As long as you express yourself truthfully, he'll hang on your every word; he'll probably also honor your sincere request to censor himself. Whatever else happens, this promises to be a good, and civilized, friendship.

You're Aquarius, He's Scorpio: If this relationship is at all prolonged, it's probably because at the time of meeting neither of you wants to be alone. It's a time when your confidence about alternatives happens to be low. The mental content of the friendship is high—you're two of the most perceptive signs of the zodiac—but you have very different sexual requirements; Aquarius can abstain for longer periods than the Scorpio who hasn't yet learned to value sublimation. If other people are pressuring you to have somebody and the wrong person happens to be available, you might cling out of a desire for social acceptance, although you would be realistic about your motives. You probably wouldn't stay with the Scorpio man beyond the first jealous cross-examination—his predictable response to your personal or professional independence.

You're Aquarius, He's Sagittarius: As with the Sagittarius woman-Aquarius man pair, the bond of a shared cause is a strong one indeed, and the jointly-held belief in a live-and-let-live relationship also promises hope for this combination.

You're Aquarius, He's Capricorn: Although he would be relieved to have you take the full weight of breadwinning off his back, he often comes across as a stodgy traditionalist. His ego may suffer a bit if you're making more money than he is, if you have a more prestigious title, or if he simply doesn't know what time to expect you home. You throw him off balance with some of your unorthodox ideas, but give him necessary moral support in his projects. He's a genius with balance sheets but sometimes needs help in understanding the human beings he supervises—help you can capably give.

You're Both Aquarius: You're both creatures of impulse, giving each other plenty of leeway to offset the oppression work can sometimes bring. Your household is run on a strictly haphazard basis, and if there's one thing you're firm about it's avoiding rigid chore assignments. Under discordant aspects you may be competitive, each trying to outdo the other in sheer craziness. You may also try to schedule too many things in too short a time, then snap at each other as the week seems to run out of control.

You're Aquarius, He's Pisces: This combination may prove frustrating emotionally for the Pisces, who craves romance and poetry more than Aquarius does. Although you may delight in his company, if your emotional involvement doesn't equal his he'll feel cheated. You may meet while working for a mutual cause, and thus have plenty in common with which to build a friendship. You're both utopian idealists. If you genuinely believe a platonic friendship would be preferable, expect to develop the relationship slowly and gradually. Know what you want— that's the most important thing—and then be honest about it. He has this fetish about pedestals, and suffers disillusionment badly.

Pisces

You're Pisces, He's Aries: You may find him rather overwhelming at first, but he can teach you that you're probably complicating your life with your own imagination a lot more than you have to. After a while you learn to keep to yourself the things you merely *suspect* are going on—you're being discriminated against, the neighbors are looking out their peepholes at the two of you, your phone is being tapped—because he'll only laugh and say, "You're just being paranoid." Maybe . . . but that doesn't necessarily mean you're wrong.

You're Pisces, He's Taurus: As with the Taurus woman-Pisces man pair, there is great hope here; both of you value refinement and tenderness, but the Taurus is less loquacious. When he *does* offer a valentine or a poem, the few choice words could move you to tears, but the process is so difficult for him he saves it for special occasions.

You're Pisces, He's Gemini: If you believe all that they say about Gemini men, you've probably been collecting clues to prove he's cheating on you. And he may be, at that! Whether or not you forgive him (assuming he's really leading a double life) depends on the way he treats you when he's actually there. Of course, if you're constantly playing Nancy Drew when he's innocent, he may say what the hell and try to salvage some fun out of it. If he is essentially a kind person, he may have gotten involved with someone he felt sorry for, and the worst that could be said of him is that he loved two women who are naturally at cross-purposes.

You're Pisces, He's Cancer: This can be a case of instant rapport, and one of you will probably talk about contact with the other in a previous life. You both have the highest hopes for a relationship—one meeting all needs on all occasions—and your chances for staying together are bound to improve if you have interests that enable you to enjoy some solitude. Try reducing your expectations by about ninety percent; reality will look considerably better.

You're Pisces, He's Leo: This pair is like Cinderella and the prince: that Leo Sun makes him patronizingly eager to "elevate" some lucky girl to a favored position. You may actually have a more impressive family tree, but if the company has him on the executive floor and you among the typists, it would be the easiest thing in the world for him to sound patronizing, even when he doesn't mean to. When first discovering your womanly pride and striking out for yourself, you'll instinctively want to keep a Leo "presence" at arm's distance lest you feel engulfed. He thinks of himself as chivalrous, so speak matter-of-factly: neither awe nor karate chops will get you the peaceful coexistence your best interests require.

You're Pisces, He's Virgo: He's so methodical and earthbound that you may have a tough day's work convincing him that daydreaming is your way of making healthful improvements in your life, that you're holding still so ideas can catch up. He's an Earth sign—a realist; what he knows is what he sees. The Virgo-Pisces axis introduces the tension between realism and imagination, economics and poetry. Another case of opposites attracting.

You're Pisces, He's Libra: This can be a loving combination indeed, as both signs have a need for sustained intimacy. Pisces, possibly in response to early programming, needs to try on various roles, while Libra needs to hear human voices around the house (his own and one other intelligent person who'd be an equal match in a stimulating debate). Both signs are ruled by planets that give a strong desire to please.

You're Pisces, He's Scorpio: There is a strong ESP-reincarnation aspect here, as seen with other Water-sign combinations. If there's any rapport at all, it's a strong one that even divorce can't quite break. If the other person does not happen to be physically present, you frequently find yourself wondering what he would say, or you just *know* he's picking up the phone this very minute. Watch out for jealousy problems; you may magnify real or imagined infidelities out of all proportion. If he's giving you cause to be anxious, he is motivated in part by a need to learn what he can and cannot get away with. If you've been more indulgent than you wanted to be, you need to be more assertive; doormats tend to bring out the worst in him.

You're Pisces, He's Sagittarius: The rulership of both signs by generous, flexible Jupiter offers great hope for this potentially conflicting pair. Maintain a policy of open-mindedness, faith, and tolerance for the other, and you can benefit each other for a long time to come. One snag to watch out for: you may disagree on questions of total honesty (Sagittarius) *versus* diplomatic white lies (Pisces).

You're Pisces, He's Capricorn: You can find some measure of peace and comfort in this relationship, but Capricorn is not demonstrative. Discussions of affection are awkward and painful for him. If you had recently suffered erratic treatment from someone else, his steadiness would make him doubly desirable in your eyes. Go slow, though. He's more comfortable that way, and you'll feel a lot better once you remove any lingering doubts about rebound love. Remember, too, that Pisces and Capricorn have different attitudes about the proportion of each day to be devoted to work. He's deadly serious about his work and the importance of putting in long hours; Pisces works more intensely but for fewer hours.

You're Pisces, He's Aquarius: Like the Capricorn, Aquarius can be frustratingly undemonstrative, at least verbally. He expects you to read his mind; if he's there, it's because he wants to be, and if he wants to be there, he must love you. He's got a delightful sense of humor and can show you spontaneous good times. Don't overdo the mind-reading act, though. He may love you but there's still another bridge to cross: cutting down on his treasured independence is a whole other ball game.

You're Both Pisces: You each understand sensitivity all too well and would rather turn headstands on ice than risk wounding your partner the least little bit. If he says he's the same way, you'd swear it was meant to be. Bear in mind that ESP is in danger of being confused with love by the mystically inclined. It might be safer to make a policy of asking questions when in doubt. If information given lovingly doesn't demolish you, the odds are good that he'd survive similar honesty, too.

5

Work and Self-Esteem

For a greater understanding of the working life so essential to genuine personal freedom, the astrologer makes a detailed study of the rulers of the sixth, eighth, and tenth houses. Since the house cusps are determined by the birth time as well as the date, this chapter, too, is organized by *rising* signs rather than by Sun signs. Regardless of the particular occupation chosen, these three houses indicate the patterns of performance of duties, income, and the esteem of superiors and the public.

The Sun sign provides clues to the ego's reactions to career developments. For instance, if passed over for promotion, Aries and Scorpio would fight back, while Libra would suggest the compromise of a transfer—but the Sun is just a small part of the story. It figures more significantly if it is located within one of the three career-related houses (i.e., if your birth time was 6-8 P.M., 2-4 P.M., or 10 A.M.-noon) or if Leo appears on one of the three cusps. I repeat: the sixth, eighth, and tenth houses indicate the patterns encountered in performing work, relating to co-workers, bringing in the desired income, and improving worldly status, *whatever the career*.

The actual determination of what that career should be is based on an elaborate assessment of the total chart, with very exact point values too intricate to detail here. Part of the process involves finding the most dominant house, as outlined earlier. Another part is finding the dominant planet. (Note: the dominant planet is not necessarily the most harmonious, but is the career key just the same; it represents the most persistent energies, which must have a constructive outlet.) For exact details on the whereabouts of all your planets and their strengths and harmonies relative to one another, you cannot get a better, more reasonable computation than that provided by Astronumeric Service, Box 512, El Cerrito, California 94530. They also do progressions, so you can find out where your natal planets have moved. Everything is presented on a printout of readable words, but they do *computations only*; the interpretation is left to human astrologers, which is as it should be.

If you already know your dominant planets and have not yet committed yourself to a career, the following table should help you narrow down your choices:

The Sun:	administration, self-employment, entertainment, creative work
The Moon:	work involving people (e.g., personnel, market research interviews, medicine) or animals, music, food, environmental improvement
Mercury:	scholarship, travel, selling, communications (speaking, spoken or written reporting, criticism, teaching, editing), work requiring manual dexterity
Venus:	work requiring diplomacy (may actually be in foreign service), fine or applied arts
Mars:	work involving athletic prowess, entrepreneurial work (founding independent enterprise), carpentry, metal or glass work involving precision cutting tools or use of fire, fire prevention, surgery
Jupiter:	professional work utilizing talent for giving encouragement (religion, teaching, medicine, the legal profession), selling, entertainment, publishing, public speaking
Saturn:	work involving talent for economy with time or money: management consulting, strategy, banking, real estate, engineering
Uranus:	scientific work involving computer technology, electronics, systematic study of people, such as psychology or astrology

Neptune: work utilizing imagination, preferably with an
                    unstructured work week: fine arts, drama,
                    poetry, fiction; advertising and pro-
                    motion; a vacation/leisure-related job,
                    preferably affording travel opportunities;
                    photography, film or photocopying

Pluto: work involving group cooperation, manag-
                    ing a franchise of a successful chain,
                    research (possibly involving chemistry,
                    radioactivity or television), investiga-
                    tion, exposé journalism, writing anything
                    that is part of a series, broadcasting,
                    the recording industry, psychic research
                    or astrology

If you have not had your chart computed for Cosmodynes (the dominant, most harmonious, and most discordant planets, signs, and
houses), the above may have given you a good clue as to what your
dominant planets are. Your occupation may utilize one outlet of the
planetary energy, while your leisure activity utilizes another outlet for
the same planet.

Remember that the sections below are conceived in terms of *rising*
signs.

Aries Rising

Work and Co-Workers: Virgo on the cusp of this house gives Mercury
rulership, hence an enormous restlessness and need for personal leeway. You have plenty of suggestions for improving procedures, but tend
to be sensitive to real or inferred criticism directed at you. It's easier for
you to rethink your methods if you do not have to explain to others the
reason for the change. While you enjoy frequent communications with
co-workers and others in the course of your work, the interruptions can
sometimes escalate to the extent where you become nervous or ill.
Intestinal disorders can be traced to nervous tensions originating in your
work. To increase your staying power and vitality, balance your day with
relaxation breaks.

Income: Mars and Pluto's rulership makes you an intense go-getter, attracted to challenging and risky sources of income. Unless there is a modifying harmonious aspect from Jupiter or Venus, you may have to be doggedly persistent when the time comes to get a raise. Once you win the desired increase you feel both proud of your own assertiveness and resentful of the necessity to hound your superiors; they should have recognized your achievements without your having to confront them with facts and figures. To protect yourself, investigate whatever insurance and profit-sharing plans may be available to you. Mutual funds could also prove beneficial.

Ambition: Capricorn on the tenth cusp gives you the stick-to-itiveness of the mountain goat, but Saturn's rulership indicates that improvements don't happen right away. As a matter of fact, the delay can be maddening for the Mars-ruled personality, but it does give you time to plan your strategy. One day, one step at a time, with your goal always in sight, is part of it. It is also a good idea to figure out, preferably on paper, just what steps are required for reaching the level you want. Further training may also be part of the plan. Investigate additional degrees or elective courses at an adult evening extension school, then see if the company you work for will help with the financing. If they do, so much the better. If not, you will at least have let the key person or people know you will be improving yourself; it could pay off at promotion time. If the organization is not large enough to promote you as far as you envision going, your research must also include alternative places to work and self-imposed deadlines. The clearer your plans, the better your chances.

Taurus Rising

Work and Co-Workers: Venus rules this house as well as the self, owing to Libra's presence on the sixth cusp. Whether or not the content of your work utilizes your fondness for the arts, your relationships with people will figure significantly in your career's development. Venus's distaste for unpleasant scenes can bring out the worst in latent bullies surrounding you, and they will try to exploit your kind nature. If the combination of Venus and the sixth house should manifest itself as an on-the-job romance, at least try to have it with someone you don't report to. Except for one instance I know of, the woman is usually the first to suffer professionally. Emotionally as well, you'd be better off separating your work life from your personal life. If the person you're in love with is also your boss, you're probably making too much of an investment in that other person—even the best of people could find the power intoxicating. The romance may be entirely on your part, so you owe it to yourself to cultivate other friendships away from your work, and to be as businesslike as possible.

Income: Thanks to Jupiter's rulership of this department of life, you could do quite well financially and win due raises at appropriate intervals. The Taurus ascendant makes you sensible and realistic—you can budget intelligently when you adopt a system—but the combination of the Venus-ruled ascendant and the Jupiter-ruled eighth house can make you colossally extravagant, too. While raises and tax refunds may come through in the nick of time to help with your debts, consider it worth your while to pay off your debts *without* running up new ones, and build up your savings instead.

Ambition: Aquarius on the tenth cusp means both Saturn and Uranus rule this department of life. For Saturn's effect read the Aries section on Ambition. As for Uranus, it governs surprising developments created by unforeseen human intervention. You may be promoted if the person previously in the job quits or is fired; you may be fired if someone who used to have the job (and is related to the boss) suddenly becomes available; a government regulation could turn events in your favor; or you yourself may give in to the overwhelming impulse to quit and never have a boss again. The nervous tension which usually accompanies a Uranus progression should not be the cause of unthinking action. When you feel the urge to be independent and the temptation gets stronger every day, instead of quitting immediately use the constructive side of Saturn's energy to investigate alternate sources of income first.

Gemini Rising

Work and Co-Workers: Scorpio on the cusp of the sixth house gives you Mars's activity and Pluto's curiosity. These two planets combine to make you abhor a nine-to-five desk job and repetitious work. Stimulation is vital to your creativity and without it you feel like a mindless automaton. Your intellectual curiosity must have a greater outlet than gossip about your co-workers' affairs, and a chance to enlist the cooperation of others brings out the best in you. If you should interview for such a job, suggest a trial period. Unless the planetary rulers are discordant, you can win the support of others with the sheer force of your enthusiasm. If you scrupulously avoid badgering when you lead your co-workers and subordinates, you can be a successful administrator with a fiercely loyal following.

Income: Saturn's rulership here is linked with delays in getting increases and the attitude that you're woefully underpaid in relation to the effort you put out. Indeed, that may well be the case. On the positive side, the regularity of your paychecks can be very reassuring. If your expenses are jumping ahead faster than your income seems to be, you could find yourself pursuing a second job. At first, just the feeling that you're doing something to lick the problem can be a stimulant that keeps you going. For the sake of your health, though, you'll want to choose a second occupation that can be managed at home and might eventually become a full-time career. When Gemini gets ambitious she can overextend herself so much that nervous exhaustion results, and so a second occupation that is flexible as well as profitable is a godsend. With thoughtful planning and pacing, eventually you won't need that first exploitative job at all.

Ambition: Jupiter and Neptune give you grandiose visions of heights to attain, and this is necessary to sustain you through dull early years in apprenticeship jobs. Jupiter and Neptune, when harmoniously aspected, give you the high esteem both of superiors and of those who observe you from afar. When you decide you're ready to make a switch, it's highly likely you will do so with the praise of those you're leaving—praise that may come as a surprise to you if you take your paycheck as the main indication of the esteem in which you are held. Another surprise may be the offer of a promotion. They may have perceived your move as a ploy to achieve just that.

Cancer Rising

Work and Co-Workers: Your personality may undergo changes from day to day, owing to the Moon's rulership of the ascendant, but the one area you see as your salvation and spirit-restorer is your work. This is because Sagittarius is on this cusp, allowing you to benefit from the attitudes linked with Jupiter. Both Cancer and Sagittarius have the gift of putting people at ease, and you require work where you can enjoy a frequent turnover of people. Unless you give in to the temptation to vent an occasionally crabby mood, the office is a jollier place because you're in it.

Income: Aquarius on this cusp makes for erratic ups and downs, while Saturn's corulership makes you very security-minded (which the Cancer personality is inclined to be, anyway). In mathematical terminology, this tendency increases geometrically by a power equal to the number of children in the family. The ability to budget and to save is a gift conferred by Saturn at its best. Uranus's corulership, on the other hand, is what brings those unstable developments merely hinted at above: unexpected legacies or refunds, severance pay, automobile insurance, bonuses, computer errors in billing or payments, to name just a few.

Ambition: Mars's rulership can make you eager for advancement on principle, almost as a reflex. You need to conduct your work *your* way, preferably as a pioneer in your given field. The personality of the Cancer ascendant can make you anxious when the opportunity to take over an operation actually presents itself, and you may go through several reversals of decision to determine your real readiness for such a step. In public you may overcompensate by adopting a tough veneer, a defense that you can retreat to in times of stress. Your sensitivity to the nuances of public opinion probably won you your position of leadership, but you must control your anxiety about the public's fickleness for the sake of your health and effectiveness. By combining the initiative of Aries with the humanity of Cancer, you'll probably pass the test with flying colors.

Leo Rising

Work and Co-Workers: You are capable of working hard for long hours—especially when the boss knows you're staying late. If you are in a job that you feel gives you less recognition and authority than you deserve and can handle, you will be anxious to be promoted fast. You are known as a hard worker, and when your time comes to supervise others, you apply the same high standards to your subordinates. You avoid boring and thankless work—unless you can get recognition for volunteering to do it. There is a remote likelihood that your desire to improve your status may be exploited with promises of privilege. It is not a situation whose repetition you would tolerate in silence.

Income: Leo's reputation for thinking big and for amassing big debts springs largely from the rulership of Jupiter and Neptune over this department of life. Before hearing the very first offer, your estimate of what you will make can be so inflated as to make a depressing letdown inevitable. In your zeal to get on with the business of getting rich, you may well neglect to check on such things as standard starting salaries in relation to skill and experience, industry standards, and the all-too-frequent practice of exploiting young postgraduate labor in low-paying apprenticeship jobs. You are particularly susceptible to the false promise of a raise after a specified number of months. If management *does* honor their word about the time interval, the amount of the raise you receive seems ridiculous after your sublime expectations. At the outset, decide for yourself if the learning experience is worth it. Whatever happens, do not make threats to leave unless you can finance the unemployment period that may follow.

Ambition: The hitch-your-wagon-to-a-star school of career advancement may seem irresistible to you, and Venus's rulership of this house can tempt you strongly to cast your lot in with the person who hired you. As with the Taurus-rising individual, your affections can be easily exploited. The exploitation (sexploitation?) is not limited to office romance, but such romances have been known to occur. When you have a boss of the opposite sex who is attractive and charismatic and you're similarly gifted yourself, you may find that there are rumors about how you got the enviable position you enjoy. If the talk is *true*, it is particularly painful for you to learn that you are the subject of gossip. Take consolation in the fact that people are going to think what they want to, and so protesting may do more harm than good. Resolve to be more circumspect and do such a capable job that those in positions to promote you will have no doubt of your very real merits.

Virgo Rising

Work and Co-Workers: Aquarius on the sixth cusp explains to a great extent the work fixation of the sixth sign: Saturn gives you endurance, the sustaining power to train and work for long hours, plus the tendency to feel guilty when you're not actually at work (to avoid alienation on the job, though, try not to make *others* feel needlessly guilty). Uranus gives the genius that enables you to find faster ways of doing things, to invent aids for speeding up performance, and to analyze the capabilities of those around you. Under discordant aspects you might become frustrated that work isn't being done fast enough. Instead of making your co-workers feel like idiots by comparison, utilize the constructive side of the Virgo nature and teach patiently and with humor. Uranus may also manifest itself in surprise developments in the job: a friend tells you about an opportunity when you need one most; someone in the position you've been hoping for suddenly quits or is fired; automation results in *your* being fired; the place you work for goes out of business or is taken over—all of these can affect your future without being a consequence of a previous act on your part. If you see each change as a liberating force rather than a destructive one, you are well on the way to success.

Income: Mars's rulership of your income suggests that nothing comes easily for you: you think of yourself as a hard worker and you regard your income as the fruit of persistent struggle. In addition, Saturn's rulership of the performance of work often goes hand in hand with "forgotten" raises; you have to remind the people with the purse-strings that you're still in there pitching. You may well feel that you're getting less than someone working half as hard or with half your qualifications. Do not present your suppositions unless you have proof—it weakens you as a professional. Instead, your first request for a raise should be based on your own performance record. If you are turned down, and for a reason you find insulting, then consult a more experienced colleague for advice or begin to look elsewhere.

Ambition: Gemini on the tenth cusp means that Mercury—a planet that is hyperactive, curious, impatient, and sometimes highly nervous—rules both the ambition and the self. Gemini may also mean you have *two* superiors to answer to, people who transmit to you conflicting, ambivalent messages toward yourself and toward one another. It creates nervous strain for you, making you feel like the taffy in their taffy pull, stretched thin and never sure whether you meet their taste requirements. There may also be ambivalence in your own mind; ambivalent feelings toward the people you work for, toward the idea of having superiors, and toward your own chances for advancement. On the one hand, you want to go as far as your intelligence will take you, yet on the other hand you're squeamish about getting involved in office politics. Your ambition to make it on talent alone would be the prime motivating force in your changing to an independent, free-lance arrangement.

Libra Rising

Work and Co-Workers: Pisces on the sixth cusp has a lot to do with Libra's reputation for laziness, as both Jupiter and Neptune sponsor belief in the curative values of leisure. To emphasize this facet of your nature is to do you an injustice, for although you tend to daydream, you have a high regard for people, their rights, and their causes. Both Neptune and Jupiter are idealistic and desirous of winning the best possible conditions for other people, and you relish the opportunity to be of help and to negotiate on behalf of others as well as yourself. Your Libra ascendant enables you to see the other side's point of view. Your greatest strength is your knack for selling your proposal in terms of the other person's self-interest.

Income: Venus, as ruler of this house as well as of the self, can make you excessively timid about asking for increases or even an appropriate salary. An employer or prospective employer can usually sense—and even exploit—your need to be liked, so be firm about separating your social-diplomatic relations from your income. It takes self-discipline and assertiveness to hold firm on issues of fair pay, but you can't let niceness be a material disadvantage.

Ambition: The tenacity of Cancer on the cusp of the tenth house can be an asset. You are sensitive to the needs of those who can promote you, but don't take too much to heart their failure to reward you immediately for your efforts. Your skill in public relations and in interpreting public opinion for your superiors can be the keys to upward mobility. The frequent fluctuations of the planetary ruler, however, make you hypersensitive emotionally to any changes, fortunate or otherwise, in your position. The higher you rise in your professional life, the more alert you are to real or possible censure on the part of present or former colleagues. You mustn't permit the envy of others to hold you back from achieving what you can.

Scorpio Rising

Work and Co-Workers: Mars rules this area of life as well as coruling the self, and so it is vital that your occupation engage your enthusiasm. (Remember that the sixth house also rules your health, and with Aries on this cusp, energies that aren't constructively utilized can result in psychogenic headaches.) When you do have the opportunity to initiate a program, you may succeed in leading others because your enthusiasm and sense of urgency are contagious. Your best bet is to sell the others on the necessity of getting the work done and to express your need for their help. Try not to succumb to the temptation to attack personalities if the work is not being done as fast as you would like; there may be extenuating circumstances. In any event, creating hostilities solves nothing.

Income: Gemini's presence on the eighth cusp indicates that the sign's famous duality would manifest itself as multiple sources of income. The Scorpio personality often becomes obsessed about debts, and Mercury's rulership of your income indicates a great deal of mental effort directed toward getting more money. Depending on the sign position and aspects of Mercury, you would require varying degrees of flexibility in any secondary jobs pursued for additional money. The reading matter on your bedside table probably favors investment advice, information on tax returns, and other guidance aimed at helping you stretch your dollars.

Ambition: The Sun—the ego—rules this department of life, and so for you a life without public recognition is only half a life. The Sun rules vitality as well; the fixity of this ruler can keep you persisting despite occasional setbacks. Goal-oriented, you habitually pick a new goal when the last one is either reached or eliminated. Since your personal prestige means more to you than money, you are in danger of being exploited with promises of status symbols and flattery. You may feel somewhat foolish if they don't come through for you, but the story probably wouldn't end badly—especially if you use that Scorpio insight to analyze your flatterers' motives. Also, if you utilize Scorpio's secretive streak and don't brag about the office or the title you're *going* to get, you'll feel little or no embarrassment should the promises come to nothing. Save your breath and let others do your boasting for you.

Sagittarius Rising

Work and Co-Workers: Venus's rulership of this house can mean exploitation of your kindly nature, a problem we have seen with Taurus-ascendant personalities also. Since you pride yourself on being a good sport, it may simply be your time that is taken advantage of as you are asked to go out of your way for someone on the job. You are less likely to be pressed into, or suspected of, a sexual relationship, simply because your sense of humor bluntly puts an end to such talk. You enjoy conviviality with co-workers and putting new people at their ease. If ever anyone can create the impression of being just one of the guys, it's you. Such people are seldom accused of being the office Mata Hari.

Income: Cancer on the eighth cusp indicates frequent fluctuations in your financial life. Cancer makes a person security-minded, although Sagittarian pride won't let your speech or thoughts dwell on need. You would be more likely to joke about the high cost of financing your polo ponies while you make your winter coat last for another season. If your early life was blissfully free of financial anxiety, the realities of self-support may seem harsh indeed. There is the self-defeating likelihood that when asking for a raise you may talk more about your needs—however truthfully—than about your performance record and qualifications. No matter what may be going on in your personal life, concentrate on what you have to offer and have *been* offering. (Let a friend tell the boss about your fight to get child support. In the most casual way, of course.) Live up to Sagittarius's high standards of professionalism by keeping the discussion businesslike.

Ambition: As with the Virgo-rising personality, when Virgo is on the tenth cusp there's a squeamishness inhibiting the efforts to rise. This is not out of character for the Sagittarius-rising person, who feels very strongly about ethics. Gossip about others is accepted as inevitable fact, but rejected as personal practice on moral grounds. Your exacting criteria make you your own severest critic, so don't let yourself brood over an occasional derogatory remark from someone else.

Capricorn Rising

Work and Co-Workers: The sixth house is ruled by Mercury, as Gemini is on the cusp. The Capricorn-rising personality is thus stimulated mentally when in a position to plan, organize, and communicate. Work utilizing strategic skill is necessary for your well-being, and you are flattered when asked to advise beginners. Discussion and brainstorming prove richly rewarding, although you have difficulty withholding criticism. You need to let your creative imagination have more leeway instead of finding immediate reasons why a plan won't work. To keep relations at the office running smoothly, do not be the first to throw cold water on co-workers' proposals; suggest instead practical ways to implement a plan, or people whose expertise could help at least as much as your own. You may be pleasantly surprised by the results of a more receptive attitude on your part.

Income: The Sun's rulership of this department of life, giving it priority in the person's scale of values, no doubt explains the Capricorn's reputation for greed, a reputation that is unjustly oversimplified. The Saturn-ruled self expends conscientious effort on the work at hand, and Saturn's logic requires that the compensation match the effort spent. The Sun rules self-importance as well as importance to the self. Since work is not exactly its own reward, the efforts to work and to improve the quality of that work ought to be recognized in logical pay increments. If need be, the Capricorn-rising person will present this bit of logic at raise time in appropriately economical language. If you are turned down in your request, you would begin a systematic hunt for a better-paying position and would be discreetly quiet until you successfully secure one.

Ambition: Venus's rulership of this house creates much the same situation as with the Leo-rising person having Taurus on the tenth cusp: you may be seduced into, or suspected of, an office romance—specifically, with your boss. The main difference between the Taurus-rising and the Capricorn-rising in this regard is in the *reaction* to such a rumor. The Taurus-rising would change the subject, emphasizing business, while Capricorn would agonize (especially if the story is true) over her own faults, tactical errors, and failure to give a more discreet impression. But all of that anxiety would be like mere pinpricks compared to the worrying that will be devoted to the probable consequences. Your best defense is a businesslike approach and attention to business itself. You may also undergo the difficulty of deciding to move to another job before anyone can fire you. If you are discontented anyway, the added motivation to find something better can accelerate your search. Remember, if you can be honest about having a better offer, you leave in a position of strength rather than in the humiliation of retreat. Think it over.

Aquarius Rising

Work and Co-Workers: Cancer's rulership of this house helps to explain the Aquarius personality's fondness for frequent change in work and for the chance to be of help to people. Whether your contact with people includes the general public or just those persons you see daily within the walls of your office, you need to have an outlet to show your understanding and concern. Your co-workers may find you the most reassuringly available ear in the place, but you do have to balance such therapeutic conversations with the work you are being paid to do. You owe it to yourself to defer some conversations to another time and place.

Income: Virgo on the eighth cusp makes you a thoughtful, shrewd strategist in your pursuit of a raise or a better-paying new job. If management rewards you more with words than with raises, your attitude would be typical of the Aquarian revolutionary: Damn the system! You most decidedly do not like being part of a system where the needy and struggling worker gets little more than a pat on the head! With Uranus as a coruler of the self, you may often find you are astonished by some of the things you say. For this reason you'd be better off keeping to yourself after a disappointing raise or you might be surprised to hear your own voice saying, "I quit!" Utilize your Mercury intelligence to devise alternative sources of income.

Ambition: Scorpio means Mars and Pluto share rulership of this house: the keen enthusiasm of Mars is directed by the strategic strength of Pluto. You have the talent to win the cooperation of your superiors, and in all likelihood you will not be victimized by the vague promises that are so often made to the obviously ambitious. Before starting you would pin the other down to definite amounts and definite dates, and if they don't come across at the promised time, no amount of inducement can make you stay. You refuse to be intimidated by people who take it for granted that they can do so, and your principles are too important to you to give up.

Pisces Rising

Work and Co-Workers: Leo on the sixth cusp makes you need work that affords recognition. You can be a capable supervisor, owing to the Sun's rulership, and a sympathetic one. You are a good listener, but be careful not to let your head be turned by the flattery of those with ulterior motives. Carefully check the references of those whom you hire to report to you. While you do not thirst after power for its own sake (unless the Sun is strongly aspected), you certainly don't want to have someone hovering over you, either. You find it easier to sympathize with co-workers and develop friendships with them if you don't have to figure out the political implications of it all. Ideally, you prefer to work self-sufficiently at an art or craft requiring your imagination. If your present job does not engage your imagination or promise glory, your mind will soon wander off to work that does, and you may seem inexplicably tired and lethargic.

Income: Venus's rulership of the cusp sign Libra indicates some hesitancy in asking for what you want. When Venus is harmoniously aspected you may be spared the necessity of asking for a raise, thanks to the liking and kindness you arouse—but don't count on it. There's still a fundamental reality to be faced: it's not to your advantage to trust that others will be fair and will take care of you; you have to take care of yourself. If need be, rehearse the best thing to say until you can speak your mind with conviction *and without apology*. What you may hear from management is an appeal to your sense of fairness, to your inclination to see the other person's problems. You are perfectly within your rights to refuse to accept such problems as your own. If you don't speak up on your own behalf, nobody else will.

Ambition: Sagittarius on the tenth cusp brings with it the benefit of Jupiter's rulership, a rulership which the personality also enjoys. Optimism and belief in your own worth enable you to roll with the punches, to take the philosophical attitude that you will be recognized for your true worth before too long; if not today, maybe next week. As a result, when you are relaxed and magnanimous toward the person who *does* win today, you can make a favorable impression on those who just might promote you next week. If Jupiter is discordant, however, your happy-go-lucky approach is likely to be mistaken for an I-don't-care attitude. There is also the temptation to trust too much to the just recognition that will come some day instead of preparing yourself with work—both your present work and the educational preparations for the next level ahead. Your training may not be paid for, but it will make a favorable impression if you make the effort of communicating with the appropriate people.

PART THREE

6

Is It Curable?
Or, What to Do until
the Astrologer Comes

An important—but avoidable—barrier that stands between astrology and people who might benefit from its guidance is fear. Skepticism is but one way of showing it. It's those who feel that "doom" is irrevocable that I most want to reach. While it's realistic to suppose that nobody's future is all roses, it's a mistake to succumb unquestioningly to the inevitability of it all.

You *can* change the twists of your future by means of controlling your thinking, and astrology* offers a system of ways to effect this. With the exception of the Sun, each planet has its own "antidote," or counteracting energy, to help you achieve stability. The Sun is the ego itself, the individual's center, and the planets around it are the environment, affecting and affected by that self. The Sun is also will power; it's the urge to make your mark on your environment *and yourself*. Apply enough of that will power and you will, indeed, make the changes you want to see in yourself. When there is a discordant aspect to the Sun, use the antidote to the other planet involved in that aspect.

When I was a student undergoing my astrological "internship," my teacher would occasionally point to me and say, "If it weren't for knowing antidotes, Tiffany would be a bitch on wheels today." And I felt as though I'd just been canonized!

The chart is the raw material you start with at birth, but who wants to go through life as a weather vane, blown this way and that by winds that are stronger than you? Surely we're not reasoning human beings for nothing. Surely we can shape and improve ourselves so that we get progressively better, more at home in our skins, as we age.

*Specifically, the school of the Church of Light (so named to ensure Constitutional protection, which it didn't have under its former name, the Brotherhood of Light. As of this writing, astrology is still illegal in California, where the Church was first established).

If you're serious about the business of making your energies work for you—and defusing those which seem threatening—you probably already know it's a never-ending process. I hope you find profit in acting upon the suggestions set forth here.

Discordant Moon: Under discordant Moon aspects everyday trivia can get in the way of accomplishment: the messes children make, neighbors in a tizzy over their problems, pets, and assorted other personalities you frequently encounter seem to be frustrating you out of sheer spite. For the duration of the aspect you may find yourself restless, difficult to pin down, oversensitive, indecisive, and too easily bored—in addition to suffering from people in your environment who are any or all of these. Being changeable under a discordant Moon aspect, you hesitate to commit yourself because you doubt you'll want the same thing two hours later. Whether your difficulty is in relating to others or in coming to terms with your own emotional fluctuations, you can improve your queasy state of affairs through an understanding of the harmonious side of Mars.

Discordant Pluto: Similar to the Moon—and sharing the same antidote, harmonious Mars—is Pluto. Pluto has been called the higher octave of the Moon, because of their shared tendency to fixate emotionally on an object and to absorb information through extrarational means; that is, often without conscious awareness or effort. Whatever the Moon is, Pluto is more so when discordant: if the Moon's energy makes you need someone, Pluto makes you downright obsessive; if Moon energy makes you need to be needed, Pluto energy is single-mindedly possessive. Relationships formed when these energies are discordant can be imbalanced in power to the point of being devitalizing. If you are not normally a possessive person, you could, during a discordant Pluto progression, temporarily become one, or you could attract someone demanding.

The therapies of the Mars antidote include forging ahead with action (the action itself may not come to much, but the feeling it gives you of doing something definite gives sorely needed confidence), competing, summarizing your problems in the bluntest terms possible, refusing to submit, fighting for rights, building something better on the foundation at hand, and creating as well as accepting challenges involving other people. Sometimes vigorous physical activity will be all that's needed. Learning self-assertion can also work wonders. If this form of therapy is new to you, seek out examples of applied courage and constructive confrontations. A book such as *The Assertive Woman*, by Stanlee

Phelps and Nancy Austin (San Luis Obispo: Impact, 1975), should have the effect of an adrenalin shot as you gain confident control of your own life.

Discordant Mercury: Mercury's discordant aspects take the form of nervousness and its associated disorders, such as stammering or fidgeting. While the intellectual curiosity is just as keen as in the case of a harmonious Mercury, the information-gathering process is handicapped by frequent distractions, disorganization, unavailability of materials, and faulty comprehension. In self-expression you may indulge in a great deal of verbiage without making your point clear. Your mind would be occupied with so many things that you become tense, say things that are misconstrued to your disadvantage, and are unable to concentrate on any one thing long enough to see it through to a satisfactory completion. Clerical errors, contracts and papers, and language present additional problems. Always hungry for new mental stimuli, you may be vaguely distressed and mentally chaotic when frustrated. Communication disappointments, such as a telephone call that doesn't come, would be blown up out of proportion.

Discordant Uranus: Similar to Mercury—and sharing the same antidote, harmonious Jupiter*—is Uranus, which is called the higher octave of Mercury. If Mercury gives intelligence, Uranus gives genius. It also, unfortunately, gives a keener edge to the nervous system, and when Uranus is discordant by progression, the shocks and surprises that enter your life can make you feel as though you've been upended and hammered into the ground.

The harmonious energy of Jupiter enables us to relax and enjoy the company of others in a leisurely atmosphere. If Mercury or Uranus is discordant, consciously reject agitation of all kinds and slow your pace. Seek the company of people who are at ease with themselves and are patient, generous, and have a sense of humor. Also see people you can help with your experience, know-how, and cheerfulness. Build goodwill by offering encouragement when needed. Maintain an upbeat disposition and your sense of humor. Accept more frequently the idea that everything will work out for the best, and don't look back. There are many "positive-think" books available today, any one of which should help when optimism doesn't come automatically. *Conscious Happi-*

---

*I've heard Jupiter nicknamed the universal antidote, so if you remember nothing else, remember Jupiter's remedies.

ness, by Samm Sinclair Baker (New York: Grosset & Dunlap, 1975), is one such book to relax with.

Discordant Venus: Venus energy provides the sweetening of life and gives us a taste for beauty in all things, including our relations with other people. In the lives of women its influence has been stressed to a grotesque extent; our programming to conciliate and to beautify has been excessive. When Venus is discordant it can damage affectional relationships with oversensitivity, overindulgence in sensual pleasures, laziness, excessive flirtatiousness, vulgarity, and an unhealthy desire to please. If you've ever been or met a doormat, Venus accounts for it. In addition, when Venus is discordant there is a tendency to make mountains out of molehills, imagining or exaggerating slights where none may have been intended.

Discordant Neptune: Similar to Venus—and sharing the same antidote, harmonious Saturn—is Neptune. Neptune is called the higher octave of Venus in that it is artistic, affectionate, and conciliating like Venus, but more so. When Neptune is discordant you can go to extremes to make the world sweeter than it seems, to the point of escaping into drink or drugs. You may also lapse into a zombielike withdrawal. This desire to have better conditions as fast as possible can make you an easy mark for con artists—if you don't actively become one yourself. When you are not a victim of deception you may deliberately perpetrate it, as, for instance, when you fake love to keep a relationship peaceful or seek relief in extracurricular affairs. During a discordant Venus or Neptune aspect, someone in your environment who knows well how you like to avoid unpleasant scenes may be unscrupulous enough to manipulate you into staying through guilt. Another problem with discordant Venus or Neptune energy is a decided hatred for physical work or structured situations of any kind.

The harmonious side of Saturn energy enables us to stabilize ourselves and to bring discipline and security into our lives. By making a conscious effort we can switch from flirtatious to businesslike attitudes, and from being conciliating to being healthily selfish. David Seabury's *The Art of Selfishness* (New York: Pocket Books, 1974) should prove helpful for anyone whose problem is excessive generosity for the wrong reasons.

Discordant Mars: When Mars is discordant be on guard against accidents, especially if you're angry or in a hurry. Cuts, burns, bruises, or other injuries are often the result of not looking where you're going. A chip-on-the-shoulder attitude is typical of this energy, as are foolhardiness, crudity, impulsive behavior, and brief sexual relationships. You can be sure Mars is discordant when you flare up easily, attack others either physically or verbally, and act upon sudden impulses without taking time to reason.

The antidote is the constructive use of Moon energy: doing something thoughtful for someone who has nothing to do with the cause of your trouble. You could also benefit from volunteering to spend time with a person or pet in need of extra care. When an argument begins, don't add fuel to it by yelling back, which would be your natural inclination. Instead, determine either to keep silent or not to raise your voice above a normal conversational tone. Better yet, speak softly if you're really angry. The other person will have to quiet down in order to hear you. Always let the other person know what your perception of the problem is, and its effect on you, without name-calling. For details on this approach, read *Between Parent and Child* by Dr. Haim Ginott (New York: Avon, 1969).

Discordant Jupiter: When Jupiter is discordant life can be a lot of fun; you're not uptight about anything. You also waste a lot of time and money, most likely on lavish display. You tend to overdo everything, and have trouble coming down to earth and working again. If you enjoy a personal or professional triumph, your ego swells past the point where you're comfortable to live with. You can't resist the temptation to throw your weight around. If you give in to the temptation to eat all that looks appetizing to you, that weight would become enormous indeed. You may indulge in too many sprees or gambles, trusting too much to the goodwill of others or to chance. The worst danger is in coasting, resting on your laurels, and believing too much that things will work out somehow.

The antidote to discordant Jupiter is the constructive use of Mercury and Uranus. Use your objectivity and your ability to analyze, to hunt for information, and to discriminate. Prepare your work, get the pros and cons down on paper, solve problems, and use logic. As we have seen earlier with Mercury, too much fretting and too little confidence can undermine your health as well as your career. With discordant Jupiter, too much confidence is a problem in a different way: you may be so lazy that your career never gets off the ground. The key is to strike a balance between active mental preparation and confidence in Her; don't overdo either fretting or relaxing.

Discordant Saturn: Discordant Saturn is the toughest of all the planets to live with; the accompanying feelings of self-pity and loneliness can escalate to the point of suicide. The operative word here is *can*, not *will*; but we still have to face the fact that there are other ways in which we can be our own worst enemies. I firmly believe that if anyone wishes us ill they don't have to do anything; they can just stand back and watch us create our own hells, which we'll do very nicely—unless we think twice. Discordant Saturn energy unchecked makes us narrow-minded, stuck in a rut, fearful, pessimistic, bitter, cold, suspicious, unable to express affection, sensitive to criticism, stingy, and envious—in addition to that villainous habit of self-pity.

The antidotes are the harmonious facets of Venus and Neptune. The last thing you want to do when you're depressed is socialize, but if you can spend an evening with casual acquaintances and force yourself to keep the subject-matter light, you're halfway back. This is the positive contribution Venus makes. You don't have to go so far as to bed-hop—and what could be more ultimately depressing than loveless, joyless sex?—but keeping communications open with other people can literally be a lifeline. If love develops so much the better, but beware of falling in love out of desperation. Women's liberation has helped women open up to other women, and has been a source of great reassurance for many. The point is, give yourself permission to experience pleasure. Harmonious Neptune energy turns your imagination loose. Give it free rein—but only about genuinely pleasurable things to do, *not* negative consequences! A book such as *How to Be Your Own Best Friend*, by Mildred Newman and Bernard Berkowitz (New York: Random House, 1971), should help. It responds to a deep need in all of us for permission to show, in tangible ways, that we like ourselves. Another guide I'd recommend is *How to Get Control of Your Time and Your Life*, by Alan Lakein (New York: Wyden, 1972), which applies equally to those who are either too disciplined or not disciplined enough. If, as often happens with discordant Saturn energy, you are so locked into habit and work that you can't think of anything pleasurable and refreshing to do, *The Pleasure Book* (New York: Stein & Day, 1975), should work wonders. And you don't need a prescription to get it!

Having seen how all varieties of energy can go haywire, you are now in a better position than ever to regain sovereignty over your own life. My personal wish for you is that you'll never lose sight of the difference between sharing and abdication.

7

"I May Not Be What I Want to Be, but at Least I'm Not What I Was": Progressions

The chart for the moment of birth shows the fundamental organization of our characters. It does not, however, stand still. Each planet progresses at a different rate, and no two years will show an identical combination of aspects. In other words, the energies that intensify to prompt events in our lives combine in different ways every day, month, and year. What we started out with moves in an orderly fashion. What we *were* carried the seeds of what we have *become*. This in turn is our bridge to the future.

The most regular of the moving bodies in the chart is the Sun, the ruler of the core of the character. You all know the Sun's sign the day you were born. What may be new to you is the concept that your Sun sign *changes*. At the rate of one degree per day, this means one degree per year of life. With thirty degrees to a sign, you can then estimate that if your birthday was the day the Sun had just gone into a sign, *you would experience a major personality change when you are about thirty years old*, when the Sun goes into the next sign on the zodiac wheel. Each sign is very different in nature from the one immediately before, and, I believe, a *reaction against* it.

Use the facing table to estimate your age at the first such change. To that age, add thirty for the age when it happens again. The second sign after your birthday sign—the reaction against the first one—restores some peace with your origins after the rebellion, or coming-of-age, phase. (Use this table, regardless of your Sun sign, to estimate your age at the time of sign change. For a more exact time, consult your local astrologer.)

The paragraphs that follow show what happens to twelve different people who have had one Sun-sign change to date. (If your sign has changed twice, read the latter part of the paragraph for your Sun sign.) *If you were born when the Sun was in Aries, and it has now gone into*

YOUR BIRTHDAY	AGE AT TIME OF SUN SIGN CHANGE
21	29-30 yrs.
22	28-29 yrs.
23	27-28 yrs.
24	26-27 yrs.
25	25-26 yrs.
26	24-25 yrs.
27	23-24 yrs.
28	22-23 yrs.
29	21-22 yrs.
30	20-21 yrs.
31	19-20 yrs.
1	18-19 yrs.
2	17-18 yrs.
3	16-17 yrs.
4	15-16 yrs.
5	14-15 yrs.
6	13-14 yrs.
7	12-13 yrs.
8	11-12 yrs.
9	10-11 yrs.
10	9-10 yrs.
11	8-9 yrs.
12	7-8 yrs.
13	6-7 yrs.
14	5-6 yrs.
15	4-5 yrs.
16	3-4 yrs.
17	2-3 yrs.
18	1-2 yrs.
19 ⎫ (the sign-	0-1 yrs.
20 ⎭ change date varies slightly	
from one month to the next)	

Taurus: You have found that rash, impulsive actions have brought you trouble and that a more subtle and diplomatic approach is called for. Maturity, for you, consists of the strength to use the best of both signs: Aries's never-say-die optimism and energy, and Taurus's consideration for the feelings of other people. Another thing you have going for you is Taurus's stick-to-itiveness. *If the Sun has gone into Gemini*: After thirty years of self-restraint, winning some and losing some, you're tired of pussy-footing and want to drum up some excitement. As Gemini rules the shoulders, arms, and hands, you may experience arthritis or bursitis after this change.

If you were born when the Sun was in Taurus, and it has now gone into Gemini: When the Sun was still in Taurus, you were quiet, shy, and uncomfortable among people. After the Sun's move to Gemini, you have an easier time conversing and may develop interests in writing, driving a car, working on one college degree after another, and sports such as tennis that emphasize use of the hands. *If the Sun has gone into Cancer*: After thirty years of frequent travel and a wide variety of mental stimuli, you have become doubly appreciative of the haven a home can be and of your family.

If you were born when the Sun was in Gemini, and it has now gone into Cancer: When you were younger you used to run around busily juggling school and friendships. With the move into Cancer you have become absorbed with forming a family and organizing your home. You may also gain a reputation in one of the healing professions, music, advertising, market research, or psychology. Be careful of your diet and get regular medical checkups. *If the Sun has gone into Leo*: You've gotten tired of job-hopping and now want to make your mark in the place where you decide to settle. The Leo emphasis indicates vulnerability in the heart and the spine.

If you were born when the Sun was in Cancer, and it has now gone into Leo: In your early years emphasis was on emotional security at home and among friends. A lack of warmth in your earliest home environment could have prompted an early marriage as an attempt to find security. You may also have begun preparation for and entered one of the occupations listed in the preceding paragraph. With the entrance into Leo you gain self-confidence and may actually be elected or appointed to a position of leadership. *If the Sun has gone into Virgo*: If you've held a responsible or powerful position during the Sun's years in Leo, you may have come to feel there was no higher rung to reach for in that ladder—and decided to study a new profession or craft. At this time you would enjoy working with your hands doing something involving intricate detail that would win you considerable praise and profit.

If you were born when the Sun was in Leo, and it has now gone into Virgo: Your earliest concerns were your self-worth and the praise and recognition you could win. You may have attempted to win this glory through athletic games or the theater. Once the Sun leaves Leo for Virgo, you become aware that in order to retain and insure what advantage you've gained you must continue to work hard and develop a detailed knowledge of your craft. *If the Sun has gone into Libra*: After the youthful glory of Leo and the thirty years of painstaking work with Virgo, you want more balance in your life. Thus the next logical stage is to taper off in your long-held profession, dabble in an art form or two (strictly as a hobby), and perhaps make a change in your marital status. Health areas to watch: the heart and spine (Leo) and the kidneys and internal sex organs (Libra).

If you were born when the Sun was in Virgo, and it has now gone into Libra: When you were younger you tended to internalize anxieties, possibly even to the extent of causing yourself severe intestinal pain. The compulsion to work hard to win approval made you especially aware of your health and diet at an early age. You wanted to anticipate even the pettiest criticism and eliminate the cause rather than have another person actually comment on it. The Sun's move to Libra would help you to relax and to ask yourself the kinds of questions that restore your sense of perspective. The influence of Libra also prompts an interest in various sorts of partnerships and your own prospects for entering one. *If the Sun has gone into Scorpio*: Your desires may be set on sexual adventures now, especially if in your youth you neglected your personal life in favor of work. The eliminative system or the genitals may be the cause of some distress.

If you were born when the Sun was in Libra, and it has now gone into Scorpio: You probably found at an early age that being nice all the time put you at a disadvantage. The younger you were when the Sun went into Scorpio, the greater the likelihood that you overdid preserving your rights. If you assert your limits without pugnaciousness, you'll stand a better chance of keeping as friends those people who thought you were nice in the first place. During this time you would have discovered sex, and had either an overwhelmingly positive or negative reaction. With Scorpio energy a person is seldom indifferent! This is a fortunate combination of signs for entering a profession that requires years of dedicated study. *If the Sun has gone into Sagittarius*: After having prepared for work in your chosen profession, you are now beginning to enjoy the reputation that comes with accomplishment. Also, you are generally more relaxed as you relish your increased income. Gone is the temporary militancy of the student. As your standard of living improves, you may also increase your intake of rich foods and drink. Get a checkup, and take better care of your liver and your weight.

If you were born when the Sun was in Scorpio, and it has now gone into Sagittarius: Your first years were very difficult, due to Scorpio's constant introspection and examination of others' motives—always assuming the intent of others to hurt, of course! After the intensity, the hexes, and the shyness in public, the freeing influence of Sagittarius enables you to relax more. Your sense of humor improves, you develop professional aspirations, and study a great deal on your own. The Sagittarian perspective and humor are very effective antidotes to Scorpio's intensity. *If the Sun has gone into Capricorn*: Alas, more introspection and self-reproach. You may also take the attitude, "So much for fun and games. Now for some *real* work!" and devote more attention to providing for your old age. The Capricorn emphasis indicates physical vulnerability in the knees, low blood pressure, and difficulty in adjusting to cold weather.

If you were born when the Sun was in Sagittarius and it has now gone into Capricorn: Childhood would have been a pleasant time, with a great deal of traveling and camaraderie. The move into Capricorn may manifest itself as a separation, literally or emotionally. If, for example, your career choice meets with parental or faculty disapproval, feelings of alienation may result. The progression into Capricorn also indicates anxiety about adequate funds for tuition, particularly likely if you have older siblings who are due to enter college first. *If the Sun has gone into Aquarius*: If you didn't succeed in getting the degree you dreamed of when the Sun was in Capricorn, you would feel freer to do so now. Aquarius has a liberating force, and after the constrictions of the last thirty years, you have new attitudes about your personal rights and new mental interests. The nervous system and ankles are vulnerable now.

If you were born when the Sun was in Capricorn, and it has now gone into Aquarius: The younger you are when the Sun moves into Aquarius, the less likely you are to become embittered by the restraints from authority figures that come during a Capricorn progression. If the change took place before college, you would have chosen an out-of-town school before your freshman year. If the change comes *during* college, you'd transfer. And drive a car. *And* take elective courses that have no "practical" value but appeal to you on a whim. If your seventh house is involved, you might marry or divorce as a declaration of independence.

When you experience such a change, you can expect to feel rather wild, but your experiences are commonly motivated by a craving for liberation. *If the Sun has gone into Pisces*: You would develop new artistic and cultural interests, and may now be able to afford the travel you've been looking forward to. You ought to have constructive work to keep you busy and get you healthily tired or you'll soon be symptom-watching. Doctors have difficulty making diagnoses with Pisces people (or others with strong Neptune aspects), so try to save your money by staying healthy.

If you were born when the Sun was in Aquarius, and it has now gone into Pisces: As a child you would have shown a quick wit and prodigious inventiveness, and you were attracted by science and mechanical gadgets. After the Sun's move into Pisces, you tend to withdraw from people into your private daydreams, while the school staff wonders why such a superior achiever has suddenly become so apathetic. The bafflements of puberty (or of coming of age, depending on the year your Sun sign changed) are part of the new introversion. Theater would be a creative outlet for a now-habitual daydreamer. Work allowing you plenty of freedom of motion would be your best bet. *If the Sun has gone into Aries*: The withdrawal and daydreaming phase gives way to more aggressive energies and a renewal of your scientific interests. An invention or enterprise you pioneer can give your career added momentum. However busy you may be, don't neglect regular eye and dental checkups. Have a general physical examination regularly, too.

If you were born when the Sun was in Pisces, and it has now gone into Aries: During the time the Sun was in Pisces, you probably were praised for being a docile, pliable child, but you would see that as a deadly handicap with your first disillusionment. When your Sun progresses into Aries, you get the nerve to talk back to anyone you feel treats you like a pushover. During the Pisces years you would begin your idealistic dreams of a creative career; with the move into Aries you show more courage and energy in going after it and training for your goal. You may also work actively for a cause. *If the Sun has gone into Taurus*: During the years the Sun was in Aries, you probably enjoyed temporary bouts of belligerence when warding off another's manipulation. As you get older and wiser and your Sun reaches a more pacifistic sign, you think maybe —just maybe—you might have overreacted, and the pendulum swings the other way. While you don't totally forget assertiveness, you are more diplomatic in your approach. You may also give in to the temptation to swallow harsh truths. It's no wonder, then, that people who have Taurus emphasis in their charts, and thus this reticence in interpersonal relations, develop throat ailments.

The Sun's sign is not the only part of a chart that changes; as the Sun crosses one of the house cusps determined by your time and place of birth, your priorities change, too. In addition to that, the Moon changes signs approximately every twenty-seven months, Mercury changes irregularly (spending approximately fifteen years in a sign, minimum), Venus spends fifteen to thirty years in a sign, and Mars is slightly slower and sometimes changes direction. Jupiter can stay in a sign for a lifetime; ditto Saturn, Uranus, Neptune, and Pluto. The midheaven's motion is the same as the Sun's. The ascendant will be slightly faster or slightly slower. To follow the progress of all of these and know the date a planet or point moves to a new sign or house, you can obtain a computer printout for eighty-seven years, starting with your year of birth. It costs approximately fifteen dollars and is available from the Astronumeric Service mentioned earlier.

As we examine the meanings of the planets in the different signs, bear in mind that whatever the successive signs each planet goes through, you never totally cease to be what you were originally. You are a combination of the new ways of evolving learned in adulthood and your old childhood habits.

The Moon

In interpreting the shift of the Moon from one house or sign to the next, such common-sense factors as present age and circumstances must be taken into consideration. The Moon's progression through the seventh house, for instance, won't bring marriage to a five-year-old— but it *may* bring a bride-doll. Details of the houses' meanings are given in Chapter 2. The Moon's passage through a house has the effect of a moving flashlight; there will be new interest and insights pertaining to the house involved, mainly because of the new illumination there. When the Moon, or *any* planet, progresses through a sign other than the one it occupied at the time of birth, its relation to the original sign of the same planet is comparable to that of a second language to your first: you acquire new ways of expressing yourself without ever completely relinquishing the old. When you read the following sign interpretations, let the phrase *"natally or by progression"* be understood, to avoid tedious repetition.

Moon in Aries: A person having this is often called a dynamo, as both planet and sign share enormous restlessness. Unfortunately, this sign often gives what I call one-way sensitivity: the person is too conscious of the effects of the environment on the self and oblivious to the reactions of others. It isn't so much a willful tuning out as a case of being in too much of a hurry to get on with the business at hand. During a progression through this sign, questions of self take on added importance. Rushing and urgency dominate daily living, so there is an added need for safety precautions. If you have a child with the Moon in Aries either natally or by progression, triple the attention you devote to commonsense precautions at home.

Moon in Taurus: There is a tendency to acquire material possessions to reinforce emotional security. This placement can also mean a danger of seeing people as possessions (one woman I know who has her Moon in Taurus actually said: "I own my husband"). On the more positive side it augurs a clearly defined, realistic approach to beginning intimate relationships, as well as to major financial undertakings. Emotional problems may manifest themselves physically as sore throats or ear problems.

Moon in Gemini: The desire to learn becomes a vital motivating force. Very often it is the influence of another person—for example, when your child starts school—that triggers in the Moon-in-Gemini person a desire to keep one jump ahead mentally. This placement may also manifest itself as dilettantism, telephonitis, or time-wasting coffee breaks. Word-of-mouth publicity can have a profoundly favorable or adverse effect on personal popularity, depending on the progressed Moon's aspects. The vulnerable areas are the shoulders, lungs, arms, and hands. Speech impediments arising during a Moon-in-Gemini progression are more likely to be emotional than physiological in origin.

Moon in Cancer: Family relationships, particularly parent-child ties, undergo severe stress. The combination of progressed aspects and the goodwill of the people involved should result in a dramatic change in the pattern of interaction. The physical setting of the home may be changed through improvement, relocation, or adjustment to the arrival or departure of a household member. Emotional stomach upsets are symptomatic of a discordant aspect when the Moon is in Cancer.

Moon in Leo: Vacations, other leisure activities, children, the ego, and love affairs would take on extra emotional significance. In childhood such a progression can mean emotional fixations on a teacher, parent substitute, or even on a game or a toy. For the adult the central emotional issues are possible parenthood, love affairs (with at least one partner who seems parental), status, and vacations. Heart flutters and back pains are the most likely psychosomatic disorders.

Moon in Virgo: The emotions turn to work- , health- , and food-related issues. When the Moon progresses through this sign after its two years in Leo (assuming, for the sake of argument, that this occurs during active adult years), self-reproach is highly likely. The play and leisure activities indulged in during the Leo phase would be termed wasteful, and resolutions to be more productive and efficient are solemnly listed. Dramatic changes in diet may occur when the Moon is in Virgo. If you find your popularity with others in jeopardy, it probably has something to do with your new-found food fanaticism or puritanism. Intestinal ailments are likely during a progression through this sign, and can make you even more exacting in your standards of diet, hygiene, and work.

Moon in Libra: There is a renewed interest in relationships; whether the person actually enters into one is immaterial. The person is enthralled by the vicissitudes relationships are prone to, and the relationship could be anybody's. Even children devote thought to partnerships as they play at having weddings and ask their parents embarrassing questions about *their* relationship. Emotional scenes about fairness as a general matter of principle are also likely to arise. The kidneys, gall bladder, and internal sex organs are vulnerable when the Moon is in Libra.

Moon in Scorpio: The double emphasis on emotional fixation can become a messy problem; it is during a Moon-in-Scorpio progression that jealousy can be most difficult to handle. It can be sexual jealousy—but it can also be a child's sibling rivalry, parent fixation, or fierce competition for a coveted prize. Coercion to pay a material or moral debt can occur. Psychosomatic disorders associated with Moon-in-Scorpio progressions can affect the nose, the eliminative system, or the external sex organs.

Moon in Sagittarius: It becomes easier and more important to relax and to let go of emotional obsessions after the debilitating intensity of the Scorpio progression. A change of companions is likely—preferably to people of varying backgrounds, who will introduce you to refreshing new viewpoints. During a Moon-in-Sagittarius progression, desire to travel in order to begin or resume advanced education may intensify. This arises in part from an interest in education, but is also motivated by a need to live in a totally different environment. Legal actions such as divorce could contribute to this eagerness to move. Material circumstances could improve dramatically, accompanied by excessive celebrating. The physical ailments linked with a Moon-in-Sagittarius progression are those following excessive indulgence: unhealthy weight gain, fatty growths or tumors, liver disorders.

Moon in Capricorn: The light-heartedness of the Moon-in-Sagittarius progression is harder to come by, as seriousness and conservatism become the order of the day. If your income increased substantially toward the end of your Moon-in-Sagittarius phase—and such timing would be fortunate—the Moon's entrance into Capricorn adds the prudence necessary to hold onto your newfound gains. Also, after the open-house period that just ended, you may feel that one of your guests has taken advantage of your hospitality. When the Moon is in Capricorn, you withdraw from contacts that aren't absolutely necessary and are fearful of being used. Chills, colds, and trouble with the teeth or joints are most likely to occur during the Moon's progression through Capricorn.

Moon in Aquarius: When the Moon progresses through Aquarius, you come out of your self-imposed deep-freeze (completely, if Capricorn is unoccupied except for that brief progression; and only partially, if there is a natal Capricorn planet and/or a longer-lasting progression). You start to act like a friend again and enjoy circulating in groups. After a severe twenty-seven months in Capricorn, a liberation movement or ideology would look especially good to you; you would welcome new ways to run your personal life. Eager to try new things and meet new people, you may live at too frantic a pace, manifested physically by such nervous disorders as tics, twitches, or wobbly ankles.

Moon in Pisces: You feel ready for more depth in the friendships formed during the Moon's progression through Aquarius. This may be due in part to a new or reawakened interest in the occult. Superficial friendships don't seem as satisfying as when you were first recovering from the Moon-in-Capricorn phase; you now want to understand as fully as possible the people who intrigue you. After some social success, solitude acquires a new positive value. You may feel vaguely at a loss for vitality, and can benefit from some self-pampering and tuning in to your true motivations (which can, all too easily, get lost in the social shuffle).

During this progression you can grow considerably by being alert to your own thoughts and motivations as they evolve—or you can become equally self-destructive by willfully blotting out your inner promptings, with assistance from alcohol or drugs. It's up to you. Besides the effects of toxic chemicals, you may experience excessive fatigue, drowsiness, or food poisoning.

The Moon takes approximately twenty-seven years to return to its original position. At about the same time, transiting Saturn returns to *its* original position, giving extra determination and desire to make a fresh start. It is at the age of the first complete Moon and Saturn cycles— anywhere between twenty-seven and twenty-nine—that we truly feel we have come of age, that we have been through it all. And in a sense, we *have*.

Mercury

Mercury's progressions trace the inclinations, strengths, and weaknesses of our intellect and its forms of expression. Mercury also indicates the gracefulness or impediments the nervous system will show.

Mercury in Aries: The mind can be so quick to catch an idea, and so loath to encounter delay in carrying it out, that the person having Mercury in this sign may well alienate those who are less quick. Deliberation over possible consequences—*anything* causing delay—is seen as stupid. Acute nervous headaches may occur in the face of frustrating postponement. Competitive as well as far-sighted, the Mercury-in-Aries person may frequently use the imperative form of a verb— without softening the effect with a *please* or *thank you*—and then wonder why others are reluctant to "cooperate."

Mercury in Taurus: This sign position produces a logical, methodical mind capable of balancing costs and long-term gains. Whatever concept or goal the Mercury-in-Taurus person works on, you can be sure that the approach will be organized and scheduled, with a full view of the financial and time requirements involved. If there is a communication problem, it is in holding back. Monosyllables are usually made to fit the occasion and this can really be maddening to more loquacious co-workers and intimate associates. If they didn't know you so well, they might think you were angry at them. Even when you *are* angry, they'd have the devil's worst time trying to pry out of you what it was that offended you. Nervous throat-clearing may occur frequently during a Mercury-in-Taurus progression and, generally speaking, written communication is more comfortable for you.

Mercury in Gemini: Shyness is no problem of yours (or has ceased to be, if your Mercury was originally in Taurus). Mercury in the sign it rules makes you alert, curious, talkative, and inclined to pursue several interests concurrently. Unless there is a Mercury-Saturn aspect to slow you down, your thoughts go so fast your words can't possibly keep up, hence occasional stammering. Organization is something of a problem for you; your varied interests are so stimulating you're often at a loss to subordinate one to the others. Your curiosity, a strength that makes you a good reporter and writer, can also be the source of myriad distractions. You hate to leave a ringing phone unanswered or to refuse to lend an ear to a colleague. Accidents involving the shoulders, hands, or arms are usually caused when a gesturing arm collides with a previously unseen object.

Mercury in Cancer: The Cancer influence facilitates learning by osmosis as well as by conscious effort. The people in your life often stimulate you to learn more about their major interests, and you assimilate their jargon easily. A discipline involving people is your first choice as a career, and your talent for listening and putting people at ease should be utilized in your profession. You express yourself best on a one-to-one basis. If called upon to address a group—particularly a group of strangers—your nervousness could manifest itself as a stomach ailment. Frequent rehearsals as well as ascertaining that the setting of your speech will afford the necessary physical comforts (a glass of water *at least*) should put you at ease.

Mercury in Leo: Your style of self-expression is dramatic, and creative writing may become a source of glory for you. A tendency to comprehend events in theatrical terms may, with discordant progressed aspects, alienate others, who dismiss you as a verbal embroiderer. Whether or not your chosen occupation is in one of the communications fields (broadcasting, publishing, advertising), you have the capability of influencing others.

Mercury in Virgo: As has been explained in Chapter 2, Virgo brings out considerably different facets of its ruling planet than Gemini does. Virgo is the more severe critic and the more persistent worker in preparing an argument. Mercury-in-Virgo may come across as quibbling, nit-picking, or nagging, but what bothers the person with this Mercury sign the most is not being taken seriously. This placement gives a genius for detail work, but it brings with it the danger of nervous upsets, specifically in the colon or small intestine, when details go wrong.

Mercury in Libra: This person has an excellent sense of what to say when, and is a born diplomat. Mercury-in-Libra is also skilled at negotiation, debate, and comparison. The association Libra has always had with justice and the concept of balance manifests itself in various Mercury-in-Libra charts as aesthetic explication (judging visual or literary symmetry, balance, or parallelism), counseling, arbitration between two equally strong adversaries, or judging from a courtroom bench. Scrupulously honest Libra often conducts the decision-making process aloud so that any hearers might benefit from the reasoning process leading to the final verdict. The person having Mercury in Libra may feel offended that not everyone wants to hear each "on the other hand" that suggests itself along the way—particularly Mars-Aries personalities, who are more interested in the bottom line.

Mercury in Scorpio: This sign of research and detection is relentless in pursuing leads until absolutely satisfied with the results. Mercury-in-Scorpio can ask precisely the same question again and again until the desired answer is given. For this reason people with this placement make good investigative reporters, detectives, doctors, scientists, psychologists, or astrologers—or writers about any of these. Unflagging curiosity is the leitmotiv of this life. Persistent as the Mercury-in-Scorpio person is in finding information, that fixity is nothing compared to the determination shown in withholding it. Any friend who has Mercury in this sign is one you can trust absolutely with your secrets. Discretion, confidentiality, and privacy are sacred to the person having Mercury in Scorpio.

Mercury in Sagittarius: A person having this Mercury sign is scrupulously, bluntly, and sometimes brutally honest. The Jupiter influence, thanks to Sagittarius, can result in an abundance of words, ideas, and principles to be wordy about. This is a fortunate placement for a person with the ambition to write or teach, but can be a drawback in everyday conversation owing to a tendency to ramble and to hog the conversation.

The person having Mercury in Sagittarius has the knack of selling anything.

Mercury in Capricorn: This sign for Mercury produces unclouded, pragmatic realism. "Shrewd" is this person's most likely self-description. Others may say that this is the person who knows the price of everything and the value of nothing. If that seems like a gross injustice, it is simply owing to Capricorn's often negative attitude (at worst) and undemonstrative nature; that which the Mercury-in-Capricorn person values most highly you will find discussed the least. Whatever the occupation chosen, there should be numerous opportunities to exercise the innate organizational skill.

Mercury in Aquarius: Both planet and sign involve the intellect and give free rein to the mind's development. New disciplines are begun and pursued in a spirit of experiment, especially those relating to science. People, also, become the object of this scientific approach. The Mercury-in-Aquarius mentality is eager to learn what makes *anything* tick. This sign's fixity enables a person to stick with a discipline long enough to use it as the basis for independent creation.

Mercury in Pisces: This mentality is the most baffling combination of the zodiac; its connections and psychic associations have a logic best known to the subconscious. Some of the unusual ideas offered by the Mercury-in-Pisces person can result in highly beautiful, emotionally powerful, at times symbolic or abstract creative works. Often preferring the realm of the creative, remote from mundane practical considerations, the Mercury-in-Pisces person is especially vulnerable to exploitation by plagiarists or collaborators. If the Sun is in Aries, basking in the limelight presents something of a dilemma; the Aries planet does like personal glory, but the Pisces Mercury likes privacy. An Aquarius or Pisces Sun would be less problematic, agreeing to obscurity as long as there is freedom to create.

Progressed Mercury spends slightly less than thirty years in a single sign, and may be slower if retrograde. Astrologers can say with conviction that it will not make a complete revolution around a person's chart within the lifetime, but *transiting* Mercury—speeding ahead at the rate of nearly two degrees a day as I write this—makes one and a fraction complete revolutions per year. In other words, each department of life gets the benefit of Mercury's intellectual focus several weeks each year, at the very least.

Venus

The sign Venus occupies, first at birth, then by progression, shows a person's particular kind of beauty and, more important, the style of expressing love. Romantic love? Yes—but not *just* that. Any enduring relationship is likely to be sweetened by an aspect to the planet ruling the affections: friends of any sexual combination, business partners, collaborators, and even owner and pet! The sign of the progressed Venus indicates one's reactions to one's own original style of loving.

Venus in Aries: The appearance is likely to be dramatic, possibly with red hair or a reddish highlight to the hair, and definitely with a fondness for bright colors. Affectionate relationships begin with enormous enthusiasm but may fizzle easily—Aries's enthusiasm is not famous for its longevity—or be demolished in a flash-fire fight. For this person, fighting can be a way of saying "I love you" or a way of testing to see if feeling is still there. Where there's fight there's hope, to paraphrase the old cliché. Unfortunately, other people aren't as swift to forget as the Venus-in-Aries person is to speak up.

Venus in Taurus: The features that may attract others are most likely to be poise of manner, beautiful skin, and a well-modulated speaking voice. The fixity of the sign gives a need for continuity and comfort in love relationships. This fixity may be taken for possessiveness, although it's a more quiet variety than that expressed by the Venus-in-Scorpio person. The person having Venus in Taurus simply settles into quiet routines involving at least one other person—and the other person may not *want* to be assumed to be available every Friday night.

Venus in Gemini: The attractive features most likely to arouse another's interest are the beauty of the hands (probably conspicuous in their gesturing) and the animation of the personality. A new acquaintance may well think, "She's the center of the action." The person having Venus in Gemini is sociable, flirtatious, and inclined to scatter her affections among several people. Romance is appealing on an intellectual level—as an idea of a pleasurable pastime with a person whose mind can keep up with yours—rather than as an intense emotional experience. You can love an adventurous companion but not a possessive one. Your upbeat disposition would be termed shallowness by someone more intense than yourself, and this would be difficult for you to bear, as your interest in the other person is usually genuine.

Venus in Cancer: Others are attracted to your unusually expressive eyes and your attitude of warm, receptive concern. Sometimes relationships may take on a protective, parental tone, and if the person having Venus in Cancer becomes interested in someone who is trying to break free of parental domination, she is likely to be rejected for reasons having nothing to do with her. Unfortunately, a person having Venus in Cancer will experience too many comparisons to the lover's parents for comfort. This person's capacity for offering emotional support is great indeed. The problems that arise are residual conflicts from the past.

Venus in Leo: The regal bearing, the aura of glamor, and the attitude that this is a person to be reckoned with will be immediately attractive to potential associates who relish challenge or need to learn authority from a living, breathing example. Under discordant aspects this becomes emotional insecurity, a feeling that you might be valued more for your external appearance than for the passionate loyalty and love of which you are capable. You don't intend to give up looking good, but you resent being taken somewhere just to be shown off.

Venus in Virgo: Exquisite, sharply etched facial features, often including a widow's peak, and a neat, tailored style of dress are the first things other people notice in this combination. The Virgo influence tends to put new acquaintances through detailed analysis, and friends or lovers who share this habit of dissection are likely to be warmly welcomed—if they meet the exacting standards. Venus-in-Virgo, like Venus-in-Gemini, values shared mental interests as cement for any relationship, but the Virgo would have more difficulty showing love for someone who is difficult to understand. (By contrast, the Venus-in-Gemini person can enjoy an enigmatic companion with an attitude of detached amusement. The Venus-in-Virgo person would instead attempt to change the other before eventually giving up in disgust.) When Virgo is the position for *progressed* Venus, the appearance may become strait-laced, prim, and businesslike after the real or imagined exploitation of the Venus-in-Leo period.

Venus in Libra: The grace in motion and the elegance and symmetry of dress style are the most noted attractions of the Venus-in-Libra person. Owing to a keen desire to be fair and gracious and to give the benefit of the doubt, the Venus-in-Libra person may overdo the compromises and nonassertiveness for which Venus is famous. Located in the sign it rules, Venus's kindly, ingratiating impulses can go unchecked unless there is an obstacle from an aspect. If this is the sign of *progressed* Venus, it indicates regret over any damages done by Virgo's critical nature, and the desire to atone for any slights a friend or lover may have suffered.

Venus in Scorpio: The Venus-in-Scorpio is a highly sexed person who exudes an aura of sexuality. Love relationships are often intense and punctuated by possessive crises. If one such scene has already destroyed a relationship, the person having Venus in Scorpio might bottle up subsequent suspicions and jealousies; but the pain is still there and so is the feeling of being threatened by real or imagined rivals. As a position for *progressed* Venus, a newly watchful and probing attitude may compensate for the overly detached demeanor of the Venus-in-Libra period.

Venus in Sagittarius: An abundant head of hair, a twinkle in the eye, and a memorable laugh are what others find most attractive in the Venus-in-Sagittarius person. A sense of humor is of paramount importance to the person having Venus in Sagittarius, and light-hearted banter as well as shared ethical principles play significant roles as aphrodisiacs. Consequently, if your partner can learn quickly and shift gears, the trusting Venus-in-Sagittarius person can be a pushover. This sign placement for Venus may also discount the importance of material things if the current love interest cannot offer them. When *progressed* Venus is in Sagittarius, the person is tired of the intensity of the Venus-in-Scorpio period, especially the painful jealousy, and tries to assume the lightness of heart of the Sagittarian nature.

Venus in Capricorn: The stark simplicity and conservatism of the total picture and the somewhat formal manner are what stand out. The Venus-in-Capricorn person is often a believer in old-fashioned etiquette, particularly when others become prematurely familiar. Steadiness, emotional security, reliability, and usefulness are important values for the Venus-in-Capricorn nature. If the friend or lover can be of use in this person's career, so much the better, but it would be unjust to assume that the Venus-in-Capricorn would not offer such help to reciprocate. Given a key position in professional life, the person having this sign placement might feel that others were more interested in her position than in any personal attributes she may have. There may also be the dilemma of mixing love with upward mobility when a boss expresses romantic interest. Keeping your life compartmentalized is probably a better idea, especially if there is reason to believe that the openness of the Venus-in-Sagittarius period was excessive and exploited.

Venus in Aquarius: Except possibly for the ankles, there is no one feature that can be singled out for special notice. Rather it is the total attitude that magnetizes attention, and the Uranus rulership of Aquarius suggests a strong charisma indeed. As with the other Air signs, love is often expressed in a detached way, and the Venus-in-Aquarius believes that the best favor one can do for someone is to allow them breathing room. There'll be no possessiveness and clutching here. If this is the position of *progressed* Venus, the policy of backing off and giving breathing room may have been a painfully learned lesson from the Venus-in-Capricorn progression.

Venus in Pisces: Venus-in-Pisces has a distinctive and somewhat remote appearance that attracts those who enjoy the challenge of winning the seemingly unattainable. As with the other Water signs, the eyes are truly outstanding features. (The Sun, Moon, or ascendant in a Water sign will also give a memorable appearance to the eyes. With Cancer the eyes have a limpid look, and seem to invite others' tales of woe; with Scorpio the gaze is penetrating and people find themselves speaking of things they hadn't meant to disclose at all; and with Pisces the attention seems to be riveted on an object a million miles away, prompting others to restore their attention.) The affections may be bestowed freely—perhaps *too* freely—to people who have little to recommend them but pitiful circumstances. The person having this Venus sign may overdo excuses and allowances for the object of the affections, with outrage surfacing later during the Venus-in-Aries progression. If th is placement follows a Venus-in-Aquarius progression, there may be overcompensation for Aquarian detachment. An exploitative person may convince you that a social conscience is meaningless if you don't prove it on a one-to-one basis.

Progressed Venus takes slightly less than thirty years to go through a single sign, and may take longer if retrograde. *Transiting* Venus moves at approximately the same rate as transiting Mercury, gracing each department of life for several weeks a year. The house Venus is in offers clues to our sources of love and friendship, and the areas we most want to beautify.

Mars

Mars's sign, natally, then by progression, shows a person's approaches to anger, assertiveness, and sex. Whether female or male, this planet will still show how you handle the most physical, potentially most violent facets of yourself. (At a recent lecture astrologer Doris Hebel expressed the theory that if you don't find a constructive outlet for your energy but expect someone else to vent it *for* you, you suffer doubly: not only because part of you is unsatisfied but because you somehow attract a person who manifests the most unpleasant forms of energy, owing to her or his resentment of having to act for two. I agree with her.)

Mars in Aries: Unless there is an aspect forming an obstacle, Mars-in-Aries unchecked can be self-destructively aggressive and overtly hostile in angry or sexual situations. The fights of a Mars-in-Aries person may end as quickly as they began, soon forgotten by the person with this sign placement, although often painfully remembered by her or his opponent-partner. If this is a progressed position, the single-mindedness and determination of Mars-in-Aries can be a welcome relief following the vague yearnings of Mars-in-Pisces.

Mars in Taurus: The Venus rulership of Taurus makes the person hold back expressions of rage or lust, often preferring to sublimate the energy into Venus-ruled creative activity. The sublimation may also, unfortunately, take the form of a sore throat. All the angry, potentially destructive things left unsaid continue to have their force in the larynx of the person not saying them. The Earth sign gives sensuality to the sex life, and the advantage of extra staying power. As a progressed position, the holding back is a result of a very real destructive lesson learned during the impulsive Mars-in-Aries period.

Mars in Gemini: With this sign there may be more talk than action. The language may often be scathing and intimidating, but the force is often dissipated in the act of talking; articulation seems to be its own satisfaction (it can also mean a plurality of sexual relationships, so eventually one of the partners gets more talk than anything else!). After a progression through reticent Taurus, letting go—verbally, at least—is welcome.

Mars in Cancer: Cancer's sensitivity often acts as an inhibiting factor for the planet occupying it, and so anger and sexual desires often are not expressed in direct ways. The inhibition could have an adverse effect on the stomach; ulcers are fairly common, as Mars rules abrasions or burns of all sorts. Fear of being unkind, especially after a progression of destructive verbal freedom in the Gemini period, is the conscious or unconscious motivation for self-censorship.

Mars in Leo: Self-confidence and authority are strong in dealing with anger and sex. Also, partners who can deal from a similar position of strength might come into your life. There may be considerable friction and competition for position of top dog when this happens, as the Leo personality likes to get recognition for authority. If both partners are secure in their strengths, the sexual side of life can be so satisfying that they're boringly ostentatious about it. Under discordant aspects conflicts and anger may take the form of heart or back pains, as well as very definite humiliations for any offender. The confidence of the Mars-in-Leo progression is a relief after the timidity and scruples of Mars in Cancer.

Mars in Virgo: Hostility and anger may take the form of relentless nagging, with the faith that by doing so one can really reform the person causing the problem. In sex the person may be obviously critical of the partner's performance and may turn the other off with talk of technical detail or hygiene. This may be a mask for one's own impotence. After a progression through the more physical sign Leo, Mars's verbal expression in Virgo may seem more civilized, by comparison, although not to the sexual partner! This energy is best used in detailed professional work; militant perfectionism finds more rewards at the office (but when dealing with people, watch it!) than in the bedroom. Intimacy and criticism coexist only in a state of truce, at best.

Mars in Libra: As with Mars-in-Taurus, Mars-in-Libra tends to hold back expressions of anger or sexual desire. The ambiguity is intense here because Libra is ambiguity itself, and there may be the added problem of one of the partners in a sexual situation being married to somebody else. The Libra effect is a diplomatic expression of sexual desire, while the Mars energy is more urgent about it. On the other hand, when succumbing to temptation there may be very real wrath to face as a consequence (such as the partner's jealous spouse!). As a reaction against the Mars-in-Virgo progression, the Mars-in-Libra hates ugly scenes and might prefer avoidance of a problem-person altogether.

Mars in Scorpio: This is one of the two home signs for Mars and the sign in which Mars's sexual nature projects most strongly. The obsessiveness of Scorpio can magnify outrages and sexual fixations, granting much more importance to the objects of these passions than they may deserve. Expressions of anger can, if they occur at all, be sarcastic in the extreme. In fact, extremes and pendulum swings can dominate the Mars-in-Scorpio life. The person having this placement *by progression* is more likely to be assertive than someone who has it natally, especially if natal

Mars is in Virgo rather than Libra. After the vacillations of the Libra period, the transition into Scorpio has an invigorating effect. If Mars is in Scorpio natally, the person who has had it with hassles is apt to hold back expressions of anger—not out of fear but out of intense self-control and the knowledge of sarcasm's destructiveness. Unfortunately, the sexual relationships the Mars-in-Scorpio person experiences may often show the bitterness and hostility of power struggles. It often seems that the choices are to struggle or to swear off sex altogether.

Mars in Sagittarius: Anger or sexual desire is likely to be expressed in a humorous, offhanded way. The benign influence of Jupiter doesn't want to express Mars energy seriously—it might hurt someone—so the desires are camouflaged in jokes. If the Mars-in-Sagittarius person isn't taken seriously, the reaction would be a shrug and an offhanded "Nothing ventured, nothing gained." This is a defense mechanism, particularly after the intense inner turmoil of the Mars-in-Scorpio years. As with Venus-in-Sagittarius, Mars-in-Sagittarius values a partner with a sense of humor; a partner who can't laugh in bed isn't likely to be invited back.

Mars in Capricorn: Saturn's influence gives the ability to express desires in a matter-of-fact, assertive way, without danger of losing control. A skilled administrator, you may make the mistake of conducting your sex life in a deflatingly businesslike manner. Another Saturn trait, self-control, may also be overdone in the face of repeated pressures from others. If Capricorn is the *progressed* Mars position, the new seriousness is the result of seeing the Sagittarian flippancy come to nothing.

Mars in Aquarius: With this placement there is probably more intellectualizing about anger and sex than there is first-hand experience. A person who has Mars in Aquarius would be attracted to someone with an enlightened, independent, and egalitarian approach to relationships, yet that same person would turn cold if the partner pulls such surprising stunts as bringing home a stranger to join them in bed. The most likely response to that would be a simple declaration of independence. The Mars-in-Aquarius would rather initiate surprises than suffer those that others inflict. This is particularly true if Mars had previously progressed through Capricorn. Mars takes pride in feistiness and Aquarius in independence, hence the combination gives the strength to do without rather than take guff of any kind.

Mars in Pisces: Pisces lends idealism to the desire for fights or for sex, and so affairs would be begun if there is any hope at all of keeping them romantic and poetic, and fights are more likely to start on behalf of someone else. If Pisces is the *progressed* position for Mars, there is a keener desire for a more intense personal experience than with the abstract intellectualizing of Mars-in-Aquarius. Once Mars is in Pisces there is a growing desire to express one's passions like the heroine or hero of the film of one's own life, although the objects of said passions may not be very clearly delineated.

Progressed Mars takes more than thirty years to go through any one sign. It is slightly slower than the Sun and moves too irregularly to say with any certainty exactly how long its passage through a given sign will be. *Transiting* Mars takes one year and a fraction to make a complete revolution around the zodiac, enlivening each department of life for one to two months at a time as it goes.

Jupiter

Jupiter's sign is an indication of how we express religious faith (if any), of our humor, and of our resiliency.

Jupiter in Aries: There may be a break with the original family religion in favor of a new religion or philosophy. The sense of humor would be lively but so would the temper if others' jokes become too personal.

Jupiter in Taurus: The philosophy is more conservative; whatever brings tangible rewards wins belief. The strong materialistic bent can inhibit the sense of humor. When the financial situation is less than rosy, the humor seems dormant. In better days the celebrating spirit may seem downright boisterous.

Jupiter in Gemini: This placement of Jupiter indicates a religious or philosophical shopper. Jupiter-in-Gemini understands several religions or philosophical trends superficially but will not make a commitment to any one on general principle. The humor is light-hearted, with a fondness for puns and riddles, and can entertain either very young children or urbane adults.

Jupiter in Cancer: Religious or philosophical principles are expressed through helping others. This is a fortunate placement for teachers of young children, as the confidence to meet a wide variety of needs exists in abundance. Perhaps the best service or charity you can offer is to teach the young the value of humor, honesty, resiliency, and faith.

Jupiter in Leo: This placement indicates belief in a benevolent deity, a belief that may be reinforced by the successful position you occupy in life. Gambles that pay off also help support your belief that somebody up there is smiling. The Leo influence indicates an outgoing, generous nature with a robust sense of humor that may successfully cover up a sensitivity to being the butt of humor.

Jupiter in Virgo: Religious faith is closely intertwined with your sound health and profitable employment. When pain comes, faith diminishes correspondingly. The Jupiter-in-Virgo person tends to believe that salvation comes through constructive work and that health is a by-product of clean living. As with Jupiter-in-Gemini, the Mercury influence gives sophistication to the wit and humor.

Jupiter in Libra: The person having Jupiter in Libra favors the ethical spirit of religion over the ritualistic letter of it and always champions those who have been treated unfairly as a way of asserting nobility. Showing generosity in dealing with a partner is another outgrowth of religious feeling. The humor is more likely to focus on issues of relationship than on individual personalities.

Jupiter in Scorpio: The guiding principles here are faith in retribution or in just reward (often the heaven/hell dichotomy) or, in the more evolved, a belief in self-discipline to overcome mundane hells. In the less evolved the humor can be crudely sexual. The more introspective Jupiter-in-Scorpio person will focus faith and humor on the desire to overcome one's faults.

Jupiter in Sagittarius: Jupiter occupying the sign it rules indicates high principles—possibly even a vocation to join a religious order—and a keen desire to communicate these principles by teaching and helping others. Humor may be used to mask the intensity of the religious feeling.

Jupiter in Capricorn: The obedience of Capricorn-Saturn's influence contributes an inclination to follow the traditional family religion, including its rituals. Right and wrong are often seen as absolutes. Humor is of the wry, self-deprecating, ironic sort, and others might not readily respond.

Jupiter in Aquarius: The rebellious, iconoclastic influence of Uranus points to a break with the family's traditional religion, and a progressive, freethinking, and democratic philosophy is usually preferred. The sense of humor is original and spontaneous.

Jupiter in Pisces: Religious beliefs often surface as philanthropies for the needy. Under discordant aspects this can escalate into martyrdom as parasites and con artists absorb the assets intended for more helpless and worthy recipients. The sense of humor is unusual, whimsical, and Pollyanna-like.

Progressed Jupiter moves so irregularly it may spend a person's entire lifetime in the sign it occupied at the time of birth. A complete cycle for *transiting* Jupiter takes approximately twelve years, or one year for each house to gain Jupiter's uplifting, expansive influence.

Saturn

Typical of Saturn's nature, this planet separates the amateurs from the professionals: the amateurs will cry doom and gloom—especially if they're inclined to be negative individuals anyway—while the professionals will call on Saturn's caution and wisdom to balance this planet's negative effects. Saturn is the energy we use to "clean up our acts." If we are self-disciplined, realistic, organized, and utilize our assets to the fullest, we have little to reproach ourselves for when the Saturn aspects gain energy. Of course, we cannot avoid certain separations from people we love, but we can forestall self-blame and guilt through alertness. For those who live wastefully and chaotically, Saturn aspects will be harder to bear. Our response to Saturn is especially indicative of our defensive measures, our self-discipline, and our level of maturity.

Saturn in Aries: Discipline in personal habits is initiated by the self rather than by another. Saturn-in-Aries is persevering and innovative, but resents the intrusion of others. Head colds may be symptomatic of overdoing it.

Saturn in Taurus: Conservatism in disposing of personal resources—including time—is the source of security for the Saturn-in-Taurus person. Depending on the strength of the aspects, this conservatism can become miserliness. Excessive anxiety about finances can take the form of throat ailments.

Saturn in Gemini: Discipline is most likely to be exercised in the area of communications, and great deliberation would precede either writing or speaking. Saturn-in-Gemini favors getting as much as possible in writing from others while at the same time committing as little as possible to paper oneself. In the chart of a professional writer, this can prompt regular work habits along with considerable mental strain in searching for the perfect word. Trouble with the lungs or with arm or hand joints may occur under discordant aspects.

Saturn in Cancer: The conservatism of the parents, internalized in the subconscious from the earliest years, may be a severe damper in the maturing adult's struggle for autonomy. Self-discipline may be motivated by the anticipation of parental dos, don'ts, and general negativity. Childhood refusals to eat, and later stomach trouble, are often manifestations of passive resistance to hovering parents.

Saturn in Leo: As a result of having had oppressive parents, the person having Saturn in Leo may be an overly bossy or oppressive parent herself. Saturn in Leo suggests intense seriousness in love relationships—a seriousness which may intimidate more light-hearted partners and delay parenthood until relatively late in life. Also, the Saturn-in-Leo person may be depressingly unromantic about scheduling time for leisure activities; few lovers can take the idea that they're either being crowded out of a busy schedule or are wasting your time. Spine or heart ailments may be the physical manifestations of a discordant aspect.

Saturn in Virgo: Seriousness about work can be too easily overdone. To plan work and meals on a regular schedule can, of course, be beneficial to both career and health, but excessive fussing over minute details can lead to overwrought nerves. This placement can also manifest itself as hypochondria, neurotic perfectionism, nagging, or illness involving the intestines. When symptoms present themselves, do not limit yourself to medical attention. Examine the part your behavior may have played in any illness you experience, but don't dwell on the symptoms and on what they might become. Relax.

Saturn in Libra: The person having this Saturn sign probably has the most difficulty adjusting to new concepts of partnership in place of the traditional role models. By placing a heavy burden of expectation and responsibility on the partner, Saturn-in-Libra often smothers whatever affection may have existed. If the relationship does survive a strong Saturn aspect, it is because responsibility has been more evenly distributed. Bladder, gall bladder, and blockages in the internal sex organs may accompany partnership problems under a discordant Saturn progression.

Saturn in Scorpio: On the positive side this somewhat morbid placement can give the person the foresight to "get the house in order" with adequate insurance, wills, and any other financial arrangements appropriate for the self and family. Saturn-in-Scorpio gives an intense and stubborn pride and inhibits sexual pleasure. There is a fear of letting go completely and of being vulnerable to another's possible exploitation or manipulation. Jealousy, clinical attitudes, emotional blackmail, and grudges taint the sexual experience further. There may be physical malfunctions in sex during a discordant Saturn aspect.

Saturn in Sagittarius: Persistence in pursuing higher education, particularly when advanced professional training is to follow a bachelor's degree, is a hallmark of Saturn-in-Sagittarius. Ironically, there may be some narrow-mindedness in religious or philosophical principles. Public expression may also create difficulties, as Saturn's style is often smug, sententious, and boring. Physical manifestations may involve low blood pressure, or low energy levels due to liver malfunction.

Saturn in Capricorn: Saturn in its home sign is a political strategist *par excellence* and can analyze the subtleties of protocol endlessly. The Saturn-in-Capricorn person will be ever alert to the reactions and opinions of a current or potential business associate or voter. Self-consciousness may be extreme, limiting personal freedom severely, but even under discordant aspects the judgment is often realistic and shrewd. A discordant progression can manifest itself as low blood pressure (if the aspect is with the Sun or ascendant), chills, or stiffness in the joints (particularly the knees).

Saturn in Aquarius: This energy tends to express itself as discrimination in choosing friends. It must have been a Saturn-in-Aquarius person who first said, "You can't pick your relatives, but. . . ." Saturn anywhere in a chart has serious and highly exacting standards, and the Aquarius influence indicates a fondness for people who are serious about a cause or ideal. Under discordant aspects there may be disappointment in people who are not so conscientious about their friendships.

Saturn in Pisces: The most advantageous use of this energy is in creative talent or in the exercise of social conscience. When there are discordant aspects to Saturn in Pisces, the problems that arise are acute guilt (often over wasted talent or time), disillusionment, excessive self-sacrifice (with pride in martyrdom), and either foot problems or hypochondria.

Progressed Saturn often stays in the same sign it occupied at the time of birth, unless it was then in the last degrees of its sign. *Transiting*

Saturn takes twenty-seven to twenty-nine years to make a complete circle around the zodiac and gives two years to each house for learning its profound lessons.

Uranus

Uranus takes approximately seven years to transit each sign and a lifetime for major progression. Like the even slower Neptune and Pluto, it distinguishes whole generations more than it does individuals. Astrologers are still studying the sign influences of these three most recently discovered planets. Probably the oldest and certainly the youngest people now alive have Uranus in Scorpio (December 10, 1890, through April 4, 1891, and November 22, 1974, through November 16, 1981, are the earliest and latest dates I have for this planet's passage through Scorpio). This particular sign gives the planet fixity and an obsessive desire for knowledge and revolutionary social change.

The way the individual relates to contemporary social and psychological changes will be indicated by the houses in the chart where Uranus and Aquarius are, and by the aspects to Uranus and any planet(s) or points in the sign Aquarius.

Neptune

Neptune is the key to our cultural myths, and its aspects in the natal chart show the extent of the individual's acceptance or rejection of these myths. Harmonious aspects enable a person to adapt; discord, on the other hand, will show up as feelings of displacement and of being hopelessly misunderstood. A person may be comfortable with a cultural ideal for years, and then a major progression or a slow transiting aspect from another generational planet (Uranus or Pluto) interferes and causes her or him to renounce it. First comes the shock of recognition as long-held assumptions are challenged; then confusion, followed by plans for change. For example, when *The Feminine Mystique* (the point from which our present feminist movement grew) was published in 1963, transiting Pluto was in Virgo and forming conjunction after conjunction with the natal Neptunes of women born in the thirties. Hence large numbers (Pluto) reassessed their lives of service (Virgo), and learned they were not alone in experiencing what Betty Friedan called "the problem that has no name" (Neptune).

Progressed Neptune moves so slowly that it will probably stay in the same sign it occupies in the natal chart. *Transiting* Neptune takes approximately fourteen years to go through a single sign. The way the individual is most affected by cultural ideals will be shown by the houses in the chart where Neptune and Pisces are located and by Neptune's aspects. Considering that Neptune rules bewilderment as well as idealism, it is just as well that our life expectancy is not long enough for us to witness first-hand Neptune's presence in all twelve houses.

Pluto

This planet's effect on a generation or on an individual is related more to peer-group pressures and comparisons than to cultural influences. Pluto rules pressure, and when Pluto is stimulated there is considerably less confusion and less blind groping than with Neptune. The Plutonian desire for drastically better living may be felt subliminally at first, but soon Pluto urges you to probe for the relatedness of it all (a Pluto pastime, remember). Then, in group gatherings (another manifestation of Pluto), the connections between interpretations as well as the connections between people gain momentum. Ultimately the demand for the greatest good for the greatest number, and action to that effect, will prevail. Pluto energy has a snowball effect; the increase in force becomes a phenomenon that seems independent of the individuals who started the sequence of events.

Progressed Pluto moves irregularly, at approximately the same rate as Neptune, if not slower; it can occupy a single sign for a lifetime. *Transiting* Pluto seldom casts its laser-beam effect on more than five houses in a lifetime. In other words, Pluto actually appears in four departments of life, plus the one house having Scorpio on the cusp.

In pointing out progressions to a client, I scrupulously avoid saying that a planet or an aspect *causes* an event. It is not planets that cause events; human decision does that. Planets are associated with certain kinds of thoughts, but whether those thoughts are acted on is where human will comes in. Step one in client counseling is pointing out the sorts of actions the planets impel us to contemplate; it is we who decide what the action will mean to us. The second step is deciding what to think. We all go through a phase of trying to be as different from our origins as possible (the first progressed sign-change). Once we gain perspective, however, and forgive our youthful indiscretions and imperfections, we can come to terms with what we have become and learn to appreciate ourselves (the second sign-change). Astrologers maintain that the best is yet to come—and we all deserve it.

8

1977-1981:
Your Astrological Future
Is What You Make of It

By now you are more fully aware of who you are, what you can do, what you want to do, what you *might* do, and, most important of all, that you are not a passive victim of destiny. You know, too, that nothing remains the same; if you delude yourself about this, you slide backward and can be victimized. If you take command of your resources and channel your energies intelligently, you can improve your outlook and circumstances in dramatic and inspiring ways. I can only hint at the changing signs and directions of the planets. To enjoy the full benefit of any planet, *you* must exert an effort. Nobody should moan to an astrologer: "It's Taurus's year and I'm a Taurus; why isn't a windfall landing in my lap?"

This chapter is a panoramic view of the years 1977 to 1981, focusing on the motions of the five slowest transiting planets—Pluto, Neptune, Uranus, Saturn, and Jupiter, in order of slowness—which have the longest-lasting and most profound effects on your development. Only to the extent that they add energy to what is already present in you can they be said to have any significant impact. Otherwise, if they manifest their energies in your life at all, it will be as forgettable mood changes.

In this chapter the estimates of the effects of these planets on you for the years 1977 to 1981 will be organized by *rising* signs. Even then, the sign-change dates you will find here must be approximate in terms of the department of life affected. When I avoid the boring repetition of qualifiers and exhortations to consult your own chart and your own astrologer, I do so with crossed fingers. Having set forth the necessary warning, I'll venture on.

Aries Rising: 1977-1981

Pluto: Pluto's retrograde motion in Libra from January 18 until June 24, 1977, suggests delay in decisions about partnership changes. The other

191

person involved may be withholding information that is yours by right, and you won't know the full story until the planet's motion turns direct. The Aries temperament is not inclined to wait for the story to unfold gradually; rather, you prefer to make the effort to find out. A direct person yourself, you demand that your partners be forthright with you. You can confront the worst truth with more ease than uncertainty and evasion. Another manifestation of Pluto's passage through your seventh house is a partner, prospective partner, client, or adviser who cross-examines *you*. Pluto is retrograde again January 21 through June 26, 1978; January 24 through June 27, 1979; January 27 through July 2, 1980; and January 28 through July 4, 1981. When Pluto is moving forward and the aspects are harmonious, it is easier to work in cooperation with another and to gain a deeper understanding of that person.

Neptune: At the start of this five-year period Neptune is halfway through Sagittarius, and so you are already familiar with a feeling of uncertainty about religious and philosophical premises. You may immerse yourself in one church or school of thought after another as you test the validity of each for yourself. Beginning or renewing higher education may be a constructive escape from a rut, but its beneficial effect on your future depends on the effort you put into it. When Neptune is going through the ninth house it's all too easy—and likely— to think that just being in school and sticking it out until you receive a diploma is enough. Neptune does, unfortunately, indicate laziness. Education, legal matters, publication, broadcasts, or other public appearances may be subject to confusion, errors, deceptions, or distortions during this period. Delays are also likely, especially when Neptune is retrograde: March 20 through August 27, 1977; March 28 through August 30, 1978; March 24 through September 2, 1979; March 27 through September 2, 1980; and March 30 through September 6, 1981. During the periods when Neptune's motion is direct and when aspects are harmonious, ideals are altruistic, imagination flows in original ways, publicity in the media is gratifying, and vacations are a pleasure.

Uranus: For most of this period Uranus continues in Scorpio, shaking up financial developments on occasions when you least expect it. Automobiles may be instrumental in increasing your debts, so make sure you are adequately covered by your insurance. Friends may cost you money or may help with opportunities to earn more. Tax audits, unexpected legacies, computer errors, or other machinery may change your financial status during this period. Delays, reversals, or errors are most likely to occur when Uranus is retrograde: February 17 through July 19, 1977; February 21 through July 23, 1978; February 25 through July 29, 1979; March 2 through August 2, 1980; and March 6 through August 7, 1981. When Uranus moves forward and is harmonious, you will enjoy beginning—or resuming—the adventure of winning an independent income. Occasional gifts will also be exciting surprises. Uranus will be in Sagittarius briefly from February 18, 1981, until it retrogrades into Scorpio March 21, 1981. It returns to Sagittarius for a seven-year stay November 17, 1981. In Sagittarius it joins Neptune, adding its revolutionary urgency to your ideals. There is also the increased probability of an interruption or transfer in your education, religious conversion, exploration of at least one foreign country, publication, public speaking, and a radical change in principles and attitudes. Deceptions may be brought to light in surprising ways, with legal action resulting.

Saturn: At the start of the period—January 1, 1977—Saturn is going retrograde through Leo, and will continue to go backward until April 13, 1977. Love affairs may become more sober, serious, and committed, although complete expressions of devotion may not be forthcoming until the planet's motion turns direct. Thoughts of the future and of having children because there won't be too many more safe childbearing years may precipitate anxiety if there is no prospective partner at hand who shares your attitude. If there is a natal aspect between Saturn and the ascendant, it will help settle the question of how the pregnancy is likely to progress: with a discordant aspect it could be painful, perhaps even involving miscarriage; with a harmonious aspect the time will be used to good advantage, combining both professional work and sound health measures to prepare for the coming child. *Do not base a decision to have a child on a reading of planetary transits.* On November 18, 1977, Saturn enters Virgo, giving new (or renewed, if you already have Saturn here) seriousness to the performance of your work. On December 13, 1977, Saturn turns retrograde, which may be experienced as delays in getting satisfying feedback for the job done, delays in getting the job done, and a decrease in the energy with which you do it. Without waiting for this retrograde period (which ends April 27, 1978), regulate your nutritional intake and try not to overtax yourself. On January 5, 1978, Saturn retrogrades into Leo; if unfinished creative work was begun during the Saturn-in-Leo transit, now is the time to complete or polish it. Saturn returns to Virgo July 27, 1978, retrogrades December

26, 1978 (for an extra dollop of guilt for all the work left undone Christmas Day!), turns direct May 11, 1979, backs up again January 9, 1980, turns direct May 24, 1980, and advances into Libra September 22, 1980. During a Libra transit relationships are seriously reassessed. If both partners have not been consistently above-board and faithful, Saturn's passage through the seventh house augurs well for the partnership's strength and security. In the event either partner has been dishonest, Saturn's effect will seem more like retribution, and total renunciation may occur. Although there will be changes in the direction Saturn moves (going retrograde again January 21 through June 6, 1981), it will not change signs until November 30, 1982.

Jupiter: Between January 1 and April 4, 1977, Jupiter will be finishing up its stay in Taurus, where its expansive effects were felt in the budget. Increases in the amount of money at your disposal are likely during such a period, but so is extravagant spending. Unless you fight the impulse to celebrate heavily, your bank balance could be even worse off than before. Between April 4 and August 21, 1977, Jupiter will be in Gemini, increasing your intellectual curiosity and communications. It will retrograde into Gemini again December 31, 1977, turn direct February 21, 1978, and return to Cancer for a longer stay (until September 6, 1978) on April 12, 1978. When Jupiter is in your fourth house, thoughts of improving and expanding the home tend to arise. There may be an increase in the family (which can include the arrival of a roommate who is not a blood relation) or an encouraging improvement in family relations, specifically between yourself and your father. On September 6, 1978, when Jupiter advances into Leo, the cheering effects will involve love affairs (you can take *or leave* a relationship with more equanimity than you would have supposed), vacations (you would enjoy a pleasure trip at such a time), creativity (you could expand your areas of creative experiment), or children (any children—yours or someone else's—would be delightful company for you). On November 21, 1978, Jupiter turns retrograde, reentering Cancer March 1, 1979. It goes direct again March 27, reenters Leo April 21, 1979, and enters Virgo September 30, 1979. This change can mean an increase in work you will be happy about, possibly a change to a professional career. Relationships with co-workers should be smoother, improved by desires for fair play. Under discordant aspects or retrograde motion you might overwork and severely endanger your health. Jupiter goes retrograde December 28, 1979, until April 27, 1980. Its entrance into Libra on October 28, 1980, should help make partnership or advisory relations more relaxed. There is an increased desire to be genuinely helpful and giving; whatever compromises may be necessary can be made without a painful feeling of sacrifice. There is at this time a greater ability to share. On January 26, 1981, Jupiter turns retrograde (until May 29, 1981), which can manifest itself as a slight complication in the equitable bargains or arrangements suggested earlier. The implementation of plans must be held in abeyance, if for no other reason than that one of the parties involved will be elsewhere physically. On November 28, 1981, Jupiter enters Scorpio, which augurs well for increases in income, tax benefits, insurance, and joint holdings.

Taurus Rising: 1977-1981

Pluto: This transit through the sixth house often gives a profound desire for a drastic change in occupation. Whether the present line of work brings too many pressures involving labor unions or pressures to be a team player—which is not easy if natal Pluto is discordant—or just plain deadline pressures, you would rather turn your back on it and work for your own causes on your own terms. You may experience delays in finding something satisfying during discordant aspects or during the following retrograde periods for transiting Pluto: January 18 through June 24, 1977; January 21 through June 26, 1978; January 24 through June 27, 1979; January 27 through July 2, 1980; and January 28 through July 4, 1981.

Neptune: Neptune's transit through Sagittarius during the entire five-year period under discussion here is likely to create some confusion in the financial status of your partner, in joint accounts, or in promises made to you about your own financial prospects. Although it may be difficult, confusing, or even boring during this period, it would be a good idea to learn about tax advantages, budgeting, the stock market, and the comparative merits of mutual funds and various kinds of bank accounts yourself, rather than trusting someone else to take care of your funds. The person you trust may at best be no more skilled at money management than you are, and may at worst abuse the privilege through unwise investment or intentional appropriation of your assets. Whatever your marital status, familiarize yourself with your state's laws on marriage, taxation, and property distribution in divorce. If you have not yet married, consider the wisdom of getting professional legal help in drawing up such premarital agreements as limitation-of-debt, forfeit-of-alimony, or whatever terms you wish to include. It may be more difficult to learn about this, or to obtain an appointment with the attorney of your choice, during the following periods when Neptune will be retrograde: March 20 through August 27, 1977; March 28 through August 30, 1978; March 24 through September 2, 1979; March 27 through September 2, 1980; March 30 through September 6, 1981.

Uranus: Except for the brief period between February 18, 1981, through March 21, 1981, when Uranus will be in Sagittarius, Uranus will spend this five-year period in Scorpio shaking up your partnership relationships. If you are currently a loner, you may impulsively join forces with another on very short acquaintance. There is a danger that you may impulsively accept the terms of others, primarily because of an ultimatum; get *your* terms up front while such talk is going on. If you protect your individual interests and enterprises, and if you write personal latitude into the initial agreement, a fight for breathing space is less likely later on. Relationships formed during this period may break up within five years. That same freedom-loving energy connected with the house of partnership can also manifest itself as an abrupt break in the relationship. The process of (or the adaptation to) the break may be drawn out during the following periods, when Uranus is retrograde: February 17 through July 19, 1977; February 21 through July 23, 1978; February 25 through July 29, 1979; March 2 through August 2, 1980; and March 6 through August 7, 1981. During harmonious aspects or direct motion, both partners may enjoy a shared revolutionary cause or simply feel unusually awake and alive as a result of having the best of both partnership and individual freedom. When Uranus is in Sagittarius—February 18 through March 21, 1981, and for the seven years following November 17, 1981—unexpected possibilities may arise for increasing your income. A promotion may be accompanied by a raise. What you would love most about the change would be the increase in autonomy.

Saturn: Saturn's retrograde motion in Leo from January 1, 1977, until April 13, 1977, may appear in your life as feelings of constraint with family members (particularly, but not exclusively, with your father). Feelings that all the responsibility and work will fall upon your shoulders often accompany Saturn's transit through this department of life. The size of your household may decrease, or family members may depress you by talk of leaving; actual changes may not occur instantly, especially when Saturn is retrograde. You may, during this period, decide to move to smaller quarters, which would be doubly therapeutic in that it occupies your time constructively and frees some of the money previously spent on overhead. Organizing a home office is another beneficial use of this energy. When Saturn enters Virgo on November 18, 1977, you may make such detailed plans for existing or hoped-for children that your partner may back away. The practical personality of the Taurus rising becomes even more pronounced when practical Saturn moves through a house associated with pleasure. When that transit occurs, extremely methodical, painstaking plans are made for everything—from a weekend away from home to childbirth. On January 5, 1978, Saturn retrogrades into Leo, indicating trapped feelings about housework. Major breakdowns, such as failure of the heating system, may occur at this time. Saturn returns to Virgo July 27, 1978, and has two retrograde periods in which to obstruct plans for pleasure— December 26, 1978, to May 11, 1979, and January 9 through May 24, 1980—before it goes ahead into Libra. Saturn in Libra—September 22, 1980, until November 30, 1982—is likely to mean harder work than before in an effort to be conscientious toward co-workers, although others may take advantage of your good intentions. When getting a physical checkup be sure the doctor pays special attention to the kidney and reproductive areas. Do not dismiss lower back pain as the natural consequence of sitting too long at a desk. It may be just that, but it's better to learn it after a careful checkup.

Jupiter: January 1 until April 4, 1977, will be Jupiter's last weeks in Taurus, and during this time feelings of contentment and well-being tend to be celebrated over a full table. In short, the period of March, 1976, through April 4, 1977, indicates extra weight gain. From April 4 until August 21, 1977, Jupiter will be in Gemini, suggesting increased income from a variety of sources and extravagance focusing on mental interests. From August 21 until December 31, 1977, Jupiter will be in Cancer, adding its enthusiastic energy to communications, short-distance trips, studies, and relationships with siblings. On April 12, 1978, Jupiter returns to Cancer, to stay until September 6, 1978. After that time, when Jupiter is in Leo, the arrival of a new lover or child may inspire you to expand your home. Relations with your father should improve during this time, resulting in feelings of generosity. On November 21, 1978, Jupiter turns retrograde and reenters Cancer March 1, 1979. At this time you might be tempted to begin or resume study of a subject involving human nature. Jupiter reenters Leo on April 21, 1979, and enters Virgo September 30, 1979. The transit through Virgo suggests more pleasure in creative work, love affairs, vacations, and relationships with children. There may be some delays or restlessness during Jupiter's retrograde period from December 28, 1979, to April 27, 1980. On October 28, 1980, Jupiter's entrance into Libra can mean an enjoyable and profitable career change. New co-workers who are by temperament more relaxed than you are, and new wisdom in relating to others on the job can bring relief to a formerly sensitive area. On November 28, 1981, Jupiter enters Scorpio, which can mean added pleasure and relaxation in partnership and advisory relations.

Gemini Rising: 1977-1981

Pluto: Pluto's transit through the fifth house can add a stability and intensity hitherto foreign to the restless Gemini personality. Gemini is notorious for valuing a casual attitude toward love affairs and pleasure, and Pluto can bewilder the Gemini by adding the desire to know what the lover does when away, which other people may be rivals, and what the consequences of the relationship might be. You may surprise yourself with the questions you hear yourself asking. Answers may not be forthcoming—not to the extent you would like—during the periods when Pluto is retrograde: January 18 through June 24, 1977; January 21 through June 26, 1978; January 24 through June 27, 1979; January 27 through July 2, 1980; and January 28 through July 4, 1981. A great deal of deliberation may also be devoted to the prospect of parenthood; the idea of a miniature copy of oneself can be irresistible. When Pluto is moving directly and aspects are harmonious, you may encounter at least one lover who promises to be a soul mate. This relationship may become an obsession for you.

Neptune: With Neptune's crossing of your seventh-house cusp, uncertainty about your future as a partner may have vague ill effects on your health: escape into sleep, dependence on medication to sleep or wake up, adverse side effects of medication or other drugs, low vitality, drowsiness, or other symptoms that are difficult to diagnose. Uncertainty as to where you stand with a specific person or disillusionment with the cultural ideal of romance can precipitate a period of escapism or spiritual searching, such as dependence on one or another of the currently popular gurus. What you really need is honest exchange with the person who is troubling you. You may get such responses as, "It's only your imagination" or "You're paranoid," but if the relationship is one you want to keep, press on. During the times when Neptune is retrograde, specific answers may not be readily forthcoming; the other person may be just as confused as you are; but the tide could turn your way if you gently make it clear that you're available should the other feel like unburdening. Neptune will be retrograde March 20 through August 27, 1977; March 28 through August 30, 1978; March 24 through September 2, 1979; March 27 through September 2, 1980; and March 30 through September 6, 1981. When Neptune is harmonious, abstract or cinematic notions of partnership prove less disruptive in your personal experience; you even congratulate yourself on your optimism and romanticism.

Uranus: The transit of Uranus through Scorpio that takes most of this five-year period indicates restlessness and dramatic change in your work. Strikes and layoffs may (if applicable) cause stoppage of work, as may personnel problems. Your work may make you so hyper that you can overwork to the point of nervous exhaustion. If you should quit a job in a company in favor of your own independent enterprise, the exhilaration of independence may enable you to work long hours without complaint or fatigue. Just the same, your system requires meals enjoyed at leisure and sufficient rest; you would not want to use the time that Uranus will be retrograde for *enforced* rest. These intervals are February 17 through July 19, 1977; February 21 through July 23, 1978; February 25 through July 29, 1979; March 2 through August 2, 1980; and March 6 through August 7, 1981. When Uranus is in Sagittarius— February 18 until March 21 of 1981, and for seven years following November 17, 1981—confusions about partnership relations should speed toward resolution. A new partner for either or both of you may function as a catalyst.

Saturn: The retrograde motion of this slow, heavy planet for the first three and a half months of 1977 may be felt as frustrations in the information-gathering processes the Gemini-rising person normally enjoys. Difficulties in reaching people by telephone or mail, delays in getting around town, and estrangements in relationships with siblings would bother you especially. Self-expression may seem more difficult than usual, and as you write either private letters or professional documents you will search for the *exactly* right word with more effort than usual. The retrograde period ending April 13, 1977, makes it difficult to gather information and formulate plans for the future. On November 18, 1977, Saturn enters Virgo, which can make family relations seem strained and confining, particularly relations with your father. Housework may seem especially oppressive. Criticism from your family (substitute roommate, if applicable) doesn't help. On September 22, 1980, Saturn enters Libra, which usually manifests itself as extra seriousness in sexual relationships or your relationships with children. Because Libra is involved, a new love relationship you may not have supposed would be meaningful becomes serious. You may consider marriage, if you haven't married already, for the sake of a child you want to have. You may suggest a marriage of convenience, with all terms stated up front—and this may prove to be more solid than some romantic marriages with no specific agreements. There may be obstructions in courtship or parenthood when Saturn is retrograde; otherwise, the continuity can prove satisfying. Saturn will be retrograde from December 13, 1977, until April 27, 1978; December 26, 1978, until May 11, 1979; January 9 until May 24, 1980; and January 21 through June 6, 1981. During retrograde periods there will be much introspection about the fairness to others of present or proposed situations or, at worst, a heavy load of expectation settled on the other's shoulders.

Jupiter: Jupiter's transit through the twelfth house fosters a new ease and acceptance of solitude where before there may have been nervousness and hurt feelings. Mercury's rulership of the first house gives the habitual restlessness, and Venus's rulership of the twelfth house can, under discordant aspects, indicate feelings of rejection. Jupiter's influence can be calming, even cheering, and solitude is perceived as having positive uses. From April 4 to August 21, 1977, Jupiter will be in the first house, where feelings of well-being will be identified more clearly and new mental interests will add energy. It promises to be a happy if hyperactive time. After a brief stay in Cancer, Jupiter retrogrades into Gemini December 31, 1977, turns direct February 21, 1978, and returns to Cancer April 12, 1978, to stay until September 6, 1978, when it advances into Leo. When in your second house (Cancer), Jupiter is experienced as wildly extravagant desires, especially when there are family members for whom you enjoy buying gifts and food. When Jupiter is in Leo your frame of mind should become more optimistic and your self-expression should seem much easier; the block of the Saturn-in-Leo period dissolves as if by magic. Relationships with siblings also improve. Jupiter reenters Cancer March 1, 1979, reenters Leo April 21, 1979, and enters Virgo on September 30, 1979. This change can mean a lessening of the critical attitude you sensed since Saturn went into Virgo in 1977. Jupiter's move into the fourth house is often realized as an I-don't-care reaction; you decide to do something that's fun and liberating for a change, the critics be damned. You may decide to do a very different sort of housecleaning: instead of dusting and scrubbing, you feel like going through closets and cleaning out the useless things that take up precious space. Throwing out or donating your long-unused clothes or furnishings to charity can be very therapeutic. Once you clear your schedule for more meaningful objects and pastimes, you can make significant progress in whatever professional work you do at home. On October 28, 1980, Jupiter enters Libra, and should help loosen up those relationships with lovers and/or children that suffered the tension, introspection, and vacillation of Pluto and then Saturn in this house. The advent of Jupiter should be a relief; you remember how to relax, and may take a highly enjoyable vacation to celebrate this reawakening in yourself. Jupiter will be retrograde January 26 until May 29, 1981, so you'd probably have a better time on that vacation if you plan it between May 29 and November 28, 1981. On November 28 Jupiter enters Scorpio, and you would tend to think of pleasure more in terms of work than vacation. If you haven't treated yourself to a vacation in a long time, don't forego the pleasure in 1981. It could be the best one yet.

Cancer Rising: 1977-1981

Pluto: The five-year transit of this planet through your fourth house, Libra, contributes a spirit of rebellion in domestic matters, particularly if there is a major progression involving Pluto. Instead of unquestioningly taking all the domestic chores upon yourself, you would prefer to negotiate for a more equitable arrangement. Libra's influence suggests a *quid pro quo* approach—I'll do this if you'll do that—for a fairer division of labor. You may also require more privacy at home during those times when it isn't your turn to do a household chore. Setbacks, or occasions for renegotiation, are likely to occur during discordant Pluto aspects or the following periods when Pluto will be retrograde: January 18 through June 24, 1977; January 21 through June 26, 1978; January 24 through June 27, 1979; January 27 through July 2, 1980; and January 28 through July 4, 1981. When Pluto is moving forward and the aspects are harmonious, the cooperation you get can make you kick yourself for not having asked for it sooner!

Neptune: Neptune, halfway through Sagittarius, may make you restless in your work and easily bored. If your imagination is not actively engaged, it will find an outlet in daydreams or, more constructively, in moonlighting work that will absorb some of the energy formerly directed toward your main occupation. If you work at two or more jobs a day, you will become more fatigued and prone to make errors. Neptune energy, during times the planet is retrograde or discordant, can all too easily manifest itself as both physical and mental exhaustion, so that you appear like a zombie on the job. If your boredom is prolonged you may indeed feel that you're there in body only. Do not be as negligent with your health as you are tempted to be with your work, as Neptune has a clouding effect and doctors would have a difficult time diagnosing your malady. Being sick would be costly and time-consuming; you'd be better off consulting your regular astrologer and looking for a more satisfying line of work. Taking a vacation may be therapeutic, but your plans to get away could be fouled up if you schedule a trip for any of the following periods, when Neptune will be in retrograde: March 20 through August 27, 1977; March 28 through August 30, 1978; March 24 through September 2, 1979; March 27 through September 2, 1980; and March 30 through September 6, 1981.

Uranus: It is in the area of love affairs, pleasures, creativity, and children that most of the sudden and surprising changes in your life and thought can be expected to occur. Even more important than changes in the supporting cast of characters in your life will be the new attitudes you adopt. Where once an astrologer might have said that if Uranus is going through a woman's fifth house her lovers might abruptly leave her, social change has now rendered such a one-sided reading suspect. The fifth-house pleasure emphasis suggests a desire for freedom, and when Scorpio is on the cusp that desire can be obsessive. With Uranus transiting through this department of life, the desire for freedom to do one's own thing becomes even more compelling. You are fortunate to have this positioning of the planets in the present and near future rather than in the past, when there was less freedom to articulate the stirrings toward independence. When Uranus is moving retrograde you may feel some inhibition impeding free communication in your relationships, but this has more to do with the person and the occasion than with your general attitude. For instance, the children in your life may have some difficulty in achieving an independence that would in turn free you. A little extra indulgence, reassurance, and gentle humor should help snap them out of their nervousness or balkiness. Uranus will be retrograde on the following dates: February 17 through July 19, 1977; February 21 through July 23, 1978; February 25 through July 29, 1979; March 2 through August 2, 1980; and March 6 through August 7, 1981. When Uranus moves forward and is harmonious, you will be capable of enjoying brief relationships in a spirit of adventure, initiating or accepting necessary breakups amicably and going ahead into happier new relationships. Creative work begun during this five-year period should be highly inventive. Uranus will be in Sagittarius from February 18, 1981, until it retrogrades into Scorpio March 21, 1981, and will reenter Sagittarius for a seven-year stay November 17, 1981. When it is in Sagittarius there should be increased opportunities for autonomous professional work, and your rate of work should speed up owing to new challenges. A friend may provide an unexpected break in your career, or may even suggest an entirely new occupation that will appeal to you.

Saturn: Between January 1 and April 13, 1977, Saturn's retrograde motion in Leo may manifest itself in exceptionally adverse financial setbacks. Where once you may have spent generously, especially on gifts for others, necessity now requires comparison shopping and other sensible economic practices. Financial planning is difficult during the times Saturn is retrograde in Leo (also January 5 until July 27, 1978), as you cannot predict which costs will rise; nor do you feel that you have adequate information about or faith in your sources of income. If you have always been financially taken care of and are unused to being self-supporting, you will have to face the relationship of cost to value in all the goods and services that your life requires more realistically than in the past. You will have to reassess your values, mercilessly weeding out the nonessentials and actively seeking the best and most durable returns for your money. If you have always been sensible, economical, and discriminating, this will be a time of added certainty of your convictions. If, however, you have been extravagant and wasteful, this transit can be a sobering, maturing one indeed. Your coming of age will be felt through dollars-and-cents symbolism. Between November 18, 1977, and January 5, 1978, and again from July 27, 1978, until September 22, 1980, Saturn will be in Virgo, contributing its practicality to your thought processes in general. At about that time you may write seriously as a professional, and the process of writing would be methodical, conscientious, and difficult. Relations with neighbors, siblings, and assorted callers may be strained, particularly when interruption of your work is at issue. On September 22, 1980, Saturn enters Libra, and you can use this energy either to accept the guilt that those who live with you would make you feel *or* you can be more firm in insisting that you won't take more than your fair share of family responsibilities. When Saturn is retrograde January 21 through June 6, 1981, you may experience the frustration of a stalemate in your domestic relations. When Saturn's motion is direct and the aspects are harmonious, you feel instead the reassuring certainty that each member of the household will be reliable and supportive and will perform whatever duties were agreed upon. Another source of security at such a time may be a move to more economical housing or a sound investment in real estate.

Jupiter: Between January 1 and April 4, 1977, Jupiter will be winding up its transit through the eleventh house and providing its generous, expansive vibrations to benefit your friendships. At a time when Saturn is going through the second house and requiring more conservative spending, you may be surprised by the generosity of even the most casual acquaintances. Their encouragement and hospitality should do much to help you through this period. Between April 4 and August 21, 1977, Jupiter will be in Gemini, during which time you may decide to turn down many social invitations, partly because you may feel embarrassed if you can't reciprocate, and partly because you see a positive value in solitude and breathing space. You could utilize the time to good advantage by doing some of that writing you may have been promising yourself in a half-hearted way. From August 21 until December 31, 1977, Jupiter will be in Cancer (prior to a brief retrograde into Gemini); it will be in Cancer again from April 12 until September 6, 1978. Jupiter's transit through your first house can have an enormously cheering, liberating effect. Your optimism and enthusiasm become more apparent, along with your capacity to forgive and accept others. You show less of the Cancerian crustiness and more of the generosity. Under discordant aspects or retrograde periods such as the March 1, 1979, retrograde from Leo to Cancer (it reenters Leo on April 21, 1979), your enthusiasms may take the form of tangible appetites and overweight becomes more likely than usual. On September 6, 1978, and again on April 21, 1979, Jupiter enters Leo, which should be felt as some lightening of the financial load. The temptation to go on a spree after a long, dry spell of watchfulness can be a strong one indeed, but you are more likely to cut your losses and come out of this period in the black if you concentrate on paying what leftover debts you may still have and saving the balance. Jupiter's entrance into Virgo on September 30, 1979, should add optimism to your outlook and communications, and relations with siblings are likely to improve. Most important, your mind should be active, productive, and hopeful; you feel more capable of enjoying your environment. Between December 28, 1979, and April 27, 1980, when Jupiter will be retrograde, your enthusiasm and its expressions may be somewhat subdued. Plans for short pleasure trips may also be hampered. Jupiter enters Libra on October 28, 1980, and this should help ease family relations considerably. Jupiter's entrance into Scorpio on November 28, 1981, should make its benefits felt in the area of love affairs, pleasures, creative work, and children. You might have a child at this time, or begin a creative project or gamble that brings you a great deal of pleasure.

Leo Rising: 1977-1981

Pluto: The transit through Libra can be a stabilizing force insofar as it adds a new activity to the mental repertoire: probing beneath surface appearances. Without this transit, Venus's rulership of the third house combined with the Leo ascendant's hunger for flattery can make you accept at face value many sweet things said with ulterior motives. Pluto's transit through the third house is felt as insistent prompting to find out where you really stand and what others mean by what they say. Your preferred reading matter would include psychology books—specializing in power shifts in relationships—or mysteries. You are also fascinated by the marital ups and downs of your neighbors and siblings. During the months that Pluto's motion is retrograde you may have difficulty learning all that you want to know. You may also decide to be perversely uncommunicative yourself. Pluto will be retrograde as follows: January 18 through June 24, 1977; January 21 through June 26, 1978; January 24 through June 27, 1979; January 27 through July 2, 1980; and January 28 through July 4, 1981.

Neptune: The area most susceptible to confusion, self-deception, deception by others, and miscellaneous misunderstandings is the fifth

house, which governs love affairs, creativity, pleasure, and relationships with children. Entering (or escaping from) a love affair may seem
like a relief or a solution, but extremely unreal expectations can threaten
the best of relationships. Subtle or even amusingly *un*subtle hints to
have a baby—hints that having a baby might be an escape from whatever
else you are doing—should be regarded with great suspicion. Parenthood may mean the end of a lackluster job, but it's certainly not the end
of *work*! Creative work initiated during Neptune's transit through the
fifth house should be distinctive and original, although the creative
process may be impeded during Neptune's retrograde period: March 20
through August 27, 1977; March 28 through August 30, 1978; March 24
through September 2, 1979; March 27 through September 2, 1980; and
March 30 through September 6, 1981.

Uranus: The transit through Scorpio is most likely to manifest itself as
domestic disturbances, including an abrupt move to a new home (owing
to eviction, transfer, or physical problems with the present home), or a
family breakup. The person who breaks away would leave with little or
no warning. The shock following this is in turn followed by a period of
moral paralysis, especially when Uranus is retrograde. There is little
insight as to what to do immediately, and so the first reaction is to do
absolutely nothing. Time helps to add perspective, and one alternative
to replacing the person who has left is, simply, not to. You might prefer
to experiment with the freedom of living alone. Finding a new place to
live may be taken care of with surprising speed, although the proceedings are apt to be somewhat less rapid when Uranus is retrograde:
February 17 through July 19, 1977; February 21 through July 23, 1978;
February 25 through July 29, 1979; March 2 through August 2, 1980;
and March 6 through August 7, 1981.

Saturn: The retrograde motion of Saturn from January 1, 1977, until
April 13, 1977, makes it difficult to plan your personal future (personal
as opposed to shared); you feel blocked in your attempts to crystallize
personal priorities. Try not to dwell on a decrease in the flattering
attentions of others. You'll feel better if you concentrate instead on
strengthening yourself and getting your health checked. Fatigue, low
blood pressure, or back pain should receive professional medical help.
On November 18, 1977, Saturn enters Virgo, which you are likely to
experience as a new practicality replacing ostentation. When Saturn is
retrograde in this house (December 13, 1977, to April 27, 1978), you
may have to double your efforts to resist the temptation to buy some-

thing to cheer you up, especially if it is advertised as a bargain. Bargains have a way of turning out to be lemons. One favor you could do for yourself instead would be to reduce your indebtedness. Between January 5 and July 27 of 1978, Saturn will be back in Leo again, indicating more of the introspection and the low morale that characterized early 1977. Saturn returns to Virgo on July 28, 1978, to stay until September 22, 1980. Saturn's entrance into Libra on September 22, 1980, adds to the seriousness and depth of the mentality, and serves as a stabilizer in decision-making. Libra on the third cusp can mean frequent vacillation and reversals. With Saturn in the third house, however, there is likely to be more confidence in the rightness of a choice, with less temptation to recant.

Jupiter: Jupiter's last weeks in Taurus, winding up on April 4, 1977, benefit the tenth house. Career efforts would have paid off between Jupiter's entrance into this sign on March 26, 1976, and its passage into Gemini on April 4, 1977. You would enjoy the high esteem in which you are held by those having the power to promote you. Higher status in the organization you work for, honors, awards, and publicity are all increasingly likely during this year. Your relationship with your mother is also likely to be more open and honest, and substantially better than before. Jupiter will be in Gemini between April 4 and August 21, 1977, and between December 31, 1977, and April 12, 1978. At that time your social life (not a synonym for your love life, which is the fifth house, but rather any combination of acquaintances and friends, however you want to distinguish the degrees of intimacy) will also pick up. Lively, communicative people may be entering your life, giving your spirits a lift. When Jupiter enters Cancer, your twelfth house, you may decide to withdraw, if only for one day a week, from the social merry-go-round in favor of an ambitious project that has to be tackled single-handedly. You may also be attracted by charitable work for children or a hospital. Jupiter will be in Cancer August 21 to December 31, 1977; April 12 to September 6, 1978; and March 1 to April 21, 1979. Jupiter's transit through Leo brings hope for higher spirits and a desire to live it up. There may, too, be considerable overeating, but this is not the solitary binge in the privacy of the kitchen that is more likely during Jupiter's passage through Cancer, but rather the convivial enjoyment of *haute cuisine* to show off to friends that you can afford and appreciate it. With this chart, doing without is somewhat less difficult: if you eat at home and prepare less elaborate, more nutritious meals, your health and shape needn't be any the worse for occasional restaurant parties. Jupiter in the first house can also mean a determination to laugh and smile for the sake of saving face, despite setbacks experienced in the various spheres of your life. Jupiter will be in Leo September 6, 1978, to March 1, 1979, and April 21 to September 30, 1979. When Jupiter is in Virgo—September 30, 1979, to October 28, 1980—the temptation to go on a spending spree should increase, along with your assets. Newly acquired prestige is likely to bring with it money in the bank. Some of the heavy expenditures may involve your work; to be a success you have to have the trappings (so you would tell yourself when deciding to go ahead with a major investment). Between December 28, 1979, and April 27, 1980, Jupiter will be retrograde. During these months you would be better off postponing major purchases; there would probably be delay in delivery or defects in the goods. Instead of actually buying, study and compare what's available. Collect and read catalogues when the acquisitive impulse overtakes you, but don't commit yourself until Jupiter moves ahead again. When Jupiter is in Libra—October 28, 1980, to November 28, 1981—mental work, communications, relationships with siblings and neighbors, and contractual agreements can prove increasingly beneficial. Even more important, your outlook should improve noticeably after the probing, brooding, and anxious decision-making of the Pluto- and Saturn-in-Libra years. When Jupiter is in the first house, the cheerfulness you show is at times a front, motivated by a desire not to depress your friends or yourself, whatever the problem may be. When Jupiter is in the third house, as it is when in Libra, the cheerfulness shown reflects a more genuine upbeat attitude. During the last month of this five-year period, as of November 28, 1981, Jupiter will be in Scorpio, indicating hope of more relaxed domestic relations.

Virgo Rising: 1977-1981

Pluto: Pluto's retrograde motion in Libra from January 18 until June 24, 1977, will most likely make its influence felt in your financial activity. You may find during this time that an object that tempts you stays in your mind until you buy it; it's very difficult to think of much else. Perversely, this tends to occur when you have to limit your spending. When Pluto's motion is direct and the aspects are harmonious you feel more freedom to buy, but you may not be altogether satisfied with the merchandise you see. If you have a very particular idea of what you want, it may not yet have been manufactured. Harmonious aspects can also mean profit from partnership (Libra). Other periods of Pluto's retrograde motion: January 21 through June 26, 1978; January 24 through June 27, 1979; January 27 through July 2, 1980; and January 28 through July 4, 1981.

Neptune: Neptune's transit through Sagittarius during the entire five-year period may manifest itself as the desire to redecorate your base of operations—both home and office. You may be vaguely aware of a feeling of wanderlust; that is, you're not altogether sure where you'd rather be, but you're not turned on by where you are. This can make the business of selecting a decor difficult. The appearance of your setting is particularly important to you at this time, as you need a refuge where you can forget the demands of your working life and preserve your balance and perspective. During this period you may also opt for dropping out and living in a foreign country or two. When Neptune is retrograde there may be delays in achieving these dreams, or even in achieving a clearer form of the dream. Note the periods of Neptune's retrograde motion: March 20 through August 27, 1977; March 28 through August 30, 1978; March 24 through September 2, 1979; March 27 through September 2, 1980; and March 30 through September 6, 1981. When Neptune is moving forward and forming harmonious aspects, you are likely to get unusually inspired ideas for improving your home life. At home you may feel—uncharacteristically—above it all, rather than up to your gut in details.

Uranus: The transit through Scorpio, for most of this five-year period, should make its presence felt in the context of your mental activities, communications, short journeys, and relations with siblings and neighbors. Surprises and reversals—invitations and cancellations—can be expected at the last minute. Your mind should be quicker than ever before and highly inventive in finding new ways to get the information you need. Interruptions from telephone calls, deliveries of telegrams, or drop-in visitors can make you more nervous than you would have supposed. Your siblings' discussions of the upheavals of your life and theirs may prove rather nerve-racking, too. During this period you may begin or resume your education as a declaration of independence, but that same independence may impel you to prefer more impulsive, whimsical reading to formalized academic studies. Your reading preferences may include any of the sciences, do-it-yourself auto repair, biog-

raphies, psychology, or astrology. When Uranus is retrograde you may
have some difficulty obtaining the material you want or fully comprehending it. Uranus will be retrograde February 17 through July 19,
1977; February 21 through July 23, 1978; February 25 through July 29,
1979; March 2 through August 2, 1980; and March 6 through August 7,
1981. When Uranus is direct and harmonious, your learning rate
accelerates—as does your impatience with regulated school courses
(being told what to read and write is another objection).

Saturn: Saturn's stay in Leo, especially when it is going retrograde, can
be particularly difficult for the person having Virgo rising. Necessary
separations, even when it's your own business interests that require you
to be away, are more lonesome than before. Whatever the reason for
your solitude, time seems to hang heavy. The need for more self-
discipline in your work (more difficult between January 1 and April 13,
1977), for solitude, or for hospital visits tends to arise when Saturn
transits the twelfth house. Disappointments occurring at this time may
be taken too personally and too seriously for your own good. This time
can be used constructively by catching up with work that you've been
meaning to do—preferably, improvements that would make your life
more cheerful or more organized. Saturn enters Virgo on November 18,
1977. As I explained in the chapter on progressions, Saturn need not
mean grief unless your habits are wasteful, undisciplined, and unpre-
meditated. Similarly, Saturn's transit through the first house doesn't
have to mean illness unless you've been remiss in your care of yourself.
While the Virgo-rising person would *think* of health care, conscien-
tiousness about work may get in the way of actually doing anything about
it. During Saturn's passage through the first house, a person usually has
to confront the painful consequences of unintelligent habits. One of
these, considering the Virgo nature, is very often excessive fretting or
hypochondria. Physical pain may, obligingly, appear in the intestinal
area. Try not to be like a friend of mine who says she gets colitis every
two years, "and the attacks are *on time*, too!" Instead, use your will
power to determine that you will *not* get your next regularly scheduled
illness. Get a medical checkup regularly, and it might also be a good idea
to taper off your work hours before your doctor forces you to. After a
retrograde period in Leo between January 5 and July 27, 1978, Saturn
will have another stay in Virgo until September 22, 1980. When Saturn
goes through Libra between September 22, 1980, and November 30,
1982, there may be a decrease in income or an increase in unavoidable

responsibilities that will require you to exercise restraint in your spending habits.

Jupiter: During Jupiter's last months in Taurus—January 1 to April 4, 1977—the problems that may accompany Saturn's transit through the twelfth house would inspire you to find a system of beliefs to sustain you through them. Travel would be another way of cheering yourself, although if there is a natal discordant aspect between Jupiter and Saturn being stimulated at the same time, you may find obstacles that threaten your desired departure. Jupiter will be in Gemini April 4 to August 21, 1977, and again between December 31, 1977, and April 12, 1978. During those months you may be cheered by recognition for responsibility you have assumed in the past, by favorable publicity, by a promotion, and/or by a more open and communicative relationship with your mother. Considering, however, the sensitive position of Saturn, you may well drive yourself all the harder. Jupiter will be in Cancer from August 21 to December 31, 1977; April 12 to September 6, 1978; and March 1 to April 21, 1979. During those intervals compassionate friends are likely to issue invitations to you and make an effort to get you to relax. With their support you may relent and give yourself permission to enjoy life. When Jupiter is in Leo—September 6, 1978, to March 1, 1979, and April 21 to September 30, 1979—solitude will become a more positive experience for you, and you will cease to feel so overburdened. Pride in individual achievement may also be a new sensation for you. You should find a certain satisfaction in meeting rather than avoiding the tests of experience. Jupiter enters Virgo September 30, 1979. When Jupiter is discordant or retrograde (between December 28, 1979, and April 27, 1980), you may feel that you are being taken for granted, but you should be able to laugh this feeling off. (Jupiter's presence in Virgo should help counteract the more sober influence of Saturn.) Saturn leaves your first house September 22, 1980, and Jupiter stays for another month, until October 28. For most of the stay in Virgo, and especially during its last month without Saturn, Jupiter can help keep your attitude hopeful and healthy. If Saturn's influence in the first house is manifested as a weight loss from ill health, Jupiter's balancing influence would add to your appetite and make you strive for a healthy stability in your weight, habits, and outlook. From October 28, 1980, to November 28, 1981, Jupiter will be in Libra, and you will probably feel a desire to celebrate your survival of recent difficulties. You deserve to! Bear in mind, though, that you will probably get better value for your money when Jupiter's motion is direct. In other words, use the January 26 to May 29, 1981, retrograde period to save up for the blast to follow. During that time have the fun of comparing travel folders. From November 28, 1981, when Jupiter goes into Scorpio, mental and written work, travels closer to home, and relations with siblings and neighbors should add to your satisfactions.

Libra Rising: 1977-1981

Pluto: The addition of Pluto to this department of life contributes a new persistence and a new fondness for probing beneath surfaces, where before there had been dilettantism and a calm acceptance of face values. Pluto began its slow progress through Libra on October 6, 1971, and will continue here beyond 1981. Pluto's influence may manifest itself as brooding, soul searching, intense questioning (given or received), emotional blackmail, and emotional fixation on partnership issues. Under discordant aspects or Pluto's retrograde motion, you would feel that a partner's emotional demands may be crowding or invading you. This formerly partner-loving sign is thus apt to find separateness newly appealing. Pluto will be retrograde January 18 through June 24, 1977; January 21 through June 26, 1978; January 24 through June 27, 1979; January 27 through July 2, 1980; and January 28 through July 4, 1981. Health difficulties characteristic of discordant Pluto aspects would involve the reproductive or eliminative system. When Pluto is direct and the aspects are harmonious, there is a happy feeling of having found a goal or cause worthy of your dedication, and people with whom it is possible to work in cooperation.

Neptune: During the entire five years Neptune will be in Sagittarius, your third house, prompting the creative imagination. In your mental work, studies, or communications, your inspiration and style should be truly original. You may at this time anticipate frequent short trips to relieve your boredom. When your mind is blocked you may seek distraction in idle telephone calls or may find you have difficulty remembering mundane details. This may irritate and frustrate those you talk to, who feel you aren't giving them your undivided attention. During Neptune's retrograde periods this problem is more likely to arise. Neptune will be retrograde March 20 through August 27, 1977; March 28 through August 30, 1978; March 24 through September 2,

1979; March 27 through September 2, 1980; and March 30 through September 6, 1981. Neptune's direct-motion months and harmonious aspects will be times of distinctive mental productivity—perhaps even including evidence of ESP—and a capacity to be detached from anything distasteful in the surroundings. The dreams and designs conceived during Neptune's transit through Sagittarius should be converted to marketable form for future profit. If you are attracted to fiction, try setting your daydreams and ideas down on paper.

Uranus: Your finances will be subject to one surprise after another as Uranus spends 1977 to 1981 transiting through your second house. Anything—a windfall, a computer error, a raise, a divorce, or the impulsive purchase of a stereo system or automobile—can mean drastic fluctuations in your bank balance. Where once you may have been dependent on the generosity of another (before Pluto's passage into the first house and before Uranus moved into the first, then the second), you now are strongly in favor of self-support. Early in Uranus's stay in the second house and when Uranus turned discordant or retrograde, you may have made some unwise investments; once you become more accustomed to having money of your own, however, you show more discretion in your handling of it. Uranus will be retrograde February 17 through July 19, 1977; February 21 through July 23, 1978; February 25 through July 29, 1979; March 2 through August 2, 1980; and March 6 through August 7, 1981.

Saturn: Saturn will be retrograde in Leo, your eleventh house, until April 13, 1977, and so you may experience separations from friends. Disappointments or long periods without communication from someone you had hoped would be more attentive are taken too much to heart. Between January 1, 1977, and November 18, 1977, you would be especially sensitive to the negligence or jealousy of others. Don't be surprised if your career requirements involve socializing more with business associates and less with other friends. Your friends may feel slighted and envious, and they may express this in oblique, ironic, even sarcastic ways which would hurt your feelings. When Saturn is in Virgo—November 18, 1977, to January 5, 1978, and July 27, 1978 to September 22, 1980—the social tensions begun during Saturn's transit through the eleventh house may cause you to withdraw into a defensive shell of self-imposed privacy. The time spent away from friends may be devoted to either brooding about real or supposed criticisms of you or catching up on constructive work. Even when your friends are not critical, their frequent expressions of gloom try your patience and repel you. You can help them with some plain, common-sense talk when they cross the line from legitimate complaint to morbid self-pity. Saturn will be in Libra from September 22, 1980, to November 30, 1982. During that time you will probably be obliged to reassess long-standing personal habits, principles, and values. If you are troubled by a decrease in your vitality or an inability to adapt to cold weather, your problem may be low blood pressure, anemia, or an infection involving your kidneys, gall bladder, or internal reproductive system. Have a thorough checkup by a physician you know and trust, and follow the regimen given you. Saturn's transit through your first house often necessitates reassessment of your priorities and the weeding out of nonessentials. Streamline your life as much as possible.

Jupiter: Jupiter's stay in Taurus from March 26, 1976, to April 4, 1977, promises some relief from financial burdens. A salary increase or a gift comes just when you need it most. During this time you may be tempted to run up bills with your credit cards, which you will feel viscerally when Saturn goes into the second house (if not sooner, when the bills come in!). Partners may be especially generous at this time. Jupiter will be in Gemini between April 4 and August 21, 1977, and from December 31, 1977, to April 12, 1978. During the time spent in this sign, you may find some satisfaction in dabbling in one philosophy after another, perhaps in the course of getting an advanced degree, or from publishing or travel. If you make public speaking appearances, your style is probably highly entertaining and witty. You can expect to become more confident in your own talent for enlightening and inspiring people as well as making them laugh. Although more of a freethinker than a religious follower, you have a *willingness* to believe in a higher being that will see you through the difficult times. When Jupiter is in Cancer—August 21 to December 31, 1977, and April 12 to September 6, 1978—efforts made toward recognition and promotion should begin to pay off. Whether or not you actually become a celebrity, you will enjoy more popularity than you've had in recent years. Another bonus should be an improvement in your relationship with your mother. You show more empathy toward her than you ever have before, and she will probably prove to be your most vocal publicist and supporter.

Jupiter's presence in Leo will seem like a spring thaw after the bleak social life you have had in recent years. Jupiter will be in Leo from

September 6 to November 21, 1978, and from April 21 to September 30, 1979. New friends, perhaps including celebrities, and newly generous friends should offer the encouragement and cheering you need. The exchange of professional favors may bring additional boosts to your spirits. Jupiter will be in Virgo from September 30, 1979, to October 28, 1980, promising relief from the anxiety previously felt in solitude. During the retrograde period from December 28, 1979, to April 27, 1980, you should confront your personal realities with courage and find pleasurable activities to sweeten your solitude. If you have undergone a separation, divorce, or parting from a lover, this would be the time you make peace with the fact.

From October 28, 1980, to November 28, 1981, Jupiter will be in Libra. Jupiter tends to bring out all the positive, ethical, well-meaning potentials of Libra. You would feel truly needed if called upon to contribute your unbiased judgment to a dispute between two friends; you thrive on being pulled into the middle of things. During this time you would really savor the happiness you find. After November 28, 1981, when Jupiter is in Scorpio, you would have a difficult time resisting the temptation to treat yourself to something extravagant. Possible plumbing trouble in your home, or doctors' bills, may siphon off some of your funds as well.

Scorpio Rising: 1977-1981

Pluto: Pluto's stay in Libra during the entire five years affects your twelfth house. During this time you tend to brood over relationships and the agonizing compromises they entail. Unlike the Libra-rising person, you have more familiarity with and comfort in solitude, and a long-term intimate relationship with a lover may make you feel claustrophobic. Those of you who are beginning your *first* intimate relationships at this time may be especially confused by ambivalent feelings. Whatever your age, you prefer to keep the details of your partnerships secret. When Pluto is retrograde you are more likely to waste your emotional intensity in stewing over past obsessions and grudges. The retrograde periods are: January 18 to June 24, 1977; January 21 through June 26, 1978; January 24 through June 27, 1979; January 27 through July 2, 1980; and January 28 through July 4, 1981. When Pluto is direct and harmonious you have the determination to overcome anything self-defeating. You may, too, be attracted to reform work in one institution or another or to cooperative humanitarian work.

Neptune: Your finances will need more study and control, as Neptune lends its confusing influence to your second house for the entire five years. Money will seem to flow like water, unless you have Mercury or Saturn in the second house natally and, therefore, keep accurate records. Other problems can include victimization by a con artist, broken promises, unrealistic expectations of your earning power, and difficulty in finding a job. The likelihood of any of these would be greater when Neptune is discordant or retrograde: March 20 through August 27, 1977; March 28 through August 30, 1978; March 24 through September 2, 1979; March 27 through September 2, 1980; and March 30 through September 6, 1981. When Neptune is direct and harmonious, you will be better able to make the charitable donations you've been meaning to, and you may profit through use of your imagination. Speculative ventures may also be profitable, depending on your natal and progressed aspects.

Uranus: If your life has seemed unusually hectic since 1974, with frequent last-minute upheavals in your plans, you can thank Uranus's transit through Scorpio. Your restlessness can make you suddenly pull up stakes, particularly if you are pursuing an intense sexual involvement. Drastic change is the common denominator of the experiences associated with this transit. During this period you may experience at least one breakup that can leave you with a nervous, loose-ends feeling. Now for the absolutely *only* instance in which I preface guidance with "If you are a woman": see your gynecologist twice a year. At least. If you act on an unexpected sexual attraction to a stranger, you'll want to make sure you weren't left with the kind of souvenir that requires medication.

When Uranus is discordant or retrograde, make a point of allowing yourself more time to do the things you have to do. In your eagerness to implement some of your inventive inspirations, you may cram more activity into a day or an hour than is healthy for you. Don't let yourself get hypernervous; take it easy. Uranus will be retrograde from February 17 through July 19, 1977; February 21 through July 23, 1978; February 25 through July 29, 1979; March 2 through August 2, 1980; and March 6 through August 7, 1981. When Uranus is harmonious or direct, you

enjoy a rapid succession of ideas, you attract people magnetically, and
are exhilarated by the independence you achieve for yourself.

Saturn: Saturn's stay in Leo until November 18, 1977—especially
during the retrograde period between January 1 and April 13, 1977—
can make you feel that your job has come to a dead end. You probably
hate having a boss, and you feel discriminated against, passed over, or
just plain unappreciated. The person you report to is stingy with feedback unless you have a complaint. During this period be as gracious as
you can while you discreetly investigate other possibilities. When
Saturn is in Virgo you'll want to consult friends for suggestions that will
help you move up professionally. Saturn will be in Virgo from
November 18, 1977, to January 5, 1978, and from July 27, 1978, to
September 22, 1980. Saturn will be in Libra from September 22, 1980,
to November 30, 1982. In your twelfth house it can add to your habitual
rehashing and brooding. In addition, you feel more resentful when
partners don't do their fair share in relationships with you, although fear
of loss is apt to impel you to keep your resentment to yourself. You
would be better off turning your thoughts to your work and letting the
past recede into oblivion. At the next disappointment speak of improving relations in the future, not of the other person's failures in the past.

Jupiter: Jupiter's beneficent effect is felt in partnership and advisory
relations, owing to the March 26, 1976, to April 4, 1977, passage through
Taurus. Whether or not such a relationship is in your life at this time,
your attitude is accepting, relaxed, hopeful, and good-humored—the
best attitude in which a relationship can grow (this does not cancel out
the foregoing section on Saturn; the two planets may trigger off aspects
on the same day, which can manifest itself in very paradoxical behavior).
If you have recently left a relationship, Jupiter's energy can help you
forgive the partner who is no longer in your life.

Jupiter will be in Gemini from April 4 to August 21, 1977, and from
December 31, 1977, to April 12, 1978, and your prospects for increasing
your income increase significantly during these intervals. You may
double your sources of income (remember, this is a dual sign!) by
moonlighting or learning a new occupation which, quick study that you
are, can soon become a lucrative enterprise. If you are a student you
could find it advantageous to apply for a scholarship during either or
both of these intervals. Writing, reporting, speaking, or an occasional
sporting bet are other encouraging possibilities. Jupiter's trips into

Cancer suggest a somewhat emotional return to the family's long-held religion. A trip to a place you loved to visit with your parents, or a visit to the parents themselves, should help you regain your perspective. Publishing, lecturing, or teaching can be satisfying outlets for you—outlets that increase your influence and popularity. Jupiter will be in Cancer from August 21 to December 31, 1977, and from April 12 to September 6, 1978.

When Jupiter is in Leo the career frustrations you recently experienced should ease somewhat, and you will make a smooth transition to a more gratifying situation. The publicity you get should be heartwarming indeed (although your mother's bragging could get downright embarrassing!) as you remember the underrated feeling you experienced not long ago. Jupiter will be in Leo from September 6, 1978, to March 1, 1979, and from April 21 to September 30, 1979. Jupiter in Virgo is likely to activate your social life, as friends try to draw you out and urge you to celebrate the fruits of your professional success with them. The time you spend with friends is apt to be devoted to constructive analysis of recent and proposed successes, and to laughter at an occasional sacred cow. Jupiter in Virgo impels criticism by satire, and when it passes through the eleventh house you enjoy this in the company of like-minded friends. Jupiter will be in Virgo from September 30, 1979, until October 28, 1980. When it goes retrograde, from December 28, 1979, to April 27, 1980, you may be more sensitive to your friends' critical humor when it is aimed at you (or you just imagine that it is). From October 28, 1980, to November 28, 1981, Jupiter will be in Libra, which can help take the heat off that solitary brooding that accompanied the transits of Pluto and Saturn in this sign. If you have been thinking that competitors or a partner may have secretly been plotting to your disadvantage, the transit of Jupiter through your twelfth house enables you to relax, to forgive the real or imagined offenders, and even to laugh at yourself. When you are alone—a state that looks better to you all the time!—you can at last do things *you* enjoy, things you may in the past have put aside in a spirit of compromise. Jupiter enters Scorpio on November 28, 1981, promising personal success in overcoming those elements of your life or personality that disturbed you in the past. You may find especially appropriate the words spoken by Katharine Hepburn (a Sun-in-Scorpio) in *The African Queen*: "Nature is what we are put here to overcome." Jupiter's passage through your Scorpio first house indicates growing courage from having done just that.

Sagittarius Rising: 1977-1981

Pluto: During this entire period Pluto will be in Libra, affecting your friendships. When Pluto is discordant or retrograde you may experience an unwillingness to socialize in groups; you prefer the company of one or two individuals you feel comfortable with, if you see anyone at all. When you consider, too, that Neptune will be in your first house (more on that later), your antisocial moods are not surprising. Pluto will be retrograde January 18 through June 24, 1977; January 21 through June 26, 1978; January 24 through June 27, 1979; January 27 through July 2, 1980; and January 28 through July 4, 1981. When Pluto is harmonious or direct, you are much more willing to be with people, particularly if you share a humanitarian cause.

Neptune: Neptune's stay in Sagittarius for the entire five years can manifest itself as a remote, unreachable quality that makes people think you're spaced out (which may be the case). When you're tired or drowsy you daydream, your thoughts drift off, and you lose minutes in your trance. Your boredom threshold is low unless you are involved in an activity such as a creative art form or an altruistic cause that stimulates your imagination to the fullest. If you feel wasted—which is likely when Neptune is discordant or retrograde—you are more susceptible to illness (such as epidemics), the toxic effects of bad foods or medicines, and psychosomatic ailments. Escapes into sleep, alcohol, or drugs are also possible. If you learned that someone had lied to you, you would ever afterward be deaf to that person's explanations. If you have defaulted on a promise or been caught in a deliberate lie, it's more liberating to face the music, pay the price, and be rid of the matter for all time than to resort to flight and be haunted by it. Neptune will be retrograde March 20 through August 27, 1977; March 28 through August 30, 1978; March 24 through September 2, 1979; March 27 through September 2, 1980; and March 30 through September 6, 1981. During times of direct motion or harmonious aspects, your creativity, ideals, and sensitivity can win you distinctive forms of recognition.

Uranus: Sandwiched between Pluto in the eleventh house and Neptune in the first, Uranus prompts independence more emphatically than usual. Quite literally between the factionalism of your social life and the self's attraction to withdrawal, you would just as soon turn your back on people as not. It can be very satisfying to say "Screw it all!" as you walk out the door by yourself. During the intervals in which Uranus will be retrograde, you would carefully conceal how nervous other people make you feel, particularly when they disappoint you by cancelling plans. Nor would you want to speak of your sexual relationships. Uranus will be retrograde February 17 through July 19, 1977; February 21 through July 23, 1978; February 25 through July 29, 1979; March 2 through Au gust 2, 1980; and March 6 through August 7, 1981. When Uranus is direct and harmonious, you will do some of your most inventive work and experience your most significant psychological insights when alone. It will be in solitude that you learn most quickly.

Saturn: The retrograde motion of Saturn in Leo (until April 13, 1977) affects your ninth house. Delays and negative responses may be expected in the areas of publishing, teaching, public speaking, and long-distance travel. Also characteristic of a Saturn transit through the ninth house are a somewhat gloomy general outlook, a moralistic attitude toward work and pleasure, ego-deflations from a puritannical person, and an awareness of the oppressive force established religion can be. You feel that your self-imposed guidelines offer discipline enough without having your life restricted further by any formal religion. Your convictions are apt to be the same regardless of the harmony of the aspects, but in times of discord the certainty of your stand may be subjected to severe challenges. You would be capable of convincing others with cogent words, but discordant aspects are felt as stagefrights, poor turnouts if you are a performer, or both. On November 18, 1977, Saturn enters Virgo. Your career may at that time seem to be at a standstill. The person to whom you report, or the general public, may seem uptight and hypercritical. If you are running for a political office, plan on working harder and putting in more hours campaigning than your opponent. The effort to overcome real or imagined criticism, or to unseat an incumbent, will seem like an uphill battle. If you have a boss who is under considerable pressure, that pressure can be relieved by nagging the living daylights out of *you*. Extra kindness and compassion on your part can do more for your professional relationship, as well as for your digestion, than the negative response that would come more naturally. When Saturn is in Libra, from September 22, 1980, until November 30, 1982, you will find yourself reevaluating your friendships. Those you have nurtured over the years and who have proven their affection will remain in your life. Acquaintances and less sincere friends will be discarded. With those friendships you want to salvage yet renegotiate, there may be some difficulty establishing contact owing to physical separation or stubbornness. This is especially true when Saturn is retrograde January 21 through June 6, 1981.

Jupiter: You may expect to feel Jupiter's transit through your sixth house—until April 4, 1977—as an abundance of work to do, plus the resilience to roll with the punches. Also possible at this time: a talent for amusing co-workers and putting them at ease, a desire to relax instead of working so hard, the necessity for an ethical decision related to your work, and further education to improve your career. Jupiter in Gemini contributes its cheering energy to your partnerships. You would enjoy talking to new acquaintances who are loquacious, witty, and enthusiastic enough to tempt you away from the antisocial funk you've been in recently. If you are currently in a partnership, this transit helps you to feel more comfortable and companionable in it. You may, if married, decide to reaffirm marriage vows in a second (anniversary?) ceremony with the same partner. Jupiter will be in Gemini from April 4 to August 21, 1977, and from December 31, 1977, to April 12, 1978. Jupiter in Cancer, affecting the eighth house, is likely to be felt as tax benefits from deductions for dependents, more debts to cover dependents' needs, gifts from parents or partners (marriage or business, if not both), increased income resulting from popularity with the public, or a cost-of-living raise. Jupiter will be in Cancer from August 21 to December 31, 1977, and from April 12 to September 6, 1978. Jupiter in Leo, your ninth house, promises an upward surge for your spirits, and any of the following may be credited for the cheering effect: religion, travel (especially if you enjoy gambling and win, or have a romantic fling), or cheers from the public for something you say via speech or print. Note the following Jupiter-in-Leo dates on your calendar: September 6, 1978, to March 1, 1979, and April 21 to September 30, 1979. Jupiter in Virgo is likely to be a happier time for you professionally than you've known in recent years. At long last comes proper recognition for the efforts you've devoted to the job, perhaps even formal promotion to a job allowing more professional latitude and more discretionary freedom. Jupiter will be in Virgo from September 30, 1979, to October 28, 1980. When Jupiter is retrograde—from December 28, 1979, to April 27, 1980—a privilege promised you with the best of intentions may be delayed. Jupiter in Libra—October 28, 1980, to November 28, 1981—offers hope of a fuller social life, as you find yourself among people more in the course of your work. The Air-sign influence combined with the light-heartedness of Jupiter help make association with others more tempting to you after the intensity of the Saturn and Pluto transits through Libra (both of those planets remain in Libra at the end of this five-year period, but, thanks to Jupiter's joining them, there's relief and hope of lighter spirits). Jupiter in Scorpio from November 28, 1981, signals a period of profound soul searching, which the fundamentally religious Sagittarius inclines toward, anyway. The Scorpio influence emphasizes the drive to probe and confront the self, and the twelfth house suggests a private, cloistered environment, perhaps even a formal religious retreat.

Capricorn Rising: 1977-1981

Pluto: Pluto's transit in your tenth house for the entire five years suggests intense competition to rise in your career. You may have to overcome the painful example of a competitor, an intensely inquisitive boss, a boss who withholds information when you ask point-blank questions, employment or salary statistics that are not in your favor, unpleasant conditions attached to a promotion, or the necessity to quit on principle. These difficulties that challenge your ambition are more likely to arise when Pluto is discordant or retrograde—January 18 through June 24, 1977; January 21 through June 26, 1978; January 24 through June 27, 1979; January 27 through July 2, 1980; and January 28 through July 4, 1981. When Pluto is direct and harmonious, you may enjoy a drastic breakthrough in your relations with your boss or your mother as you relate cooperatively on a one-to-one basis and work for a mutual cause.

Neptune: For the entire five years Neptune will be in your twelfth house, Sagittarius. As the Capricorn nature can assume other people's responsibilities as well as your own, you feel as though you are carrying on under considerable sacrifice single-handedly and altruistically, and that your dreams have to be put out of sight in favor of the needs of others, in favor of reality. When you are home alone after a day's work, however, you not only crave but need some time to be alone and unreachable. Whatever you consciously postpone in favor of others' real or imagined needs, you mustn't fail to confront what your choices can mean to you. If you discount your imaginative gifts and lose sight of what you once dreamed of doing, the unused energy may surface as a psychosomatic ailment or an unhealthy addiction. You would be better off doing your thing alone for part of every day (although when Neptune is retrograde the results may not be altogether what you had in mind) than living as a martyr with self-defeating forms of escape. Neptune will be retrograde March 20 through August 27, 1977; March 28 through August 30, 1978; March 24 through September 2, 1979; March 27 through September 2, 1980; and March 30 through September 6, 1981. When Neptune is direct and harmonious, you are successful in keeping your creative work a secret until such time as you feel ready to release it to the world. The work would proceed smoothly, under benefit of inspiration, and you become increasingly confident of your talent for single-handed imaginative work. You may enjoy further glory from helping a charitable institution.

Uranus: The five-year-plus transit through Scorpio during the period under consideration here indicates that your social life will be undergoing one surprising change after another. The Capricorn-rising person can get stuck in ruts or depression, and so it is a blessing to have the intervention of others to blast you out of some of your assumptions. It is likely to be through a friend rather than a book that you first become exposed to revolutionary thought. Capricorn conservatism may prompt you to resist at first—you have to assimilate the implications slowly and deliberately—but you will notice changes in your perspective. When Uranus is discordant or retrograde, you may experience difficulty in comprehending a friend's ideology, or someone's erratic behavior may turn you off entirely. You prefer advance phone calls to drop-in visitors, and are not likely to enjoy last-minute developments. Uranus will be retrograde February 17 through July 19, 1977; February 21 through July 23, 1978; February 25 through July 29, 1979; March 2 through August 2, 1980; and March 6 through August 7, 1981. When Uranus moves forward and is harmonious, you can win new friends easily, accept at least a portion of their ideologies as common ground, and understand people's motivations with little or no effort.

Saturn. Saturn's transit through your eighth house can be very difficult to put up with (it ends November 18, 1977), as it involves delays and inadequacies in your income. When something is owed to you, you may experience difficulty in obtaining payment, particularly during the retrograde period between January 1 and April 13, 1977. Somehow the regularity of your income doesn't seem as consoling as it used to, and thoughts of what the neighbors have—advantages you must for the time being deny yourself—can be salt in the wound. So, too, may the partner's financial obligations, poverty, or stinginess. To get through this time you have to make up your mind not to waste thoughts on keeping up with the Joneses. When Saturn is in Virgo—from November 18, 1977, to January 5, 1978, and July 28, 1978, to September 22, 1980—your somewhat gloomy attitude may be relieved via a trip that combines business with a much-needed change of scene. Be cautious in your diet when in strange surroundings. With extra work in a critical job, you can succeed in winning respect in the media as an expert in your subject. Saturn in Libra affects the tenth house, and you are likely to feel more tense than you should. If your boss or the general public is weighing and balancing your contributions up to that time, you may erroneously assume they are finding you wanting—that's the fault of the Capricorn-rising's self-effacing pattern. You may be called upon to explain in detail some of the past decisions you have made, but that's not necessarily cause to panic. During this time of evaluation you may learn you've got the respect and support of others; they're taking you more seriously than they have before. Your relationship with your mother may also be problematic at this time, due to your excessive dependency. The retrograde period from January 21 through June 6, 1981, may bring delays in learning what others think of you. Perhaps the only way to survive a period of suspense is to put the question out of your mind entirely. Distract yourself with something unrelated. Saturn will be in Libra from September 22, 1980, until November 30, 1981.

Jupiter: The last months Jupiter will be in Taurus—ending April 4, 1977—will benefit your fifth house. New satisfactions that arise in your love life, the delight of a child, a pleasurable vacation, or progress in your creative activities keep your spirits up when your friends' erratic behavior would otherwise have you climbing the walls. Jupiter in Gemini may mean a second occupation, one that you may enjoy even more than the first. If you go to school in addition to your regular day's work, the feeling that you're really getting somewhere would keep you high and thriving on what would otherwise be a taxing situation. Jupiter will be in Gemini between April 4 and August 21, 1977, and between December 31, 1977, and April 12, 1978. Jupiter's stay in Cancer can help relieve some of the tensions in an overly dependent partnership relationship. Where before you may have looked to your partner to be as protective as a parent (or vice versa), with Jupiter's advent into the seventh house you can relax, enjoy expressions of gratitude, and even laugh at yourself. Jupiter will be in Cancer from August 21 to December 31, 1977; April 12 to September 6, 1978; and March 1 to April 21, 1979.

Jupiter in Leo can mean the financial relief you've been awaiting eagerly for the last several years. Any combination of the following would be most likely to occur when Jupiter is in your eighth house: sizable monetary recognition for your worth in your profession, tax refunds, or the generosity of a partner. Jupiter will be in Leo from September 6, 1978, to March 1, 1979, and from April 21 to September 30, 1979. When Jupiter is in Virgo—September 30, 1979, to October 28, 1980—your mental attitude should perk up considerably. Although the Earth-sign emphasis adds the skepticism of someone who's been stung in the past ("I'll believe it when I see it," you'd say), you *do* feel more hopeful, without altogether knowing why. Public applause, a trip, and credit for expertise in your work all serve to improve your outlook. Jupiter in Libra augurs well for your professional reputation as well as for your relationship with your mother. Doors seem to be opening up for you, and you will have the feeling that you were right to hang in there and express support for those people you conscientiously stuck by—they will be your enthusiastic supporters in the months to come. Jupiter will be in Libra between October 28, 1980, and November 28, 1981, from which time it will be in Scorpio. Jupiter's transit through your eleventh house can mean a restoration of faith in the friends whose erratic behavior in recent years brought upheaval into your life. You express more trust in them now, stemming from a feeling that you've finally adjusted to their peculiar methods and from your desire to put an end to frictions and forgive.

Aquarius Rising: 1977-1981

Pluto: Pluto's years in Libra have their effect on your ninth house. You may discover a strengthening religion or philosophy and, after considerable deliberation, convert. If your desire is to break with the established faith you grew up with, the issue that finally decides the matter would have something to do with marriage and the equality of relationships. Other possibilities of this transit through your ninth house include: opportunities to make a series of public appearances to advocate a cause, court action, vacillations about citizenship (likely to arise in the event of marriage to someone of another nationality), interfaith marriage, opportunities to speak on radio or television, and the desire to publish a series of related works. When Pluto is retrograde or discordant, any debate—

internal or otherwise—may seem deadlocked, and you may rehash past experiences when you responded less than courageously to an ultimatum or to emotional blackmail. Delays in trips or broadcasts are also likely. Pluto will be retrograde from January 18 through June 24, 1977; January 21 through June 26, 1978; January 24 through June 27, 1979; January 27 through July 2, 1980; and January 28 through July 4, 1981. When Pluto is direct and harmonious, you feel that your philosophy or faith has given your life new focus, and you would want to help others find themselves with the same certainty. Travel would also give you the feeling you have a new lease on life. In public appearances you can be very convincing as you proselytize for your cause. The intensity of your conviction sells the material more effectively than the polish of your rhetoric.

Neptune: Confusions, evasions, misunderstandings, and defaults in your friendships are apt to arise during Neptune's stay in your eleventh house. These snags, which could alienate most people, can instead inspire the Aquarius-rising person to double expressions of friendship. There is also the likelihood of opening your home to all sorts of dropouts and transients among your acquaintances and friends, allowing a place for them to crash. When Neptune is discordant or retrograde, communicating with friends proves especially difficult. At best, they seem spaced out. At worst, they may deliberately lie or con you. Neptune will be retrograde from March 20 through August 27, 1977; March 28 through August 30, 1978; March 24 through September 2, 1979; March 27 through September 2, 1980; and March 30 through September 6, 1981. When Neptune is harmonious and direct, a philosophy (such as Eastern mysticism or transcendental meditation) learned through a friend may bring you new peace of mind, creative work shown to a friend can lead to an opportunity for professional success, and a friend you idealize may justify your faith.

Uranus: Uranus's erratic brand of excitement shows itself in your professional life. Both honors and dismissals—when you least expect them—can occur during this lengthy transit. Through the intervention of another person, you may be catapulted into a position giving you more prominence and more publicity than you would have thought possible. There may be a layoff, a strike, or replacement by automation (also ruled by Uranus) to complicate your career. Your own strong independence will become more obvious to others than it had been before and you may break with whatever established group you have been working for, preferring to work for yourself. The process of affirming your own freedom may be delayed during the retrograde periods: February 17 through July 19, 1977; February 21 through July 23, 1978; February 25 through July 29, 1979; March 2 through August 2, 1980; and March 6 through August 7, 1981. When Uranus is harmonious and direct, the publicity you win for your inventiveness should help further the cause of your personal independence. The improvement in your relationship with your mother would be another plus, although you'd rather have more independence.

Saturn: Saturn's transit through Leo until November 18, 1977, can manifest itself as a feeling of constraint in partnership relations as well as in anxiety when meeting strangers. If your partner is more uncommunicative than usual—especially during the retrograde period extending from January 1 to April 13, 1977—you feel that you're single-handedly keeping the relationship going. Also, at this time your partner may have to assume more responsibility for past actions or attachments. Reexamination of your relationship is painful for you and may result in a separation. Saturn's stay in Virgo—November 18, 1977, to January 5, 1978; and July 27, 1978, to September 22, 1980—can help you get your budget under control, although the times Saturn is retrograde can be wasted on self-pity and blaming your problems on your inadequate income or your partner's responsibilities or stinginess. These retrograde periods occur December 26, 1978, to May 11, 1979; and January 9 to May 24, 1980. Try putting these intervals to better use by getting organized and formulating plans for supplementing you income. Saturn will be in Libra from September 22, 1980, to November 30, 1982 (with a retrograde period extending from January 21 through June 6, 1981). This transit through the ninth house is likely to be felt as a serious reexamination of your guiding philosophy. Disillusionment with principles or with a religious-philosophical leader may occur under this newly objective scrutiny. Disappointments in publishing, public speaking, court actions, or travel are also likely to occur in any combination during this transit.

Jupiter: The final months Jupiter will be in Taurus—ending April 4, 1977—will see the relaxation offered by family life easing strains experienced elsewhere. Also at this time you may consider a move to more spacious quarters, and may improve your relationship with your father. Jupiter's intervals in Gemini may well speed up your love life; the temptation to have two or more concurrent affairs may prove irresistible! Encounters with children should be enjoyable, particularly children old enough to sustain conversation. Answering their challenging questions and entertaining them with stories may spur your own creativity. Jupiter will be in Gemini between April 4 and August 21, 1977, and between December 31, 1977, and April 12, 1978. When Jupiter is in Cancer you may succeed in achieving a new level of professionalism in your work, with new opportunities to work with people. The new joys your work affords can help relieve emotional health problems. Jupiter will be in Cancer from August 21 to December 31, 1977; April 12 to September 6, 1978; and March 1 to April 21, 1979. Jupiter in Leo suggests relief from the recent tensions in partnership relations. If your relationship has survived the Saturn transit, you may have reason during Jupiter's intervals in Leo to celebrate a new pride in your partner. Honors, promotions, and other ego-gratifications can give either or both of you the desire to give generous gifts, entertain together, forgive past injuries, and make up for past problems by treating each other with indulgence and tolerance. Jupiter will be in Leo from September 6, 1978, to March 1, 1979; and from April 21 to September 30, 1979. Jupiter's transit through Virgo can mean financial relief, a gift or legacy put to practical use, debts for the sake of education or travel, or newly allowable tax deductions for work-related expenses. Jupiter will be in Virgo from September 30, 1979, to October 28, 1980, with a retrograde period from December 28, 1979, until April 27, 1980, during which you may be tempted to spend money you haven't received yet, money that is promised to you but delayed despite the best of intentions. When Jupiter is in Libra, partnership-related trips may arise, as well as public appearances for public relations purposes. Court actions in which you are involved may be settled justly, although not entirely on your terms; still, you would see the fairness of the final determination and be willing enough to compromise. Previous disputes on religious issues can now be approached in an open-minded spirit and you are able to be more relaxed and good-natured in philosophical debates. Jupiter will be in Libra from October 28, 1980, to November 28, 1981. During the retrograde period from January 26 to May 29, 1981, you may experience delays in trips or speeches, postponements or continuances in court actions initiated by the opposing side, and some backtracking in assessing your stand on a principle. From November 28, 1981, when Jupiter will be in Scorpio, you may benefit from a promotion that definitively establishes you as a professional, giving you more career freedom than you've ever enjoyed. The publicity surrounding your ascendance would also be profoundly gratifying.

Pisces Rising: 1977-1981

Pluto: Pluto's slow transit through your eighth house can, under discordant aspects or retrograde motion, be felt as a struggle to learn the truth about joint finances. The apparent vulnerability characteristic of the Pisces ascendant may prompt a protective partner to withhold information on finances to "spare" you the mundane details. This is more likely to occur in a marriage partnership than in business. If your partner has definite plans for your joint income (or just for *your* assets) or has mismanaged the funds, the struggles about money can seem like a fight to the death. Emotional blackmail may also arise, and you end up feeling blameworthy somehow. Pluto will be retrograde from January 18 through June 24, 1977; January 21 through June 26, 1978; January 24 through June 27, 1979; January 27 through July 2, 1980; and January 28 through July 4, 1981. When Pluto is direct and harmonious, you enjoy a team solidarity in building joint accounts, and you show persuasive power in collecting what is owed you.

Neptune: A boss, sensing your grandiose dreams of personal glory, may raise your hopes with promises of promotion—promises and schemes that are likely to go unfulfilled. When you hear promises and schemes that call for blind faith on your part, discount ninety percent of them. "I'll believe it when I see it," is the best policy you can have, as well as a habit of asking for specifics. Be prepared to exit in no uncertain terms if employers do not deliver at the promised time or if they do not give you precise answers to your questions. You don't, after all, want to give anyone the impression that you can be exploited. When Neptune is discordant or retrograde, it is difficult to get specific information from those in positions to promote you, and to formulate your goals; your vision of the future is cloudy. You may also have a disillusioning experience involving your mother. Neptune will be retrograde March 20 through August 27, 1977; March 28 through August 30, 1978; March 24 through September 2, 1979; March 27 through September 2, 1980; and March 30 through September 6, 1981. When Neptune is harmonious and direct, you may enjoy success in preserving your privacy; the goals, imaginative work, or utopian visions you are promoting may be adequately publicized, but your personal circumstances may stay conveniently obscured.

Uranus: Uranus's transit through your ninth house can mean an impulsive change of religion (if you encounter a charismatic person who persuades you that the new principles can turn your life around), last-minute trips, or unexpected opportunities to express yourself in public (including court actions, unfortunately). When Uranus is retrograde or discordant, the changes are more likely to be nerve-racking as you are caught off-guard. Uranus will be retrograde February 17 through July 19, 1977; February 21 through July 23, 1978; February 25 through July 29, 1979; March 2 through August 2, 1980; and March 6 through August 7, 1981. When Uranus is direct and harmonious, your intensity in self-expression can turn the tide in persuading others to see issues your way. Although you may be on the receiving end of a lawsuit, your charisma can save the day. Public appearances for the sake of your chosen ideology can also turn out to your advantage.

Saturn: When Saturn is in Leo, your sixth house, especially when it is retrograde (January 1 to April 13, 1977), you may feel trapped in your present job, bored by the structured hours and repetitiousness of the work itself, and increasingly reluctant to do the usual tasks at all. You become depressed when you think of privileges that are extended to those who seem less imaginative, though they rank higher than you. If you feel chest constrictions or back pains, they are probably psychosomatic, stemming from ego-frustrations, though by all means double-check with your doctor. Saturn enters Virgo November 18, 1977, and is likely to show up as a cramp in partnership relations. Although your partner may depend on the income your work brings in, do not make the mistake of blaming your partner for your hatred of what you're doing. The relationship is more likely to survive this strain if instead you ask for the practical advice your partner is capable of offering. It would be far too easy to use this energy for criticism of one another, nagging, and rehashing nit-picking irritations. You can avert this danger by working with your partner to clarify future plans. After a retrograde trip into Leo (January 5 to July 27, 1978), Saturn has another passage through Virgo (until September 22, 1980) and another chance to clean up leftover partnership problems. When Saturn is in Libra—until November 30, 1982—unpleasant truths about partnership funds must be confronted. If there has been mismanagement or unscrupulous appropriation, you must deal with that during this Saturn transit. At the very least, even if your partner has been totally aboveboard in financial delaings, there may remain within you a deep discontent with your assets, perhaps resulting from an envy of other people. This is a time for balancing the checkbook and the budget, tightening the reins, and paying debts. Try to reduce the number of things your money has to buy. During the retrograde period from January 21 through June 6, 1981, you may have to go back through your checkbook or ledger more than once to find an error in calculation, and some amounts due you may not be delivered promptly.

Jupiter: During Jupiter's last weeks in Taurus—winding up on April 4, 1977—you may find renewed self-confidence through praise received in correspondence or via telephone. The faith of your siblings helps, too. If you have done some creative writing, this may prove a good time to send your work to carefully chosen markets. Jupiter in Gemini, your fourth house, can mean a desire to work at home writing or to have a second base of operations, a more spacious place, in which to seek refuge. Your life at home becomes more relaxed, in direct proportion to your satisfaction with mental work. The more appreciated you feel, the more communicative you become. Jupiter will be in Gemini April 4 through August 21, 1977, and December 31, 1977, to April 12, 1978. During the intervals Jupiter is in Cancer, you feel more relaxed, trusting, and generous in your love relationships. Your lover may seem more like an overgrown child, but your inclination is to indulge his childish needs and to encourage as much laughter as possible. Also at this time you may feel an increased desire for children, particularly if you don't yet have any. Your sentimentality may grow to epic proportions, so I must repeat: *Do not base a decision to have children solely on planetary transits*. If you are a professional in one of the creative arts, you may find that parenthood can place a severe strain on the creative rhythm you've enjoyed up until the present time. Take all the relevant factors into account before committing yourself: the other parent, costs, career interruption, life-style. Jupiter will be in Cancer from August 21 to December 31, 1977; April 12 to September 6, 1978; and March 1 to April 21, 1979. Jupiter in Leo suggests increased pleasure in your work, freedom to do truly creative work, work in a creative art form perhaps intended for a juvenile audience, or a career in entertainment. Relations with co-workers and employees are likely to become more supportive and relaxed. Jupiter will be in Leo from September 6, 1978, to March 1, 1979; and April 21 to September 30, 1979. Jupiter in Virgo—from September 30, 1979, to October 28, 1980—manifests itself as a greater capacity to relax in partnership relationships, and as honesty and openness. If you have not yet formed a partnership, you may at this time be tempted to begin one with a person you meet in the course of your work.

If you have shared professional interests and if the other person is more practical than you believe *you* are, you would have high hopes for the stability of the relationship. When Jupiter is retrograde, between December 28, 1979, and April 27, 1980, you or your partner may complain of being taken for granted, but the underlying goodwill can keep the problem from becoming a serious one. Jupiter will be in Libra from October 28, 1980, to November 28, 1981. During that time increases in your income may tempt you to celebrate ostentatiously, motivated in part by your desire to show off and in part by your overwhelming feeling of relief. You are more likely to emerge from this phase solvent if you keep to earlier stringent plans to curtail spending. Try saving instead so that you can then support a long-dreamed-of period of freedom from structured jobs. Avoid major credit purchases when Jupiter is retrograde from January 26 to May 29, 1981, as the item you are buying may be haphazardly put together and the income you are counting on is likely to be late or somewhat less than you expect. From November 28, 1981, when Jupiter will be in Scorpio, your optimism for the future should be perceptibly stronger, a blend of faith in benevolent unseen forces and a new-found faith in your own strength.

PART FOUR

9

Her Kind of
Housework Was Different:
Evangeline Adams

Evangeline Adams' crusades—from legalization of astrology, to writing books exemplifying such luminaries as Carrie Chapman Catt, to astrological adoption work—have long aroused my curiosity and gratitude. For thus giving me ideas of how I may be of service to others, she deserves the tribute of an entire chapter here, as I proudly introduce her to you: a shining example of the "second oldest profession."

Today it's a common occurrence for an astrologer to see clients openly, to learn their real names, and even to advertise in the *Yellow Pages*. Before 1914 this wasn't the case. Men came with hat brims down and collars up and women came veiled, many taking elaborate pains to conceal their identities. Fortune-telling laws prohibited astrological advice; practitioners had to go underground.

The first time Evangeline Adams was brought into court, in 1912, the judge dismissed the charges against her. She was not satisfied with personal acquittal, however. Her second arrest occurred in 1914, when Detective Adelle Priess came to her anonymously and posed as a client to gather evidence against her. Adams engaged Clark L. Jordon as counsel and insisted on going to trial. She offered to calculate and analyze in the courtroom the chart of a person unknown to her. Judge Freschi provided the data, and as a result of that reading he wrote in his decision:

> The defendant raises astrology to the dignity of an exact science.
> She has given ample proof that she is a woman of learning and culture, and one who is very well versed in astronomy and other sciences. Her chart here, as made out, may be verified, as she stated, in the books and records of astronomers for years. . . .

> When the defendant prepared her horoscope of the complainant and calculated the relative positions of the planets of her birth, raising this horoscope on the well-known and fixed science of astronomy, she violated no law.[1]

The unknown person was the judge's own son.

From that time on astrologers practiced their profession as freely as those in more orthodox lines of work.

Less anonymous than her colleagues, Evangeline Adams did what she knew best, risking imprisonment for years before the precedent-setting trial that was the culmination of her ambitions.

Very little is known of her personal life, unfortunately. Her autobiography deals mainly with her professional life and the foibles of clients she had known, and no one has published any personal reminiscences of her.

Of her early years she has written that her father died when she was fifteen months old; her mother single-handedly brought up Evangeline and her three brothers in Andover Hill, near Andover Theological Seminary, Abbott Academy (a girls' school), and Phillips Academy (for boys).

Her introduction to astrology was a by-product of a serious illness she had been recovering from for months. The family physician, Dr. Whiting, introduced her to Dr. J. Heber Smith, a professor of medicine at Boston University and at that time the leading diagnostician of New England. Astrology was instrumental in his achieving that stature, and he used the science in connection with his medical work. As a matter of routine he began a visit with a patient by asking for the complete birth data. He disputed the 7 A.M. birth time Evangeline gave him; it could not possibly be right, as the zodiacal sign on the ascendant at that moment indicated a person of much slighter build and fairer complexion.

"But, Dr. Smith, my mother said it was seven o'clock."

"She ought to know. But if you had been born at that time you would have been very beautiful." With that, he proceeded to calculate a chart for his estimate of her birth time—half-past eight. Years later, when Evangeline Adams had almost forgotten that interview, she found an old diary of her father's in the attic of her brother's house in Chicago. In it her father had recorded the birth times of all his children. The entry next to her name read "8:30 in the morning."

If Dr. Smith had been trying to recruit a devoted and hard-working student, he couldn't have done a better job. He told her, "You are not only a born astrologer and should take up the study of the science, but you should go a long way with it. Fear was left out of your horoscope. I doubt if you fear man, God, or devil," and that clinched it for her. From then on she pestered him to take time from his lectures and medical practice to give her lessons.

Initially she refused to take money from the friends who were her first clients. One said, "We'll see your shingle yet," but she rejected the idea. Astrology was not highly regarded then—especially among the Boston friends of her family. Eventually, though, she had nerve enough to begin her practice on a professional basis from a studio in the Hotel Copley in Boston. But she still had a hazing to go through first.

Legal persecution was easier for her to bear than the persecution by her family. Even after her trial, she was still a black sheep: "Naturally, I regarded the legalization of astrology as the finest thing an Adams had done since the signing of the Declaration of Independence. But the Adamses didn't think so!"

When she was eighteen and her brothers had gone off "boy-like" to make new lives for themselves, she had the responsibility of supporting herself and her mother, the only member of her family to give her any sympathy in her pursuit of astrology. (Her influential relatives, who could have helped, did nothing for her. They were mortified that a descendant of President John Adams should be "dabbling in heathenism.")

Before astrology became a full-time job for her, she earned her living as a secretary in the office of Lord & Webster, wholesale flour and grain merchants. Mr. Webster was her uncle by marriage, and Mr. Lord proposed to marry her. She thought that her secretarial job was safe. However, her family, including her employer's wife, became so agitated about her astrological work that they harassed her, her out-of-town brothers, her mother, and her mother's nurse. They made her life so miserable that she consulted a lawyer, who informed her that inasmuch as she was paying all of her own and her mother's bills, she was within her rights to inform her relatives that they were barred from her house. In view of the fact that her employer's wife was the "ringleader in the family circus," she resigned her job and dedicated herself to astrology on a full-time basis, at which time Dr. Smith printed her first professional cards.

While still in Boston, through Dr. Smith she met a Dr. George S. Adams, who was then head of the state hospital for the insane at Westboro, a highly respected institution. Dr. Adams, like Dr. Smith, was secretly a practitioner of astrology, and he timed everything at Westboro according to charts. Since he charted every patient at the time of admission, he had a vast collection of interesting charts, and Evangeline horrified her family still further by spending her spare hours in the insane asylum, studying charts and meeting patients—even those in the violent ward.

Many years later the head of the state institutions for the insane in New York said to her, "Eighty percent of the people in our insane asylums could be 'snapped back' if someone like you would only talk to them."

"Thank you," she replied, "but I have enough trouble 'snapping back' those that are out."

From a study of her own chart, she learned that conditions favored her astrological work from about the middle of March 1899, so she set off alone for New York on March 16. The first hotel she went to, the Fifth Avenue, was managed by a family friend. Everything seemed fine until she mentioned her intention of doing astrology readings in his hotel. His reaction was horror and rejection, although her relatives had always patronized his hotel whenever they were in New York. After the legalization of astrology, the man invited her back, but at the time she found herself alone, homeless, and insulted "on the sidewalk of Madison Square." She described herself as "righteously indignant . . . mad clear through."

> Of course I didn't know that I was committing a social error by carrying my own bag in so fashionable a neighborhood; but I should have experienced a certain wicked pleasure if I had known. I was in a mood to defy assistance and the world.[2]

The hotel that eventually accepted her and her work was the Windsor. Given a choice of rooms, she decided on the more expensive suite on the first floor rather than the room on what was later to be called the "fateful fifth." She paid her first day's twelve dollars, which she could ill afford, at eight o'clock on the evening of Thursday, March 16, 1899.

The manager, Warren Leland, said to her, "Tomorrow will be Friday, a bad-luck day. You'd better give me a reading now."

When she laughed, he insisted. "I want to be your mascot."

As she calculated she studied the combination of planets, and warned him of danger on the morrow. All he could think of was the stock market. The astrologer asked him what had happened on the other two occasions when similar conditions existed in his life. He remembered only two small fires. Then he talked some more about stock market operations. He was so impressed with her that he sent guests to her until long after midnight.

He came to see her again the next day, and she was unable to conceal the chills his impending danger caused her to feel.

"You're chilly in here; I'll have the porter make a fire in your fire-place." He pressed a button four times, then opened the door—and the "greatest hotel disaster of all times, the famous Windsor fire," was in full blaze. The fifth floor was gone and the others were flaming. Only the first floor remained intact, so Ms. Adams rescued her more valuable papers and left the hotel. From outside she saw the facade fall across Fifth Avenue and bodies jumping from the upper windows. It was not until the next morning, when she saw the newspaper account of the fire, that she learned the extent of the loss to Mr. Leland: not only was the hotel gone; so were members of his family, including his wife and his favorite daughter (his other daughter was on a visit away from home at the time). There had been some help in fighting the fire—volunteers were marching past in the St. Patrick's Day parade that afternoon—but the fire blazed on, from three in the afternoon of the seventeenth, when it started, until after one-thirty the following morning.

The *New York Times* account of the fire stated that it was caused by a smoker's match, which was thrown out of an upstairs window and ignited the curtains. In that first day's coverage it was reported that fourteen people had died and still more were injured. For days afterward more and more bodies were found in the wreckage.

"I would have given anything I possessed at the time if my prediction had not come so terribly true. But the stars had decreed otherwise," said Evangeline Adams. They had also decreed, in her own chart, success for her. In the days following Mr. Leland was her best publicist, telling reporters that the fire had been predicted by Evangeline Adams of Boston.

The sources disagree on Evangeline Adams' year of birth, ranging from 1865 to 1873. The only chart I've seen for her was printed with the date of February 8, 1868, 8:30 A.M.[3] Since we have already seen authentication for the time, let us accept the rest—until someone with more accurate information gets in touch. The following is the closest Evangeline Adams comes to being specific about her own chart:

> I was born under the influence of the human sign Aquarius with more than the usual number of planets rising in my chart; the Sun and Mars, which give courage; Mercury, which gives mental understanding; Neptune, which gives spiritual understanding; Venus, which makes possible the telling of ugly truths in palatable form; and Jupiter, which should provide the priceless gift of tolerance.[4]

The chart shows Mars in the house of friends; the Sun, Mercury, and Jupiter in the twelfth (secrecy as well as work in institutions); and Venus and Neptune in the first (the self). Pisces, ruled by Neptune, is on the ascendant; this double rulership by Neptune, along with a strong twelfth house, explains why her private life is so difficult for a contemporary biographer to learn about. The same spiritual energy that gives the astrologer insight also gives the craving for privacy common to many practitioners; enlightened colleagues and students can know one *too* well!

Her autobiography, *The Bowl of Heaven* (New York: Dodd, Mead, 1926), was her first book and the only one to contain any anecdotes about her own life. Her in-person practice seemed to be based for the most part on horary charts (calculated for the time of a question rather than the time of a person's birth), if the brevity of the time she devoted to each client is any indication. Dealing with an individual birth date, the half-hour allotted could not have enabled her to do more than a quick across-the-page estimation of aspects.

A typical work day consisted of a morning devoted to letter-answering and other paperwork lasting through lunchtime, and an afternoon of one visit after another, with each visit limited to thirty minutes. Sometimes this extended into the evening hours and included interruptions of her dinner by demanding clients who refused to accept a secretary's no.

The percentage of written or oral readings cannot be known. By a happy stroke of fortune, a sample of a written reading was made available to me by a client of mine whose mother had requested a reading for her child from Evangeline Adams during the first year of my client's life. The subject, to be referred to as J, is perhaps the only person to be charted by both Evangeline Adams and myself.

The format is a blue-covered book of thirty-six double-spaced 5½-by-8-inch pages, without the chart diagram. Adams refers to J in the third person, sometimes as "she," other times as "it!" Either Adams was scrupulously avoiding gender pronouns on these few occasions (which is hardly likely, coming from someone who called planets "he" and "she") or she regarded very small children as neuter.

The birth data had been discreetly omitted from the manuscript by Adams, so it is impossible to tell whether the birth time supplied was from memory or from a document, as the time subsequently told *me* was; and it is also impossible to tell whether the differences in the two charts—differences in the house positions of Neptune and Jupiter—resulted from differing sources of the time or from mathematical error. In the first (Adams') chart, Neptune is in the midheaven and Jupiter is in the house of siblings. The effects would be, respectively, bosses who are deceptive and siblings who are happy and generous. The chart done by me has Neptune in the house of friends and Jupiter in the house of the father (and housework): deceptive friends and a jovial father (plus an I-don't-care attitude about housework). J will have to decide for herself which fits her life more exactly.

The main reason for examining the manuscript was to determine the possible effect on a young person's morale. Would Adams suggest arbitrary interpretations and close off others simply because J was born female? No. Although more career details could well have been added, her attitude was laudable. The words of advice especially worth passing on may have been part of every child's reading; if not, they should be:

> She should not be made self-conscious or to feel that she is inferior. . . .Be sure that she is not made to feel that she is 'queer,' but rather that she has gifts and possibilities which, if used to advantage, will make her a very superior person;

and:

> If she were obliged to constantly adapt herself to the views of others, it would not only have a disastrous effect on her health, but bring to the fore the most inharmonious side of her disposition. It would be most unwise to crush her individuality.

"One of the first things I learned from astrology was that I was in love with the wrong man," said Adams. Since astrologers are themselves human and need the more objective insights of experienced colleagues, Evangeline was fortunate to have had the guidance of Dr. Smith when faced with the prospect of a marriage of her own (she had received and declined several proposals before her first and only marriage, at the approximate age of fifty-five, to a man thirteen years her junior).

Two of the men who proposed to her before she met the man she was to marry would have been termed "good catches." The first—her employer, Mr. Lord—she didn't love. The second—Sir Franklin Simmons, the sculptor—was more difficult to refuse, as they were congenial and shared an enthusiasm for astrology. One deterrent was Sir Franklin's

> mid-Victorian idea about women and their jobs. He wished to take me away to his beloved Rome, to install me as chatelaine of his beautiful *palazzo*, and introduce me to a life of pleasurable leisure. And leisure didn't appeal to me. I had just moved from my hotel because I couldn't stand seeing so many women sitting about doing nothing, to Carnegie Hall, where I knew everybody was working and trying to accomplish something in life.[5]

The deciding factor was the astrological indication in the man's chart of discordant relations with women.

Even though some couples she advised had obviously done a poor job of finding a mate, she did not provide introductions ("My practice is astrological—not matrimonial," she said). In one case only did she make an exception. The woman

> happened to see the horoscope of a young man and she knew enough about astrology to be interested immediately. "I would like," she said, "to see the owner of that horoscope."
>
> So it was arranged. The man came over from Boston and met her in my studio. Nothing happened right away. But about two months later the young man was leaving the Commodore Hotel to take the Knickerbocker for Boston. . . . Suddenly he felt the urge . . . to again see the lady who had been attracted by his horoscope. He went to the telephone and called her up. It was then twenty minutes to one. She told him that she had an appointment at one o'clock, but that if he'd come right up, she would see him for a few minutes. He gave up his train and came to see the lady. Two years later they were married.
>
> Did it turn out happily for him?
>
> I hope so. I was the woman![6]

They were married on April 12, 1923, when the bride was approximately fifty-five and the groom, George E. Jordan, Jr., forty-two. He had been a manufacturer in England but gave up his business to devote his life to the study of astrology with her. The announcement of their engagement printed in The *New York Times* on April 7 included the information that he was a Cancer, she an Aquarian, and that they were guiding their new life in accordance with the stars.

The only anecdote relating to their life together told by her in her autobiography, was of an evening when four young men came over for talk and refreshments. It was the last night of an accident-prone period for Mr. Jordan, which he had managed to survive in comfort, having been forewarned. After hours of talk, as Mr. Jordan was opening a bottle a fragment of cork hit him in the eye. The four men attempted first aid and Ms. Adams headed for her studio to calculate the outcome of the moment's accident. Even her husband, accustomed as he was to living with an astrologer, was rather shocked by what seemed like desertion, but he calmed down when she reassured him that the damage wouldn't be permanent.

Another item describes an incident that could have taken place in her own marriage. She termed amusing the story of the man who wanted more than anything to be a cook:

> His stars indicated that he would be successful in anything he touched. But he was born under Cancer—which means that he thought a lot about good things to eat. . . . An awful husband, you might think? For some women, yes. But he happened to marry a professional woman, who was too occupied with her own work to care who went into her kitchen or what came out of it. This was the Cancer man's opportunity. In his spare time, he has taken over the entire management of the household. At night, he comes home laden with caviar, hand-picked chickens, Stilton cheeses, and fat, juicy steaks. And the wife, after a hard day at her desk, staggers into the dining room and eats what he has cooked. He is fulfilling his destiny, and both he and she are happy.[7]

In the chapter "Why Most People Come to Me," she wrote that early in her practice the questions were dominantly marital. "But with the increasing divergency of women's interests, even my feminine callers' reasons for consulting astrology have taken on a great variety." Reprinted in the autobiography is a letter from a woman planning a trip to Europe. It closes with a question about profiting from the stock market, a question "more frequently in . . . masculine correspondence."

Men and women were equally represented among her clients, although more women came in person because they had more free time. It may be correctly inferred that if women began with questions of love and switched the subject to money, with men it was the reverse. Whatever the sex of the caller, sooner or later the question of love came up. The current planetary conditions indicated not only the probable outcome of the questions but the subject matter; sometimes an entire mailbag dealt with the single question of wages.

On the question of fallibility she uses the feminine pronoun to refer to the astrologer in general, although the first astrologers she knew personally were men:

> The stars make no mistakes. They are divine. But the astrologer is human—and although she is dealing with a strictly mathematical problem, she may make mistakes. I claim infallibility for the stars. I do not claim it for myself.

In actual practice, a reading is only as accurate as the data on which it is based; the mathematical skill of the astrologer and the astrologer-client rapport are additional variables.

The experience she recounts to illustrate this involved a young woman who gave her the data but not the name of the man she wanted to marry. The planetary aspects for that date indicated a cold, insensitive person. When the client heard that description, tears came to her eyes, but she listened, then quoted her astrologer's reaction to her fiancé later. The next day a man whom Ms. Adams had often read for and knew to be a fine person rushed into her studio and said: "What do you mean by telling ——— that I am no good?" Ms. Adams laughed until she cried. Masculine vanity had prompted him to subtract seven years from his age—and he had picked the worst possible year.

After the legalization of astrology, Evangeline Adams believed that her most significant contribution to astrology lay in astrologically planned parenthood, so that the childbirth process and the family's life in the time following would be as smooth as possible. ("I have no sympathy with the present grin-and-bear-it school of obstetrics, in which the father does the grinning and the mother does the bearing.")

Her name for it was "astrological eugenics," and her aim was to avoid needless tangles rather than suffer them.

Another project she devoted years to was matching homeless children to adopting parents. A woman whose job it was to place children with families would give the birth dates of the babies to be adopted, and, in some cases, also the dates of the prospective parents, and the astrologer would describe the home environments in which the children would best develop.

Evangeline's outlook was a happy one, as summed up in the final chapter of *The Bowl of Heaven*:

> As for me, I have seen all my ships come into the safe harbor toward which they have been guided by my stars. I am a happy woman—happier than I was when I began the work to which I have devoted my life.[8]

From the vantage point of 1926, her ambition lay in the direction of more research and less consultation. The results of her research were published in her three texts: *Astrology: Your Place in the Sun* (1928); *Astrology: Your Place Among the Stars* (1930); and *Astrology for Everyone* (1931).

Most of her writing is scrupulously neutral. Sometimes her feminism would show, and at other times masculinist bias would, surprisingly, rear its ugly head.

> If a woman, you must guard against being too dictatorial in your relations with men. Forget that you are the pioneer, the leader—at least, appear to forget it. Men will be attracted to you by the brilliant rays of your favoring Sun. Don't let them be driven away by the overaggressiveness of the war-like Mars.[9]

If toning down Arien abrasiveness in personal relationships makes sense, it is sense that men should have been urged to adopt, too.

At the same time that she was actively cross-referencing her charts for use as examples in her books she was also broadcasting three times a week on WABC Radio, starting in 1930, which brought four thousand chart requests a day from an enthusiastic public.

The reviews of her books ranged between praise and grudging admiration. In 1928 Charles Willis Thompson wrote in his skeptical and derisive review of *Astrology: Your Place in the Sun* that he had read the physical description of his sign, Pisces. It was so accurate that he wrote, "I cannot imagine where Miss Adams saw me."

She died November 10, 1932, of heart disease, after an illness of only three days. Her estate, valued at more than ten thousand dollars, was left to her husband, who was with her when she died. Included in the estate was her property in Yorktown Heights, Westchester—a remodeled Friends' Meeting Hall, with its pictures and her "astrological business, papers, and books."

Funeral services were conducted on November 14 at 11 A.M. by the Reverend Dr. Randolph Ray of the Church of the Transformation, on Twenty-ninth Street in Manhattan. The eulogy was by Frank Gillmore, president of the Actors Equity Association. Sidney Blackmer, the actor, was an usher, and a judge was one of the pallbearers. Evangeline Smith Adams, former outlaw, would have loved it.

Evangeline Adams' Unfamiliar Quotations

"When the Moon is in Aries, the women in the life of the native are brilliant, passionate, headstrong, and impractical. They are often intellectual and capable of immense initiative . . . in the case of a man, he will find it very difficult to control them."[10]

To Aquarian women: "You are any man's equal—and know it. Your husband may as well understand that fact."[11]

On the Moon in Gemini: ". . . much better in the case of women . . . for the lack of ordinary feminine qualities often makes for success. Queen Victoria, Frances Willard, and Patti . . . were able to concentrate upon the mental side of their work."[12]

"The violence of Mrs. Pankhurst, again, is undoubtedly due to (Mars in Scorpio). . . . Her undoubted nobility of character and the altruism of her violent action indicate the vision conferred by the trines of Neptune and the Sun, which the sextile of the Moon directs toward the masses of women."[13]

"Inescapable limitation is manifested curiously in the career of Rosa Bonheur, whose sex shackles her. Sturdily she laid hold of all that Saturn trined by Mars could give. She never faltered in purpose and we know the splendid measure of her success."[14]

"Men as leaders have always commanded the admiration of woman-kind. Women as leaders have been accepted rather recently and some-what reluctantly by mankind:
"In business, both sexes find a wonderful field for some of their best Aries qualities. The sign gives great executive ability, plus the personal-ity necessary to carry authority in dealing with associates and subordi-nates. The Aries man, or for that matter, the Aries woman in business never says die."[15]

"Libra lovers too often fail to satisfy and hold the object of their affections. . . . The Libra lover treats his beloved as if she were a beautiful vase—and there are few women in this world content to be a vase, even a beautiful one. As for masculine vases, the type is well-nigh extinct!"[16]

"Let us consider Mrs. Carrie Chapman Catt, heroine of that 'Votes for Women' campaign which now seems so far back in the distant past, and still head and front of all movements for the advancement of the feminine side of the human race. She was born on January 9th, when the Moon was in Pisces in conjunction with Neptune and Mars. No wonder she had the vision to foresee the emancipation of women and the courage to fight for it! No wonder, too, with her favorable aspect of Mars, that she has now turned her energies into the fight against war! . . . She has Mercury, the planet ruling the mind, in the forward-looking sign Sagittarius, and friendly to Neptune, the God of vision. Mrs. Catt has always been in advance of her times. . . . She also has Venus in Sagittarius, a most impersonal sign, which frees her from many personal temptations and leaves her free to lavish her nature on the world. . . . 'Woman of the year.' . . ."[17]

"[Men] fall into a certain husbandly formula for treating wives, and act on it blandly throughout their married lives, as if they believed that every woman was just like every other woman."[18]

NOTES TO CHAPTER NINE

1. Evangeline Adams, *The Bowl of Heaven* (New York: Dodd, Mead, 1926), pp. 54-55.
2. *Ibid.*, p. 36.
3. Stephen Erlewine, *The Circle Book of Charts* (Ann Arbor, Mich.: Circle Books, 1972), p. 61.
4. Adams, *Bowl of Heaven*, p. 58.
5. *Ibid.*, pp. 153-54.
6. *Ibid.*, p. 152.
7. *Ibid.*, p. 195.
8. *Ibid.*, p. 215.
9. Evangeline Adams, *Astrology for Everyone* (New York: Dodd, Mead, 1931; reprint ed., New York: Dell, 1972), p. 37.
10. *Ibid.*, p. 149.
11. Adams, *Astrology for Everyone, op. cit.*, p. 270.
12. Adams, *Astrology: Your Place Among the Stars, op. cit.*, p. 153.
13. *Ibid.*, p. 326.
14. *Ibid.*, p. 387.
15. Adams, *Astrology for Everyone, op. cit.*, p. 31.
16. *Ibid.*, pp. 103-4.
17. *Ibid.*, pp. 227-28.
18. *Ibid.*, p. 259.

10

Of Women and Birthdays

The dates and odd-sized portraits in this astrological gallery are offered first and foremost as stimulants for the curious. I hope they may serve additionally as role models for the undecided and inspiration for the discouraged.

Aries

Joan Crawford and Bette Davis are mentioned jointly here not only because both are movie stars who have made a strong impact in forming our images of exciting, courageous women in their choices of screen roles, but also because there are planetary aspects that are the same in both charts. Both Aries, born thirteen days apart in the same year, they have semi-squares between their Suns and the Venus-Mars conjunction in Taurus: problems arose from passive as well as aggressive behavior. Two more fortunate shared aspects are the trines between Mercury and Neptune (dramatic talent) and between Jupiter and Saturn (enduring admiration from fans).

Lucy Komisar is the author of *The New Feminism* (written for teenagers), *Down and Out in the U.S.A.* (a history of public welfare published in 1973), and *The Machismo Factor* (published in 1976). She is an Aries with ascendant and Moon in Capricorn. Mercury is in Aries conjunct her Sun in the house of money, hence her success in supporting herself with her writing. Mars in Gemini in the fifth house also rules her third house (thinking, writing) and her reputation. As Aries is volatile and capable of losing enthusiasm quickly, she is fortunate to have the Capricorn strength as well, giving her perseverance to see ideas through to completion. Other assets include trines to the ascendant from Saturn (stability), Uranus (independence), and Neptune (imagination).

Joan Crawford	March 23, 1908
Diana Ross	March 26, 1944
Doris Day	April 3, 1924
Dorothea Dix	April 4, 1802
Bette Davis	April 5, 1908
Billie Holiday	April 7, 1915
Lucy Komisar	April 8, 1942
Lucy Ellen Sewall (physician and feminist)	April 9, 1837
Clare Boothe Luce	April 10, 1903
Eudora Welty	April 13, 1909
Bessie Smith	April 15, 1898
Isak Dinesen	April 17, 1885
Edith Summerskill (British feminist)	April 19, 1901

Taurus

Bernadette Devlin received a government scholarship to Queen's University of Belfast (majoring in psychology), became the youngest member of the British House of Commons, and published her autobiography, *The Price of My Soul*. Although she won a seat in the British Parliament, her ambition is not politics. "Five years from now I don't see myself as a politician. I hope instead to be a very good psychologist." This is borne out in her chart: the Sun makes only four aspects—very few for a sustained political career—whereas the Moon (in diversifying Gemini) makes six aspects, giving her a greater interest in private problems, as well as popularity among the voters, who sense her empathy.

Mary Wollstonecraft was perhaps the first known author of a feminist treatise, *A Vindication of the Rights of Woman*, which was published in 1792. She was the first to apply the words *legal prostitution* to marriage. When her out-of-wedlock daughter's father, Gilbert Imlay, had the effrontery to send Wollstonecraft to Denmark, Norway, and Sweden to clear up his financial problems there (which freed him to enjoy his new mistress at home), she accepted because she enjoyed travel and welcomed the challenge of conducting business like a man. Accompanied by her baby and nurse, she set out for Scandinavia, where she wrote of her experiences in letters that were published in *Letters Written*

During a Short Residence in Sweden, Norway, and Denmark. She also wrote *Thoughts on the Education of Daughters*, an early autobiographical novel entitled *Mary, A Fiction* and the fragments of an incomplete novel which her husband, William Godwin, attempted to piece together after her death.

The Sun is surprisingly weak for one whose fame has lasted nearly two hundred years. The conjunction to the Moon, a neutral aspect that affords energy and intensity, and the discordant aspects to Neptune and Pluto, are more easily understood in the context of her unhappy personal relationships, in which she showed appallingly little self-respect. Pluto, her dominant planet (with eight aspects), enabled her to overcome the unhappiness of her upbringing as the oldest daughter in a family of six children. Pluto's sign, Sagittarius, indicates the relief offered her: first, the job as governess to a titled Irish family, then as writer and editor for publisher Joseph Johnson. Her most harmonious planet, Mercury in Taurus, is conjunct and parallel Venus (enabling her to romanticize her life in fiction and letters), trine and parallel Jupiter (praise for her writing), and sextile revolutionary Uranus (which facilitated speed, too; *Vindication* was written in only six weeks).

Charlotte Brontë	April 21, 1816
Queen Elizabeth II	April 21, 1926
Elaine May	April 21, 1932
Baronne de Staël	April 22, 1766
Bernadette Devlin	April 23, 1947
Shirley MacLaine	April 24, 1934
Barbra Streisand	April 24, 1942
Ella Fitzgerald	April 25, 1915
Mary Wollstonecraft	April 27, 1759
Catherine the Great	May 2, 1729
Henry Blackwell (feminist and husband of Lucy Stone)	May 4, 1825
Audrey Hepburn	May 4, 1929
Margaret Rutherford	May 11, 1892
Daphne Du Maurier	May 13, 1907
Margot Fonteyn	May 18, 1919
Nellie Melba (Australian opera singer)	May 19, 1861
Sigrid Undset	May 20, 1882

Gemini

Terri Tepper is the founder of the Center for a Woman's Own Name,* dedicated to keeping women informed of their options. Adoption of the husband's name in the United States is merely customary, not compulsory. The center was founded when Ms. Tepper, seeking information from other states on legal regulations and procedures, placed an ad in the February 1973 issue of *Ms.* Thinking that readers might not respond to an unknown individual's name, she invented the name of the center. People thought she was *offering* information, and sent her their requests. As a result, Ms. Tepper set up a network to provide such information. With the help of Diana Altman (of Name-Change in Massachusetts), legal consultant Priscilla MacDougall, and Jane Burrell in New York, she has been working to influence public policy at state and federal levels. Also, Ms. Tepper has published fact sheets and a booklet, periodically updated, including legal precedents, guidance for establishing the name you choose, and quotes from letters by women who have kept or returned to their premarriage names (Ms. Tepper herself has resumed her original name, with legal help from her husband, attorney Lawrence Weiner). A Gemini with Leo ascendant, she is avidly interested in questions of personal identity, of which one's name is a key symbol. The Sun's sign placement makes the mind and verbal expression quick and to the point. The Sun—the ego itself—rules the house of the self, the first house. Leo's fixity shows firmness of purpose on matters of identity. The Sun is one of five planets in the eleventh house: social issues as well as friends are important in her life. The other four planets in this house are Saturn (strength and moral support) and Uranus (progressive attitudes) in close conjunction with one another and the Sun, plus Mercury (communication) conjunct Jupiter (good luck through friends, and friends in the legal profession). The predominantly harmonious aspects to Jupiter in Gemini indicate wit, a sense of humor, and generosity—which is obvious, considering the extent of the homework she has already done above and beyond the call of duty.

Elizabeth Rich is both a stewardess (one of the founders of Stewardesses for Women's Rights) and an author. *Flying High* is a guide for those considering becoming flight attendants, and *Flying Scared* deals

*261 Kimberley, Barrington, Illinois 60010.

with highjacking. Both her Sun and ascendant are in Gemini, the dual sign that gives so much mental and nervous energy that one career isn't enough. This vitality is reinforced by a Grand Trine in Air signs, involving her career, creativity, and personal strength. Her Scorpio Moon in the house of work and co-workers makes her empathy with her sister stewardesses genuine and intense; and thanks to her Moon-Jupiter conjunction, her efforts toward drastic reforms in the airlines' treatment of its women employees should prove gratifying.

Dorothy L. Sayers is included here partly because her life was unusual—she was a classical scholar from childhood, a translator of Dante, a playwright, a detective novelist, and an advertising copy-writer—and partly because of her achievement in detective fiction: the creation of Lord Peter Wimsey, whom I would call the greatest male feminist in fiction. Lord Peter's deductive exploits are sustained through thirteen novels, as well as a volume of short stories published under the collective title of *Lord Peter*. The four novels of greatest interest to feminists are those showing Lord Peter's relationship with the author's alter ego, Harriet Vane, the detective fiction writer whom he saves from the gallows after she is accused of poisoning her lover: *Strong Poison, Have His Carcase, Gaudy Night*, and *Busman's Honeymoon*. Ms. Sayers had not only the Sun in Gemini but also the Moon (skill in winning the public's interest in her characterizations), Pluto (series writing, detection), and Neptune (fiction, intrigue, advertising copywriting); the last three are in very close conjunction. Also in close conjunction are Mercury and Venus in Cancer, both of which trine Uranus in Scorpio (detection again!), enabling her to earn an independent living with her writing, and to sustain a mystery plot and a believable love story without sacrificing either.

Mary Cassatt	May 22, 1845
Queen Victoria	May 24, 1819
Peggy Lee	May 26, 1920
Julia Ward Howe	May 27, 1819
Isadora Duncan	May 27, 1878
Beatrice Lillie	May 29, 1903
Terri Tepper	May 29, 1942
Cornelia Otis Skinner	May 30, 1901
Marilyn Monroe	June 1, 1925
Rosalind Russell	June 4, 1911
Ruth Benedict (anthropologist)	June 5, 1887

Judy Garland	June 10, 1922
Millicent Fawcett (British suffrage leader)	June 11, 1847
Jeannette Rankin (congresswoman)	June 11, 1880
Dorothy L. Sayers	June 13, 1893
Harriet Beecher Stowe	June 14, 1811
Malvina Hoffman (sculptor)	June 15, 1887
Katharine Graham (publisher, *Washington Post*)	June 16, 1917
Duchess of Windsor	June 19, 1893
Lillian Hellman	June 20, 1907
Francoise Sagan	June 21, 1935

Cancer

Mary Baker Eddy founded the Christian Science Church, the *Christian Science Journal*, and the *Christian Science Monitor*. Following the birth of her son by her first marriage (of three), she was troubled by back pain for years. Faith healing helped, but she believed it didn't go far enough. The healer who generously taught her what he knew succeeded in transforming matter; her persisting idea was to ignore matter altogether. Her faith was put to the test when, following a fall she suffered one night, her doctor told her that she either wouldn't survive or would be permanently bedridden. She asked only for a Bible. That same day friends saw her walk out of her bedroom. The growing number of people who espoused the new faith were organized into the Christian Science Association, for which Ms. Eddy obtained a church charter for legal protection. The original church was disbanded by her when she feared it was degenerating into a personality cult. After a test period of solitude, she reorganized the church, beginning with the First Church in Boston, to be called the Mother Church. To protect the Church from factionalism and egocentric pastors, she wrote a manual on organization. As a result, at each service there are two readers, a woman and a man, who read alternately from the Bible and Ms. Eddy's text, *Science and Health*.

Sagittarius—the "religion sign"—is on the ascendant, and her Uranus-Neptune conjunction in Capricorn in the first house gave her a persistent faith in transcending matter (Neptune—transcending; Capricorn—matter), tested by the crisis of an accident (Uranus) and by criticism from newspapers and orthodox religions, who attacked her because she was a woman. Her third-house Pluto (healing) forms a harmonious aspect to the Jupiter (religion)-Saturn (hardship) conjunction in pioneering Aries. The latter conjunction also forms a harmonious aspect to the ascendant, hence her religious faith, challenged by personal hardship, eventually transformed her life for the better and was preserved beyond the end of her life.

Warren Farrell is one man who goes to N.O.W. meetings to work, not to meet "girls." A writer, Mr. Farrell's articles have appeared in various publications, including *Cosmopolitan* and the *New York Times*, and in 1974 he published his first book, *The Liberated Man: Beyond Masculinity: Freeing Men and Their Relationships with Women* (New York: Random House). *The Liberated Man* is a passionate and thorough work guaranteed to make a dent in all but the most rigid of minds. It is an exploration of unhealthy standards of masculinity and of the ways in which we can all make our lives more human and free from stereotypes. Mr. Farrell is also a lecturer, a consultant on feminism to industry and colleges, and a leader of consciousness-raising groups.

The third house, Mercury, and the signs Gemini and Virgo, are particularly important in the chart of a writer. Mr. Farrell's third house is ruled solely by the Moon (as Cancer is on the cusp of this empty house), a factor impelling him to write about human vulnerability. His Moon is in Aries in the twelfth house, hence he does his writing alone and with enthusiasm. The harmonious aspect between the Moon and Saturn has been used to good advantage in communicating clearly, whether the subject is history or cooking, and in sustaining discussions on delicate personal issues. Gemini and Virgo rule his money and his work. The domestic influence of Cancer is emphasized in his life not only by virtue of the Sun's presence in this sign, but also because Jupiter is there, an indication that his benevolent influence will be happily welcomed.

Anne Morrow Lindbergh	June 22, 1906
Warren Farrell	June 25, 1943
Pearl S. Buck	June 26, 1892
Helen Keller	June 27, 1880
George Sand	July 1, 1804
Susan Glaspell (playwright)	July 1, 1882
Gertrude Lawrence	July 4, 1901
Ann Landers	July 4, 1918

Abigail Van Buren	July 4, 1918
Wanda Landowska (harpsichordist)	July 5, 1877
Ann Radcliffe (novelist)	July 9, 1764
Dorothy Fields (lyricist)	July 15, 1905
Mary Baker Eddy	July 16, 1824
Barbara Stanwyck	July 16, 1907
Margaret Smith Court	July 16, 1942
Phyllis Diller	July 17, 1917
Lizzie Borden	July 19, 1860
Natalie Wood	July 20, 1938

Leo

Helen Thomas has progressed from cub reporter for United Press International to chief of UPI's White House Bureau—the first woman to hold that position. She has covered every administration since Franklin D. Roosevelt's, and published her personal impressions in her book *Dateline: White House* in 1975. ("The Presidency awed me, but Presidents do not. . . . Some have stood the test better than others.") With Neptune, the Sun, Venus, and Jupiter in Leo, it is no surprise that she has not only attracted the friendship of those in power, but has achieved positions of leadership herself: first as the chief of UPI's White House Bureau, then as the first woman president of the White House Correspondents Association. The trine between her Aries Moon and her Sun-Neptune conjunction shows positive recognition of her drive, as well as the importance she attaches to compassion in her writing. Her Grand Trines to the Mars-Saturn conjunction in Scorpio—from Pluto in Cancer and Uranus in Pisces—enabled her to find success and independence through nerve and self-discipline.

Myrna Lamb is the author of the plays *What Have You Done for Me Lately?* and *The Mod Donna*. Her rising sign is Virgo, her Moon sign Sagittarius. Mercury, ruler of her midheaven and ascendant, trines the midheaven, hence the praise she received in the press. Uranus, ruler of her work, squares her tenth-house Jupiter in Cancer. Thus, the cast of *Mod Donna* became an irritant to her, as members of the company disagreed strongly with the premises of the play. The eleventh-house Sun makes harmonious aspects to the third-house Moon, to Mars (which prompts her incisive style), to Jupiter (satire and success), and to Uranus (radical thinking). All of this energy should keep Ms. Lamb writing for many years the witty plays that have become her hallmark.

Amelia Earhart was the first woman to fly across the Atlantic—first as a passenger, in 1928, and then, on May 20, 1932, as a solo pilot. The latter flight and her solo flight from Honolulu to California are considered her greatest achievements. Her choice of career is no surprise, considering that she had more planets in the Air element—her Moon, Pluto, Venus, and Neptune were in Gemini—than in any of the three others. The discordant aspects between Neptune (flight) and the Sun and Saturn hint at the mystery surrounding her last flight in 1937, when she and her navigator, Fred Noonan, disappeared. The most popular conjecture is that she was on an espionage mission and was executed by the Japanese; thirty-nine years later her fate still remains in the realm of conjecture.

Amelia Earhart	July 24, 1897
Bella Abzug	July 24, 1920
Jacqueline Kennedy Onassis	July 28, 1929
Emily Brontë	July 30, 1818
Myrna Loy	August 2, 1905
Myrna Lamb	August 3, 1930
Helen Thomas	August 4, 1920
Lucille Ball	August 6, 1911
Mata Hari (Dutch spy)	August 7, 1876
Carrie Jacobs Bond (American composer)	August 11, 1862
Lucy Stone (feminist)	August 13, 1818
Maria Montessori (educator)	August 13, 1870
Ethel Barrymore	August 15, 1879
Edna Ferber	August 15, 1887
Julia Child	August 15, 1912
Mae West	August 17, 1892
Jacqueline Susann	August 20, 1926
Dorothy Parker	August 22, 1893

Virgo

Without Margaret Sanger's dynamic crusade to make birth control a part of every woman's life, most of the achievements by women of this century would never have materialized. After witnessing the death of a woman who had given herself one unskilled abortion too many in 1914, and the pathetically undernourished condition of the family's existing children, Margaret Sanger began her uncompromising fight to give women control over their own bodies, a fight she remained actively involved in until 1960 (she died in 1966, at the age of eighty-seven). The first person to dispense specific information on contraceptive methods, she suffered harassment from both church and state. Under the Comstock Law her pamphlets and her newspaper, *Woman Rebel*, were considered pornography and not fit to be sent through the mail. She left her three children in the custody of their father and set out for Montreal, then Europe, rather than stand trial when she believed it was the law and not her work that was at fault. Her exile lasted more than a year, ending when her husband was threatened with a jail term unless he revealed her whereabouts (which he loyally refused to do). Soon after her return the charges were dropped. Sanger's crusade survived several jailings and confiscations, and was helped along by her speeches and her books, which include *The Case for Birth Control* (1917), *Motherhood in Bondage* (1928), and *My Fight for Birth Control* (1931).

The close conjunction of her three planets in the health-oriented sign Virgo—Venus, the Sun, and Uranus—is the only hint that she had the intensity required for a fifty-year fight. Her success—from her intelligence, determination, and compassion—got a boost from her Grand Air Trine of Mercury (Libra), Saturn (Gemini), and the Moon (Aquarius), respectively. Her anger at "motherhood in bondage" is represented astrologically by the semi-square of Pluto (in Gemini) to Mars in Cancer. Jupiter, also in Cancer, made its presence felt as her success in changing the law pertaining to planned parenthood information, her travels to help countries more heavily populated than her own (notably India and Japan), and her ideal of children's rights: "The first right of every child is to be wanted, to be desired, to be planned with an intensity of love that gives it its title to being."

Barbara Seaman is the author of two books, *The Doctors' Case Against the Pill* and *Free and Female*, and has recently contributed to such publications as *Ms.*, the *New York Times*, the *Washington Post*, and the *Village Voice*. Soon to be published is a book on the dangers of hormones, written with her husband, Dr. Gideon Seaman. Her active output and success in achieving publication are linked with her active fifth and ninth houses. Her creativity is ruled by a well-aspected Jupiter in Scorpio—popularly called the "sign of sex"—and by Venus, and the process of reaching the public is ruled by Saturn, Uranus, and the Moon. The Moon in Aquarius rules her Cancer ascendant. Jupiter and Neptune corule her career, reputation, and strivings. This means large-scale ambitions, plus a desire to help others grow.

However beneficial and far-reaching her writings on sexual liberation have become, Ms. Seaman sees her investigation into women's health care as her major contribution. The Library of Congress identified her as the first writer to focus on the sexism women encounter as they are faced with such abuses as unnecessary surgery. With Venus and Neptune conjunct the Sun in Virgo, empathy with the disadvantaged impels her to produce accurate work that should immeasurably improve the well-being of women.

Jacqueline Michot Ceballos was public relations coordinator for N.O.W. and president of the New York City chapter. She is now a partner in the public relations firm of Ceballos & Phillips Communications. Her other enterprises include the New Feminist Theater, promotion of the production of *Mod Donna* and the feminist literary magazine *Aphra* (all of which gained from her Mercury-Neptune conjunction in Leo). In 1970 she founded the New Feminist Talent, a speakers' bureau, to fill the many requests for accomplished and informed feminist speakers. The planet closest to the midheaven is Neptune; her visions and aspirations are humanitarian, far-reaching, and limitless. Publicity work and public relations are her means, and she is gifted in these enterprises. Her eleventh-house planets form harmonious aspects to Jupiter in the third house; consequently her encouragement of her friends should yield mutual benefit.

Sophia Smith (first benefactor of Smith College)	August 27, 1796
Elizabeth Seton (first American-born saint)	August 28, 1774
Anna Ella Carroll (military strategist)	August 29, 1815
Mary Godwin Shelley (author of *Frankenstein*)	August 30, 1797
Lily Tomlin	September 1, 1936
Amy Marcy Cheney Beach (composer)	September 5, 1867
Frances Wright (feminist social worker)	September 6, 1795
Jane Addams (founder of Hull House)	September 6, 1860
Queen Elizabeth I	September 7, 1533
Grandma Moses	September 7, 1860

Elinor Wylie (poet)	September 7, 1885
Jacqueline Michot Ceballos	September 8, 1925
Barbara Seaman	September 11, 1935
Claudette Colbert	September 13, 1907
Margaret Sanger	September 14, 1883
Kate Millett	September 14, 1934
Agatha Christie	September 15, 1890
Lauren Bacall	September 16, 1924
Greta Garbo	September 18, 1905

Libra

Eleanor Roosevelt's public career began in World War I with her work in the Navy Hospital. After the war she turned her energies to the Consumer's League, the Women's Trade Union League, organized units of Democratic women, and her husband's campaigns to be governor and, later, president. When her husband became president in 1933, she became the first wife of a president of the United States to maintain a career of her own, the first to hold regular press conferences, and the first to travel by plane (logging about fifty thousand miles a year). Her daily newspaper column, *My Day*, begun in 1935, continued until her death in 1962. She made many personal appearances as a speaker, and spoke on the radio as well. In April 1945, after President Roosevelt's death, Mrs. Roosevelt attended the United Nations Conference in San Francisco and in December of that year became one of the four United States delegates to the United Nations General Assembly, a position she held until 1952. During that same interval she served as president of the United Nations Economic and Social Council's Commission on Human Rights.

Like Mary Wollstonecraft, her Pluto is her strongest planet, enabling her to overcome the initially low self-esteem associated with a weak Sun. Although born into a materially comfortable family, she had much to overcome nonetheless: her father's alcoholism (Neptune corules her fourth house), her mother's criticism of her plainness (Virgo is on the cusp of the tenth house), an intimidating mother-in-law (the Sun, a ruler of the ninth house, of in-laws, forms a discordant aspect to Pluto), an unpredictable voice (Uranus conjunct Mercury), and her husband's preference for her secretaries (Saturn semi-sextile her sixth-house Neptune)—all of which added up to agonizing shyness. It was not until her husband's paralysis began (Uranus was in her tenth house and his first) that her career really began. Uranus's aspects in her chart are a conjunction to Mercury (she worked to improve her speaking voice), a semi-sextile to Jupiter (opportunities to travel and speak publicly), a square to her seventh-house Saturn (conflicts between being out in public and caring for her husband in person), a trine to Neptune (independence through substituting for her husband and through idealistic causes), and a trine to Pluto (the repetition of public appearances reinforces her strength and independence). The trine between her Cancer Moon and Scorpio Mars also came to her aid when she was needed and had to rise to the occasion. The harmonious aspects between Mars and her Libra Sun, and between Pluto in Gemini and her Libra Mercury, found fulfillment in her writing and diplomatic work, which is the ideal Libran challenge.

One of the most colorful figures of the early days of American feminism was Victoria Claflin Woodhull. She started out as a young con artist in her father's traveling medicine show, participating in a spiritualist act. After a brief marriage in her teens, she and her sister Tennessee (later known as Tennie C.) opened the first stock brokerage firm to be owned and run by women (with the help of Commodore Cornelius Vanderbilt, who loved Tennessee almost as much for the séances she conducted for him as for her beauty). Mrs. Woodhull branched out into publishing with the controversial *Woodhull & Claflin's Weekly*, which supported women's rights, miscellaneous other progressive causes, and the candidacy of a woman for president—specifically, Victoria, in the election of 1872. The women of the Suffrage Association, notably Susan B. Anthony and Lucretia Mott, supported her at first, but eventually withdrew after her public advocacy of free love. In 1877, after her second divorce and the Beecher-Tilton scandal (she published news of the affair between Rev. Henry Ward Beecher and the wife of his friend, Theodore Tilton, in her weekly), she moved to England with her sister, parents, and children, where she married again. She established a new journal, *The Humanitarian*, which was progressive but less controversial than the old *Weekly*, and ran it with the help of her daughter, Zulu Maud. In the last four years of her life (she lived to be eighty-eight), she was afraid to lie down lest death have an advantage. On the morning of June 9, 1927, she was found dead in her chair.

Mercury's three harmonious aspects and one neutral conjunction helped her reputation as an engaging speaker and persuasive writer for her causes. Even if the country had been ready for a woman president in 1872, she would not have won, owing to an unaspected Pluto and a Moon-Saturn conjunction in Scorpio; the division within the party and her own sexual attitudes militated against her.

Neptune in Aquarius formed a harmonious aspect to Uranus in Pisces, adding magnetic appeal to her personality and popularity for her brokerage firm. Ahead of her time in every venture she pursued, it is sadly ironic that by the 1920s she was indifferent to the fact that the social changes she had continuously pleaded for—free love and stigma-free divorce—were becoming part of everyday life.

Victoria Claflin Woodhull	September 23, 1838
Brigitte Bardot	September 28, 1935
Faith Baldwin	October 1, 1893
Bonnie Parker (bank robber)	October 1, 1910
Eleanora Duse	October 3, 1859
Emily Post	October 3, 1873
Carole Lombard	October 6, 1908
Helen MacInnes (novelist)	October 7, 1907
Helen Hayes	October 10, 1900
Eleanor Roosevelt	October 11, 1884
Molly Pitcher (American Revolution heroine)	October 13, 1754
Katherine Mansfield	October 14, 1886
Helen Hunt Jackson (novelist)	October 15, 1830
Laura Nyro	October 18, 1947

Scorpio

Billie Jean King is widely known as a tennis champion, winner of victories at Wimbledon, Forest Hills, and Houston (that Houston match against Bobby Riggs would have made a rich woman of me, but no friend of *mine* was about to bet on the opposition). Aside from that highly exciting match, Ms. King stands out among women tennis players as an agitator for better conditions and equal prize money for women. Her eighth-house planets are the Moon and Neptune in egalitarian Libra, which serve to indicate how ideals are directed—toward the tangible recognition of victory, equally tangible for both sexes. Ms. King was the first woman to win one hundred thousand dollars in a single season, and she achieved this in both 1971 and 1972. The pleasure of competition for its own sake is shown by the seventh house, containing Jupiter and Pluto in Leo. In addition, the fifth house (sports) is dominant: Uranus, Mars, and Saturn are there in Gemini. The planets give her intensity on or off the court, and Gemini contributes versatility and fast reflexes.

Jupiter has the added outlet of her magazine, *Women Sports*, created to give women athletes the coverage they deserve "as athletes who happen to be women, not as decorations or sideshow attractions in the real world of sports."

Ti-Grace Atkinson, a former officer of NOW, is a Scorpio with Gemini ascendant and Moon. Radical Uranus, ruler of the philosophy guiding her life (and philosophy was the subject of her Columbia doctorate), is in opposition to the Sun (reputation). Although a discordant aspect, an opposition to Uranus is usually enjoyed by the person having it; controversy adds excitement to the lives of all involved.

The main priority of Ms. Atkinson's life is the performance of her work. Her Sun is in this house (her sixth), along with her Venus and Mercury, which are conjunct in Sagittarius (philosophy, publishing). Venus's extremely close proximity to Mercury in blunt Sagittarius gives a gift for memorable phrasing, for example, "Love is the victim's response to the rapist." Her most recent publication is *Amazon Odyssey*.

Belva Lockwood (lawyer and suffragette)	October 24, 1830
Mahalia Jackson (gospel singer)	October 26, 1911
Elsa Lanchester	October 28, 1902
Ruth Gordon	October 30, 1896
Marie Antoinette	November 2, 1755
Marie Curie	November 7, 1867
Joan Sutherland	November 7, 1929
Joni Mitchell	November 7, 1943
Katharine Hepburn	November 8, 1909
Ti-Grace Atkinson	November 9, 1938
Marie Bichat (French physician)	November 11, 1771
Maude Adams (actress)	November 11, 1872
Princess Grace of Monaco	November 12, 1929
Marya Mannes	November 14, 1904
Petula Clark	November 15, 1932
Amelita Galli-Curci (opera singer)	November 18, 1889

Brenda Vaccaro	November 18, 1939
Selma Lagerlof (Swedish novelist and poet)	November 20, 1858
George Eliot	November 22, 1819
Billie Jean King	November 22, 1943

Sagittarius

Margaret Mead has Mercury and Uranus in Sagittarius in close conjunction to the Sun; thus, before becoming an anthropologist, she contemplated the classic Sagittarian callings of law and religion. The Uranus-Aquarius (Moon and Venus) aspects also exerted considerable influence, and their outlets of psychology and anthropology won out as career choices. Sagittarian energy then manifested itself in a doctorate, publication, and travel. Her arrival in Arapesh in December, 1931, marked the beginning of the field work celebrated by advocates of sex-role change: the Mountain Arapesh people of both sexes placed a premium on gentleness and nurturing; deviants who were violent were avoided. The field work which followed was with the Mundugumor, a tribe of fierce men and women, highly sexed, aggressive, and rejecting of children: parents disappointed in the sex of their babies tossed the still-alive infants into the river. Her subsequent study was of the Tchambuli, whose expectations of the sexes reversed the pattern that is familiar here. This work (which she later described in *Sex and Temperament* and *Male and Female*) provoked such questions as What if there were other kinds of innate differences—differences as important as those between the sexes, but that cut across sex lines? and What if human beings, innately different at birth, could be shown to fit into systematically defined temperamental types, and What if there were male and female versions of each of these temperamental types?

Nancy Borman, a reporter, is a Sagittarius with Scorpio ascendant and Mercury. Along with Mercury in the first house are her Sagittarius Sun and Jupiter. As both Scorpio and Sagittarius are signs of satire (with Scorpio the more caustic of the two), Ms. Borman was an excellent contributor as well as managing editor of the parody called *The Now York Times*. She is now an editor of the feminist newspaper *Majority Report*.

Louisa May Alcott	November 29, 1832
Anna Comnena (Byzantine historian)	December 1, 1083
Mary Martin	December 1, 1913
Maria Callas	December 2, 1923
Anna Freud (psychoanalyst)	December 3, 1895
Agnes Moorehead	December 6, 1906
Mary, Queen of Scots	December 7, 1542
Willa Cather	December 7, 1876
Emily Dickinson	December 10, 1830
Annie Jump Cannon (astronomer)	December 11, 1863
Helen Frankenthaler (artist)	December 12, 1928
Dionne Warwicke	December 12, 1940
Jane Austen	December 16, 1775
Margaret Mead	December 16, 1901
Liv Ullmann	December 16, 1939
Charlotte Curtis	December 19, 1928
Jane Fonda	December 21, 1937

Capricorn

Simone de Beauvoir is an internationally known, prolific writer of both fiction and nonfiction, but perhaps her single most important work is *The Second Sex* (1949). Thorough in scope and precise in style, it delves into ancient as well as modern history and literature to analyze woman's predicament.

Mlle. de Beauvoir's Scorpio ascendant is but one clue to her rebellious nature. The third house combines Venus in Aquarius—the astrological reflection of her subject matter (the feminist sensibility, progressive ideas about humanity). Aries's rulership of her creativity promises vivid output, and Mars's placement in Pisces enables her to be as sensitive and profound as she is dynamic. The conjunction of Mars and Saturn is most constructively used as self-discipline to see a project through to completion, an attribute not normally characteristic of Mars and Aries. Saturn, the planet associated with longevity and seriousness, was activated in the production of her recent success, *The Coming of Age*. Libra rules her friendships and well-wishers. Its ruler trines Pluto from its position in the third house, so she succeeded in winning the admiration of the entire women's movement through her writing.

Betty Furness was President Johnson's special assistant for Consumer Affairs in 1967 and 1968, and in 1970 was appointed chairman of the New York State Consumer Protection Board by Governor Nelson Rockefeller, which position she quit in 1971. She subsequently wrote a column for *McCall's* and became New York City's Commissioner of Consumer Affairs. She currently reports on consumer issues on NBC's "NewsCenter 4," often taking action on behalf of those who write to her.

The Neptune-Pisces energy ruling her early work in movies and refrigerator commercials is outweighed by the Saturn-Capricorn energy of business. With Saturn and Pluto in consumer-oriented Cancer and an idealistic Sagittarius Moon, she would enjoy positions enabling her to resolve complaints and to champion the causes of those who need her.

Clara Barton	December 25, 1821
Rebecca West	December 25, 1892
Marlene Dietrich	December 27, 1904
Mary Tyler Moore	December 29, 1937
Betty Furness	January 3, 1916
Joan of Arc	January 6, 1412
Loretta Young	January 6, 1913
Carrie Chapman Catt (feminist)	January 9, 1859
Simone de Beauvoir	January 9, 1908
Joan Baez	January 9, 1941
Gwen Verdon	January 13, 1925
Ethel Merman	January 16, 1909
Shari Lewis (puppeteer-ventriloquist)	January 17, 1934
Jean Stapleton	January 19, 1923

Aquarius

The revival of feminism in the United States probably began in February (Aquarius!) 1963 with the publication of *The Feminine Mystique*, by Betty Friedan.

Ms. Friedan is an Aquarius with Sagittarius rising, introducing her iconoclastic ideals to the public via publications and lectures. Her Capricorn Moon gives durability of purpose and is also conducive to boredom with domesticity.

In her third house (writing) are Mars in Pisces and Venus in Aries. This combination gives her a sharp writing style on behalf of the underdog (Pisces) in marriage (Venus), with suggestions for striking out (Mars, Aries) into more challenging life-styles. Mars also rules her outlook on domesticity: impatience. When she conceived the 1970 Women's Strike for Equality, she gave women a battle cry as well: "Don't iron while the strike is hot!"

Public expression in all its forms is dominant in Ms. Friedan's life. Mercury, Jupiter, and Saturn rule her ninth house. Jupiter rules her religious thinking too. In 1973 she went to the Vatican to deliver her suggestions personally to Pope Paul, then wrote about the visit for *McCall's*. The emphasis on the ninth house indicates frequent travel, speeches, teaching jobs (she is presently at Yale), writing assignments, and opportunities to broadcast. In 1976 her second book, *It Changed My Life*, was published.

Although an independent, she is not an extremist or an isolationist. In a 1975 interview with Tom Snyder she spoke happily of "new possibilities for love," not of man-hatred; of joy, not bitterness.

Germaine Greer is the author of *The Female Eunuch*. Like Simone de Beauvoir, she gives a historical and cultural perspective of male exploitation and hatred of women. Throughout, though, she offers a specific solution: refuse to marry; break the neurotic pattern.

The Sun, ruler of her Leo ascendant, is in her sixth house, indicating work as the source of self-esteem and autonomy. The Sun-Moon square shows personal pain to be the source of publicly advocated bachelorhood; enforced domesticity is no life for a woman. The disillusionment with and the contempt for dishonesty in love indicated by the Venus-Neptune square is articulated brilliantly in her carefully documented chapters on gentle cajolery and "pussy power" as a con. The Pluto-Mars harmony must have been activated when she appeared on two Dick Cavett broadcasts. On one, when she was guest hostess, she interviewed a rape victim. On the other she talked with Cavett. When he relayed to her Norman Mailer's surprise at finding her attractive, she smiled and said, "I would have been surprised to find *him* attractive."

Jurate Kazickas is a feature writer based in New York, a former Vietnam correspondent, and is perhaps best known for her partnership with Lynn Sherr on the annual (since 1972) *Liberated Woman's Appointment Calendar*, the source of many of the birth dates in this chapter. An Aquarius with Moon and ascendant in Leo, she has certainly had ample opportunity to use all the perseverance her chart affords (including ten aspects to Saturn) to pursue and organize the birth and event dates that make each year's calendar a surprise.

Ann Sothern	January 22, 1912
Edith Wharton	January 24, 1862
Santha Rama Rau	January 24, 1923
Angela Davis	January 26, 1944
Colette	January 28, 1873
Germaine Greer	January 29, 1939
Ayn Rand	February 2, 1905
Gertrude Stein	February 3, 1874
Betty Friedan	February 4, 1921
Evangeline Adams	February 8, 1868
Amy Lowell	February 9, 1874
Leontyne Price	February 10, 1927
Virginia E. Johnson (sex researcher)	February 11, 1925
Eileen Farrell	February 13, 1920
Susan B. Anthony	February 15, 1820
Judith Anderson	February 16, 1898
Marian Anderson	February 17, 1902
Helen Gurley Brown	February 18, 1922
Yoko Ono	February 18, 1933
Jurate Kazickas	February 18, 1943

Pisces

The life of Edna St. Vincent Millay was as intriguing a work of art as the lines she wrote, lines such as:

Oh, oh, you will be sorry for that word!
Give back my book and take my kiss instead.
Was it my enemy or my friend I heard,
"What a big book for such a little head!"

She wrote philosophically of the impermanence of love; not as a wronged woman but as one who does the leaving—unusual for the poetry of a woman.

Her sympathy with suffragism began in 1915, when, as a student, she heard Inez Milholland give a speech at Vassar. (Inez Milholland's husband, Eugen Boissevain, was later to fall in love with and marry the young poet, in 1923, seven years after his first wife's death. He gave up his exporting business to devote himself entirely to keeping house for his creative wife.) Oppression had never been a problem at home, however, as her divorced mother gave her steady encouragement.

Fame began when Ms. Millay was twenty, with the publication of "Renascence." She lived in Greenwich Village when artistic rebels from all over the country were migrating there in search of freedom. Many of the rebels in the Village before World War I were women escaping from the shackles of their sex, eager for professions and emancipated living. Vincent, as she was called since childhood, stopped her romances short of marriage, fearing not so much unhappiness as domestic contentment. This shows in the chart as a square between her Sagittarius Moon—domestic happiness—and Saturn in Virgo—work. She was afraid she would lose her motivation to write poetry, and only Boissevain's devotion and feminism could convince her otherwise. She did no housework at all after marriage, except for preparing her country retreat for habitation, until she was widowed. She once explained that if she had to "live in a mess, or live in a neat room and give up writing, I prefer the mess."

Although she was America's leading lyric poet of the twenties and a Pulitzer Prize winner in 1922, she had to supplement her income with other writing. The satirical articles and poems she produced toward this end were published under the pseudonym Nancy Boyd (a strategy characteristic of Neptune-Pisces energy at work) to avoid giving the impression that they were as serious as the Edna St. Vincent Millay poems. Having a Jupiter-Saturn opposition, she wanted a clear separation between her satire and her serious works. The mischievous Jupiter side of her nature, however, could not resist adding to the collected works of Nancy Boyd a preface by Edna St. Vincent Millay: "I take pleasure in recommending to the public these excellent satires, from the pen of one in whose work I have a never-failing interest and delight."

Lynn Sherr is a television reporter (Pluto corules her ninth house) and a chronicler of feminist achievement, with Jurate Kazickas, in the annual *Liberated Woman's Appointment Calendar*. Her Venus-Mercury conjunction in Aquarius in the twelfth house adds energy to the research that impresses fans as a labor of love. The harmony between Mercury and her Pisces Sun in the first house adds inspiration to find little-known facts about unjustly obscure people. Her third house is dominant, with a close conjunction of Saturn, Uranus, and Mars in Taurus, further enabling her to be enterprising and persistent in her search for new material.

Edna St. Vincent Millay	February 22, 1892
Alice Hamilton (physician)	February 25, 1869
Ellen Terry	February 27, 1847
Joan Bennett	February 27, 1910
Joanne Woodward	February 27, 1930
Elizabeth Taylor	February 27, 1932
Mary Lyon (educator)	February 28, 1799
Geraldine Farrar (actress)	February 28, 1882
Svetlana Stalin Alliluyeva	February 28, 1926
Lynn Sherr	March 4, 1942
Elizabeth Barrett Browning	March 6, 1806
Lillian D. Wald (founder, Henry St. Settlement)	March 10, 1867
Dorothy Schiff (publisher, *New York Post*)	March 11, 1903
Liza Minnelli	March 12, 1946
Rosa Bonheur (painter)	March 16, 1822

11

What Makes Samantha Run?

The survey in this chapter was compiled from a poll of forty women—dynamic, intelligent, and liberated career women, married and unmarried, urban and suburban, and ranging in age from twenty to forty-five. The reason for the survey was to discover what common personality traits prevailed among the women sampled—women who, I suspected, could not find comfort and guidance in traditional, sexist astrology—as my aim has consistently been to offer today's contemporary woman a dynamic astrology that is suited to her needs and wants. Instead of the widespread practice of telling women what they *should* be, I want to tell women what they *are* and what they *can* be.

In the course of collecting the timed charts I needed, I found a remarkable degree of astrological sophistication in the women polled; not only did they ask about Sun signs, but about Moon, ascendant, and other planet signs as well. All forty knew their exact birth time (on which the rising sign is based) and expressed interest in the extent to which they appeared typical, and eagerness to learn the result of my findings. The following were my conclusions.

Rising Signs

There was a tie for the lead in this category (six women each had rising signs of Gemini, Leo, and Scorpio), and each of these signs will be placed on the ascendants of each of three charts (Figures 1, 2, and 3).*

*If the total picture for each ascendant adds up to the Sun-sign portrait you're accustomed to finding for the sign in question, that's because general Sun-sign readings are based on a presumed, admittedly arbitrary, sunrise birth. What you're getting here are the fundamental reasons why Geminis are quick-witted, Scorpios highly sexed, and so on. Gemini rising has as many obvious Gemini qualities as a Sun-in-Gemini, if not more.

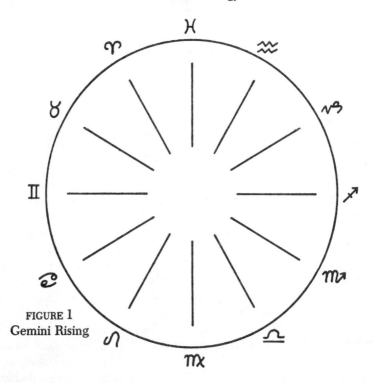

FIGURE 1
Gemini Rising

Gemini on the ascendant, also known as the first-house cusp, indicates a keen mind and curiosity, restlessness, varied interests, and spontaneity.

Cancer on the second-house cusp can bring frequent fluctuations and anxiety about having enough money to guarantee creature comforts.

Leo on the third cusp indicates a high priority for mental activity and keeping on the move physically as well as cerebrally. This is one of the reasons Gemini is said to be strongly mental; the other, more publicized, reason is that Gemini's ruler, Mercury, is the planet of the objective mind.

Virgo on the fourth cusp can mean keeping an office at home, a home that is hygienic and neat; the likelihood of having domestic help; and a critical father.

Libra on the fifth cusp indicates gracious hospitality, fairness with children, and vacillation about love or creativity.

Scorpio on the sixth cusp can mean investigative talent; a person with such an asset ought to find a job that affords an opportunity to employ it.

Sagittarius on the seventh cusp points toward a generous husband; someone in higher education, publishing, religion, broadcasting, or work involving travel; it can also mean a business collaboration, a blithe I-don't-care attitude about marriage itself, and a live-and-let-live lifestyle within marriage.

Capricorn on the eighth cusp implies difficulty in collecting what is owed, a hatred of being in debt, financial hardship resulting from discrimination (for example, in getting raises or credit), or tax trouble.

Aquarius on the ninth cusp can mean a radical philosophy far ahead of its time, a break with one's original religion, impromptu journeys, and probable charisma as a teacher or as a broadcaster.

Pisces on the tenth cusp (or midheaven) is a very complicated influence: high hopes, promises made and broken—promises both to and by the individual; a reputation for creativity or oddness; accusations of laziness when a nine-to-five job is refused. A distorted image of the mother confuses the career choices still more. Pisces here can mean great disillusionment. When Jupiter is discordant, there is a conflict between marriage and career.

Aries on the eleventh cusp suggests the leadership of friends; friends who themselves are leaders; daring, athletic, aggressive, or controversial friends.

Taurus on the twelfth cusp denotes artistic interests—or romance—pursued behind closed doors. Solitude is welcome unless Venus or planets in this house are discordant.

Leo on the ascendant is an indication that the personal life has top priority with the individual. The stronger the Sun, especially when there are discordant aspects, the more insistent one will be about self-determination.

Virgo on the second cusp suggests precision with budgeting and income from editing, writing, teaching, or crafts.

Libra on the third cusp can mean diplomatic skill, a logical mind, legal aptitude, and a fondness for socializing.

Scorpio on the fourth cusp connotes a hostile home atmosphere, punctuated by inquisitions and brooding silences; rebellion against domesticity; and a coercive father.

Sagittarius on the fifth cusp can represent a cavalier attitude toward love, a spirit of adventure, fondness for gambling (which can also extend

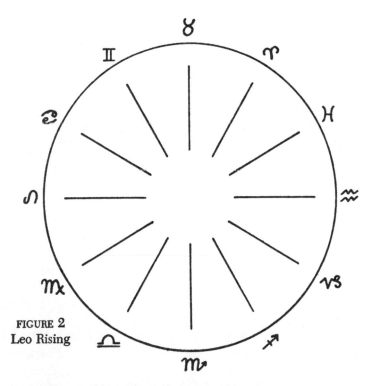

FIGURE 2
Leo Rising

to taking too many chances with pregnancy), abundant and joyful creative output, and generosity with children.

Capricorn on the sixth cusp symbolizes perseverance in the execution
of work, investigative ability (like Scorpio), and a feeling of oppression
or of being discriminated against on the job.

Aquarius on the seventh cusp signals an unusual husband or marriage
arrangement, pressure to get married or to work at the marriage—with
surprising responses to these varieties of pressure, sudden breaks and a
consequent utopian plan to redefine and/or avoid marriage.

Pisces on the eighth cusp indicates an unrealistic plunge into debt—
very likely as a result of charging to celebrate a promised raise that
doesn't come through, getting money through creative work, a gift, or a
legacy.

Aries on the ninth cusp indicates a caustic style of public expression,
crusading for a cause, a philosophy espousing confrontation, and agitation for reform.

Taurus on the tenth cusp can mean a reputation for steadiness, creativity or both; fame, along with the desire for it, can last and grow over a lifetime.

Gemini on the eleventh cusp suggests witty, intelligent, nomadic, or younger friends.

Cancer on the twelfth cusp points toward emotional fluctuations, anxieties about security and about children, fondness for music to make solitude pleasant.

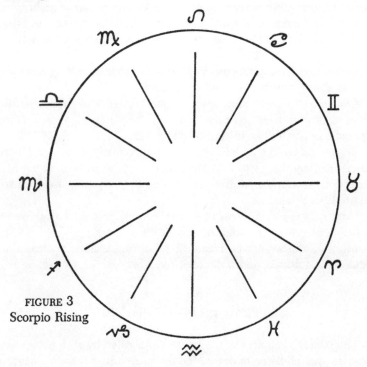

FIGURE 3
Scorpio Rising

Scorpio on the ascendant indicates a willful, rebellious, secretive nature capable of intense loyalty. Scorpio is good at reading hidden meanings and innuendoes. The Scorpio-rising personality can be very highly sexed unless checked by a strong aspect from Saturn.

Sagittarius on the second cusp can mean extravagance; publishing, teaching, broadcasting, the law, medicine, or religion are indicated as sources of income. This temperament spends money freely for a good time, to help a friend, or for a worthy cause.

Capricorn on the third cusp implies seriousness as a general approach to life, perseverance in mental work, older or conservative siblings, a retentive memory, and the ability to dig for information.

Aquarius on the fourth cusp signifies an erratic father or an oppressive one, a stepfather, an unusual home, oppression from housework, and a rebellious attitude about doing chores.

Pisces on the fifth cusp alludes to unusual (or perverted) lovers, partners who are lazy or con artists or both, victimization by pro-romantic and pro-motherhood propaganda, and dramatic ability.

Aries on the sixth cusp suggests quarrels on the job, particularly about duties. On the positive side, tasks are initiated enthusiastically and quickly, and energy expended unstintingly.

Gemini on the eighth cusp implies the chance of getting money via verbal ability, mechanical skill, or selling.

Cancer on the ninth cusp means an emotional style of public speaking; fluctuations in religion, philosophy, higher education, and travel; sporadic opportunities to address the public.

Leo on the tenth cusp indicates determination in pursuing ambitions. Generally, anything less than top billing is a disappointment not to be tolerated in silence. Motivation comes, in part, from the mother's example or doubts.

Virgo on the eleventh cusp can signify intelligent, analytical friends, possibly people in editorial, health, or office work.

Libra on the twelfth cusp can, like Taurus, mean pleasantness and comfort in solitude, and a discreet love life.

Planetary House Rulerships

The planet locations and the house cusps ruled by each planet were studied and tabulated to determine the total influence each planet had on each house.

The houses where the Sun most frequently appeared were the first (the personal life, personality, priority for the self, self-esteem), and the second (money).

The houses where the Moon most frequently appeared were the twelfth (keeping emotional problems private, perhaps even hidden from the self), the first (compassion for the underdog, restlessness, low boredom threshold), and the second (financial affairs in constant flux).

The houses where Mercury most frequently appeared were the first (keen mind, articulate expression, mechanical ability or manual dexterity), the second (another indicator of frequent financial changes), and the twelfth (a good placement for writers who have to do much of their work alone).

The houses where Venus most frequently appeared were the twelfth (good for artists, also for keeping secrets about affectional matters), the first (physical attractiveness, diplomacy, sometimes excessive modesty and timidity), and the fifth (tenderness with lovers and children, artistic ability, a tendency to take the line of least resistance in love situations, and creativity in the visual arts).

The houses where Mars most frequently appeared were the fourth (vitriolic home life, a quarrelsome if not violent father, rebellion against domesticity), the eleventh (daring or aggressive friends), and the sixth (work involving initiative, problems with employees or co-workers, struggles to get desired duties).

The houses where Jupiter most frequently appeared were the seventh (luck with, or indifference to, marriage), the second (luck with money, abundant expenditures), and the fifth (luck, abundance, or indifference with love or children, a willingness to take chances in life).

The houses where Saturn most frequently appeared were the ninth (oppression by orthodox religious and educational institutions, frustration in communicating with the public), the fourth (a strict, oppressive father; hardships at home, such as in furnishing or maintaining same; hatred of housework), and the eleventh (holding on to friendships, self-pitying friends).

The houses where Uranus most frequently appeared were the tenth (unconventional mother or approach to self-promotion; surprises and shocks through gossip or the press; a reputation as an eccentric, since Uranus is the most radical and progressive of all planets), the seventh (unconventional husband, attitude toward marriage, circumstances surrounding the marriage, sudden breaks), and the ninth (progressive, radical philosophy; a break with the family's traditional religion; charisma in public expression).

The houses where Neptune most frequently appeared were the fifth (good for creative work in drama or poetry, but less fortunate in love; illusions and disillusionment with love, sex, and motherhood), the eighth (great expectations about income, with disappointing results; a partner who lies or makes well-intentioned but unkept promises about money), and the tenth (unwillingness to do drudgery; lies and empty promises about promotions, job titles, status).

The houses where Pluto most frequently appeared were the fourth (coercion into and rebellion against housework, a domineering father), the sixth (good for research work, attempts to win the cooperation of co-workers or employees), and the twelfth (secret enemies undermining efforts, good for solitary research work).

Shifting our vantage point somewhat, now to the houses and the two or three planets most frequently ruling them, we see:

The first house:	Mercury	(intelligent, articulate, restless)
	Sun	(forceful personality, self-determining)
	Venus	(attractive, gracious)
The second house:	Mercury	(financial changes, income through mental work)
	Jupiter	(luck, generosity)
	Sun	(money is important as an indicator of status)
The third house:	Saturn	(persistent, can dig for facts, may write of oppression)
	Mars	(quick mind, can be caustic)
	Venus	(can be diplomatic, may write about social developments)
The fourth house:	Mars	(conflicts at home, hostile father)
	Saturn	(hardship at home, oppressive father)
	Pluto	(rebellion at home, coercive father)
The fifth house:	Jupiter	(abundance of lovers, humor in love and creative work; adventurous spirit)
	Mercury	(intelligent and articulate lovers; writing talent)

	Venus	(drifting into love affairs; affection in love, artistic talent)
The sixth house:	Mars	(quick worker, quarrels on the job, struggles for desired duties)
	Jupiter	(good-natured in doing work, perhaps overqualified for the job, forgiving nature with co-workers)
	Mercury	(good for mental work, but secretarial work may be offered, too)
	Venus	(good for artwork and for smoothing over personal problems on the job)
The seventh house:	Jupiter	(indifference to marriage, luck with partner)
	Saturn	(oppressive atmosphere, loss or sacrifice through marriage, older partner)
	Mars	(quarrels; sexy partner)
The eighth house:	Mercury	(getting money through writing, lecturing, editing, selling)
	Jupiter	(pulling out of financial scrapes at the last minute; income through publishing, professional work, humor)
The ninth house:	Saturn	(oppression from traditional religion; a stubbornness about bringing this to light)
	Jupiter	(ethical rather than ritualistic philosophy)
The tenth house:	Jupiter	(luck with popular opinion, promotions, and good press; also humor at the individual's expense, honest mother)

	Saturn	(would feel—and, all too possibly, *be*—discriminated against; conservative mother)
The eleventh house:	Mars	(daring, argumentative, aggressive friends)
	Saturn	(clings to friendships; friends might be older or oppressed)
	Mercury	(intelligent friends)
The twelfth house:	Venus	(secretive about romance; discreet for friends' sake; likely to do artwork when alone)
	Mercury	(energy to do writing, other mental work, mechanical work, or a craft when alone; behind-the-scenes planning)

The houses in descending order of strength (determined by the planet count for each house) are the fourth (the home and father), the first (the personal life, the self), the tenth (ambition, the mother), the second (money), the sixth (work, co-workers, and health), and the twelfth (solitude and secrets) equally; the seventh (marriage and partnership); the ninth (public expression, religion, and higher education); the eleventh (friends and acquaintances); the eighth (source of money, partnership money); the fifth (sex, creativity, children); and the third (writing, studies, communication, siblings).

Aspects

For each possible combination of planets to aspect (the midheaven and ascendant are treated as planets), the charts were divided into four categories: harmonious, discordant, neutral, or no aspect at all. The following pairs indicate the most frequent combinations; the pairs not listed below did not appear in the majority of charts:

Sun-Venus, harmonious (48 percent): Since Venus is never more than forty-eight degrees away from the Sun, the aspects between these two are limited to the semi-sextile, a mildly harmonious aspect of thirty degrees' distance; the semi-square, a mildly discordant aspect at forty-five degrees; or a conjunction, harmonious owing to Venus's influence, if less than ten degrees apart. Either way, the harmonious combination of these two planets gives sweetness to the disposition and artistic tastes. Physical attractiveness is also linked with Sun-Venus aspects.

Sun-Mars, discordant: Exactly fifty percent of the charts have this: obstacles arising from a macho mentality, problems with aggressiveness, knocks to the ego, and a temper ready to fight back.

Sun-Jupiter, harmonious (55 percent): This indicates a desire for goodwill, generosity, fairness, and humor.

Sun-Midheaven, harmonious (35 percent): This indicates hope for the recognition of ability and a healthy desire for such recognition.

Moon-Uranus (38 percent): The Moon rules perception on an unconscious level, and Uranus is one of the "Psychic" planets—hence, extraordinary and rapid perception. Also, the Moon is our clue to the individual's attitudes toward people in general, and Uranus is the planet of independence. The combination of these two planets in a harmonious aspect shows a belief in the fundamental ideas of women's liberation and a desire to incorporate such progressive ideas into everyday life. This aspect also gives the power to influence others.

Venus-Jupiter, harmonious (40 percent): This is an excellent indication of a genius for winning and pleasing friends, for positive thinking, and enjoyment of living.

Venus-Neptune, harmonious (40 percent): This aspect is most frequently associated with artistic ability (Neptune energy conceives the design, and Venus gives the taste and skill to execute it), social utopias, and romantic success through mystery and artifice.

Venus-Pluto, harmonious (43 percent): This is an indication of friendly cooperation with groups of people. This aspect gives idealism and a desire to help further a cause that should bring the greatest good to the greatest number. (And women constitute a majority of our population!)

Venus-Midheaven, harmonious (40 percent): Success could come through art as well as through beauty and social grace. With this aspect in a woman's chart, achievement is played up rather than appearance (although the latter is bound to get comments anyway).

Venus-Ascendant, harmonious (40 percent): Another indication of aesthetic appeal, which will probably come as a shock to detractors who choose to think of liberated women as shriveled or unwashed hags.

Mars-Saturn, discordant (48 percent): These are the two malefics: Saturn, the planet of hardship, oppression, discipline, insecurity, and fear; Mars, the planet of arguments, aggression, and battle. The people I polled, however, are glad to have the energy—this aspect—which gives them the guts to fight and sustain their efforts. The negative side of this aspect, which so often is the main interpretation, is a vicious cycle of frustration, fighting, and more frustration. But for the sake of balance, the positive advantage of having energy with which to work and fight must also be given attention.

Uranus-Neptune, harmonious (50 percent): Both planets are visionary and utopian, with Uranus adding impatience for radical changes. Neptune, even when harmonious, has such high hopes for better conditions that disappointment often results.

In the other fifty-two possible planet-point pairs, the majority show no aspect at all, if only by a small margin. The most notable small-margin case is Saturn and the midheaven, which in forty percent of the cases combine discordantly. The most-repeated aspect between this pair was the opposition, and two such cases were intensified by a parallel into the bargain. This is perhaps the strongest sign of sustained ambition possible: ambition crystallized by frustration.

Generally speaking, most charts have balancing factors to stabilize the personality and the life; in these forty charts, frustration was balanced by thirteen cases of Grand Trines. (Grand Trines are the most dramatic indications of good luck, but any trine is a blessing.) One chart had Grand Trines in two elements: Fire (enthusiasm) and Water (emotional depth). In all, there were two Grand Fire Trines, three each of Air (intellect) and Water, and six in Earth. The Grand Earth Trine gives an extraordinary practicality and grip on reality. In every one of the Grand Earth Trine charts in this study, there is at least one of the idealistic planets (Jupiter, Uranus, Neptune). Thus, the individuals involved are not without beautiful, far-sighted ideals, but they think in terms of the best way to implement plans *now*.

Houses

In any chart the angular houses—the first, fourth, seventh, and tenth—are the houses with the most energy and power; the more planets a person has in these houses, the more vitality they have. In the forty charts the total number of planets in this group is 150, or 37.5 percent.

Next in energy—and in emphasis here—is the succedent group, or the second, fifth, eighth, and eleventh houses. The total number is 128 planets, or 32 percent.

Third and last is the cadent group—the third, sixth, ninth, and twelfth houses—with a total of 22 planets, or 30.5 percent.

Also to be hoped for in the chart of one who desires independence at *least*—and leadership at *most*—is a majority of planets in the eastern hemisphere—or left half (houses ten through three)—of the chart. The more planets in this half, the more self-sufficient one is and the more one shapes one's own environment. A slight majority in this hemisphere showed up in the samples: 215 planets, or 53.75 percent. (When the majority is in the other hemisphere, one is more influenced and victimized by other people and by circumstances.)

Another way houses are categorized is by four triplicities:

Life (capacity for, and importance of, pleasure): houses one, five, and nine;

Wealth (potential for material success and status): houses two, six, and ten;

Association (importance of dealing with and enjoying other people): houses three, seven, and eleven; and

Psychic (perceptivity, interest in spiritual subleties and the occult): houses four, eight, and twelve.

The Psychic group has a slight lead, with 109 planets to Life's 106. Wealth and Association follow with 101 and 84, respectively. One manifestation of this dominance of the Psychic energy is the sophistication of the women subjects mentioned at the beginning of this chapter and their willingness to probe astrology beyond the Sun-sign level.

Signs

As with the ascendants, there was a tie in the leading Sun signs between Leo and Aquarius. This is hardly surprising, as Leo has a flair for leadership, self-containment, and drama (all of which are utilized in the women's liberation movement), encouraging and organizing other participants, taking the initiative in demonstration planning and lobbying, and devising aesthetically memorable vehicles for communicating feminist aims. Aquarius is the sign of the social crusader ahead of her time, fighting City Hall to make the administration adopt her advanced ideas.

The leading Moon sign is Capricorn, the sign of the ambitious goat single-mindedly climbing to the top of the mountain. This is not surprising, partly because of that drive to climb and partly because the Moon, in its detriment here, does not freely express so-called feminine domestic talents.

Mercury most frequently appears in Leo, which is not harmonious with Mercury's nature: Mercury is detached and analytical, conflicting with Leo's passion and eagerness to proceed (remember, Leo is a Fire sign).

Venus is most frequently in Sagittarius, which is said to be the bachelor sign in that it has many enthusiasms and cerebral interests (such as philosophy, law, teaching) and does not confine itself to one individual, who would more likely than not establish limitations.*

The two equally leading signs for Mars are Gemini and Scorpio. Gemini, as a filter for Mars energy, gives a razor-sharp mind and inclination for rapid, caustic speech. Scorpio makes the individual very highly sexed, passionate about ideals as well as emotions, rebellious, and likely to hold a grudge forever.

One of the two equally leading signs for Jupiter is Capricorn, which is rather unfortunate, as the sign and planet are extreme opposites in nature: Jupiter is expansive, generous, and trusting; Capricorn is stingy, selfish, and suspicious. One way this combination manifests itself is as a desire for free professional advice. The Jupiter energy gives luck in getting it, but the Capricorn, the sign of frugality, alienates the professional in the process! The other leading Jupiter sign is Pisces, one of its "home" signs, which gives an extraordinary sensitivity to others' needs and the ability to get along with people. It also gives a broad-minded viewpoint, a willingness to gamble, a taste for unusual forms of fun, and a desire to benefit all of humanity.

Saturn is in Aries in as many as twenty percent of the charts. This is

---

*It is interesting to note here that the second most frequent Venus sign is Virgo, which for a different reason can do without romantic activity as easily as Sagittarius: it is so critical—sometimes even downright prudish—that few partners could measure up to the standards exacted.

fortunate in that it steadies Aries's often fleeting enthusiasm, although it can also limit success, bring delays, and decrease self-esteem and daring.

The three outlying planets—Uranus, Neptune, and Pluto—did not figure in this tabulation, as they are so slow-moving that they can stay in one sign for half to a whole generation, and would distort the entire study if calculated.

Compared to the other Uranus signs, Taurus is dominant. Taurus, a pragmatic Earth sign, limits but stabilizes psychic and erratic Uranus.

Neptune's main sign is Virgo, where again we have a visionary-realist balance. With Neptune in Virgo there is ambivalence between faith and skepticism.

Pluto is most frequently in Leo. It is the planet of sustained obsession, in a sign also known for fixity. Leo is associated with role-playing, leadership, sex, love of children, and adventure, all of which the Pluto-in-Leo generation of women (June, 1939, through December, 1952) is managing to overhaul. Pluto in Leo gives the conviction that child-bearing and rearing must be reconsidered in light of changing roles. On the other hand, the previous generation, having Pluto in Cancer (the motherhood sign), was obsessed with child-rearing, the issue of progressive education *versus* the school system, and full-time motherhood.

When the total planet placements are figured for each sign—and this is where it's especially important to omit Uranus, Neptune, and Pluto—the strongest signs were Taurus; then Aries, Leo, Capricorn, and Pisces with equal strength; Scorpio and Sagittarius, also equal; Gemini; Cancer and Aquarius equally; and Virgo.

Of the element groups, the one with the highest total was the Fire-sign group. Earth, Water, and Air followed in that order—or, the qualities of enthusiasm, practicality, sympathy, and intellectual detachment.

Dividing the signs another way—into groups of movable, fixed, and mutable signs—the dominant group was the fixed, followed by mutable and movable. The emphasis on fixity is a very heartening indication that the women's movement is not a flash in the pan. The mutable signs show adaptability, and the movable signs show initiating genius. To illustrate how these three different groups work together: the movable signs (Aries, Cancer, Libra, and Capricorn) present the ideas and organize the fixed signs (Taurus, Leo, Scorpio, and Aquarius), who follow through with research and development; the mutable signs (Gemini, Virgo, Sagittarius, and Pisces) add the finishing touches and do the promoting.

Slicing the zodiac still another way—into the three degrees of emanation (or the first, second, and third quartets of signs in zodiacal order, Aries through Pisces): if the first four signs—Aries, Taurus, Gemini, and Cancer—had the largest total, the individual would forge ahead, doing what she wanted without heeding the advice of others. With the second four strongest—Leo, Virgo, Libra, and Scorpio—she would weigh her desires in the light of suggestions and act upon a judicious compromise. This emphasis was the case in our combined forty sample charts. Were the last four—Sagittarius, Capricorn, Aquarius, and Pisces—strongest, our composite woman would be very much the follower if not counterbalanced by other indications of self-determination. For instance, of the eleven charts that have these last four signs dominant, seven are balanced by a majority of planets on the eastern half of the chart.

Lastly, to show how ridiculous and dispensable gender labels for signs are—if you aren't convinced already—the total of Fire and Air signs—the "masculine" signs—came to *less* than the total of the "feminine" signs in these women with ambitions more "manly" than "womanly." The total percentage of planets in the "feminine" group is fifty-one percent.

Knowing a "composite" or "typical" liberated woman's personality is but a starting point. From there each individual must use her given energies in the most beneficial and rewarding ways. To do this we need the help of a modernized, sexually liberated, astrological discipline—and this discipline must be part of the solution, not the problem.

12

Can a Leo Subjugate an Aries? Ha! (Letters from My Files)

I get more questions about relationships than anything else, and that's probably the only one I'd ever answer with a monosyllable.

Questions about Sun-sign combinations show up in every day's mail. These combinations tell how egos will mesh with one another in continued association; but egos are only part of the picture.

In the questions that follow, identifying birth data will be omitted for two reasons: first, as indicated above, Sun signs reveal but a small percentage of the whole relationship, and second, to protect my clients' anonymity.

My partner, a Libra, and I, a Sagittarius, are forming our own business and would like to hire someone to train to be a diversified assistant (editorial) as well as a secretary. What sign should we hire?

Since teaching is involved in your choice, look for someone whose Moon sign is in either the Fire or Air element. It's important that the person be receptive to his or her teachers' personalities.

I am an unemployed Aquarian, running around on interview after interview with still no commitment. What sign should I hope my boss will be?

This is a very tricky business, because if you ask at the interview you'll lose instantly. (You don't, after all, want to be dismissed as an astrology nut!) The clues that follow should help you recognize the boss who would suit you best at this stage of your development, but it's up to you to tailor your responses accordingly to win the job of your choice:

ARIES: A vigorous, hearty person who'll stress enthusiasm more than anything else—and hers will be highly contagious. On the negative side: she wants the work done *yesterday*.

TAURUS: A calm, steady person who'll be very patient about training you, and who will respect your matter-of-fact questions about salary and benefits. On the negative side: she conceals her anger until she feels she's been pushed too far, and then it will probably be too late. Don't take advantage of her good nature.

GEMINI: She may do most of the talking during the interview, and would make you feel at home thanks to her warm and informal manner. If you get the job she'll keep you informed every step of the way, and you'll really learn the whys and wherefores of the business. On the negative side: follow-up could well be difficult, as the pace is fast and she'll have plenty of irons in the fire (but if you're alert and can keep up with her, you'll do fine).

CANCER: Her office will be a home away from home and will look like one, full of plants and things to eat on display in open dishes. She's persistent, perceptive, and sensitive to people. Don't be surprised if she sends you home at the first sign of a cold, or suggests remedies. On the negative side: she could worry a subject to death, or get too involved in office politics.

LEO: She'll be warm, cheerful, sometimes theatrical, and would delegate plenty of responsibility to you. On the negative side: she could be your worst enemy if she thinks you want to replace her.

VIRGO: She'll be a patient, methodical teacher with an uncanny tolerance for the most minute detail. Neatness counts, and this would show up in her appearance (rosy and healthy), her diction, and the arrangement of her office. On the negative side: a perfectionist, she gives in to the temptation to be overly critical. Don't come into the office with a run in your panty-hose!

LIBRA: She's gracious, diplomatic, and will make every effort to give you a fair chance. On the negative side: she can be a real prima donna.

SCORPIO: She manages to conduct an interview without seeming to make an effort; you just find yourself telling her what she wants to know—if not more. She knows exactly what she wants and likes; you won't have to wonder where you stand with her. On the negative side: her criticism can be stinging, like the Virgo's. If she doesn't love you, she'll hate you— nothing in-between.

SAGITTARIUS: She's breezy, likes to laugh, and has a strong feeling for fair play. On the negative side: she is ingenuously unaware that her sense of humor can be hurtful unless you make it obvious that she's offended you.

CAPRICORN: She'll be thorough yet concise in talking terms, and would anticipate your questions. If your credentials boast high-status schools or awards you'll stand a good chance with her. Once you're in, work hard and don't watch the clock. On the negative side: that's the crux of it—she often gets on the negative side and relies on her assistant to prop up her morale. You'll have to sell her positive thinking. She suffers laziness badly; pull your weight and you should win her unswerving loyalty.

AQUARIUS: She may fill the interview with seemingly irrelevant personal questions, but it's simply because people fascinate her; she wants to see how your mind works in a spontaneous situation. She'll be friendly and willing to give you training, independence, and contact with the public. On the negative side: her remarks may throw you off balance, but if you're quick-witted she'll respect you.

PISCES: She's a good listener and is as willing to learn from you as you are to learn from her. She's creative—a genuine original—and you could learn a lot indeed. On the negative side: she may be absentminded, so you'll have to compensate and be more organized and more capable with follow-up and assorted mundane details than you've ever been before.

Is there any way of telling who in a love relationship loves more?
Yes, and I can do this thoroughly only when the birth times of both are documented. I can tell, too, if it isn't love at all—which I've seen in the cases of several married couples. For the sake of simplicity I won't give a convoluted technical description of what it is I do to find this, but I want to add that in studies of relationships I *always* study exactly what it is each person loves—or hates, fears, or resents—in the other. The planet under stress is the key. (Page 290)
If the aspect between Venus in one chart and any planet in the other's is harmonious, the emotional satisfaction will be the greater. Where the aspect is discordant, the love feelings will still be very much in evidence, but there are likely to be emotional bruises.

I am a lawyer, an Aries born at sunrise, and my problem is this: I did some unpaid legal work for a close relative a couple of years ago, and since word got around I've been besieged by family requests to do endless time-consuming favors gratis because of the love they know I have for them. Or did have. I don't want to alienate these people permanently, just to put a stop to these encroachments on my free time and to exploitation of my good nature. Help!
Saturn rules the house of the regard people have for you, and Saturn can really be stingy. Also, Venus, ruler of your house of clients, introduces that element of love you mentioned, giving you a desire to keep relations open. Try saying with a smile that your office will send a bill in the morning. The usual reaction to that is, "But you *love* me!" At that

The Sun:	self-assurance, authority, the ego, ambition
The Moon:	compassion for the vulnerable, changeability, adaptability, musical talents or tastes, domestic and culinary aptitudes and ideas
Mercury:	the style of thinking and self-expression
Venus:	appearance, refinement, kindness, social poise
Mars:	sex appeal, competitiveness, fast pace of living, directness, decisiveness, courage
Jupiter:	humor, fairness, generosity, religious and philosophical beliefs
Saturn:	responsibility, discipline, talent for getting organized and working efficiently, reliability, thrift, moral strength
Uranus:	independence, inventiveness, progressive ideals
Neptune:	creative imagination, sensitivity to others' thoughts and feelings
Pluto:	cooperation and sufficient interest to probe—in the face of resistance—how the other really feels
Midheaven:	career accomplishments, ambitions, reputation
Ascendant:	personal style, mannerisms, approach to living, appearance

point you can feel perfectly justified in saying, "If you don't love me enough to offer to pay me, I don't love you enough to give my time." You have my heartfelt empathy! It happens to astrologers all the time!

I've always been a frank and open person. Just about anyone who knows me can tell you that. All of a sudden I find myself tongue-tied with the man I've been seeing recently. I'm censoring myself all the time. Will I be this way long? Will I soon be more relaxed again? I hope you won't tell me to give up the man, because he's the only reliable man I've ever known at a time when I'm starting to go for more than "kicks."

Saturn in the man's chart is in exactly the same degree and sign (Capricorn) as your Jupiter. Jupiter in Capricorn isn't all that free-and-easy to begin with, but when another person's Saturn is in an exact conjunction, it's a definite inhibiting force. It isn't just a temporary progression; it's in your natal charts, so the relationship won't get much better than it is now. On a day-to-day basis, this constraint can be a real depressant. If you gradually see less of him, your friendship can be a reassuring platonic one (you two can probably give each other valuable business help, too). PS: Unless the charts show a real disaster, an astrologer should never urge a drastic decision on you such as giving up a person in your life. We can only outline the conditions surrounding the alternatives. The final decision rests with you.

Can you tell a person her or his life expectancy?
Maybe I can, but I won't. While an astrologer has an obligation to tell the truth, there is also the obligation for discretion. We don't tell the whole truth if the prophecy can be destructively self-fulfilling. Besides, we can be wrong. The death we see may not be the death of the client but of someone else—and it may not even be a physical one; just the death of a way of life.

My marriage is more like the setup of Felix and Oscar in "The Odd Couple"! My husband, a Sagittarian, is a great live-and-let-live companion, but he's so sloppy it's driving me nuts! I'm a Virgo, a real dust-hunter, and I can't stand to see the mess. I have a full-time job, too!
This issue is the main reason why strongly Virgo personalities have trouble with Sagittarians, who are notorious for indifference to detail. Try avoiding the cleaning, too, and see how long it takes before he cares enough to do something about it. In any event, don't spend so much time at home running your finger along the window sills! Follow your husband's example and learn to relax more. Get out of the house and *do* things besides go to your job. And what you don't see won't bother you.

My husband promised that we would always be honest with each other, so that we would have a marriage that was better than his marriage with his first wife. But when I ask questions about things that affect us he gets angry, calls me nosy, rolls his eyes, and doesn't give me a straight answer. Why?
As you do not have the birth information on the ex-wife, I cannot say what you have in common—besides *him*, of course. As Jo Coudert wrote in *Advice from a Failure*, there are two kinds of people in this world: the angry and the guilty. As a Capricorn with Venus in Capricorn conjunct your Sun, you are more the guilty sort—that is, you internalize

the blame and guilt others may find it convenient to throw at you. It seems that women are more accustomed, through conditioning, to accepting guilt, while men are more likely to get angry. In terms of your husband's chart: he is a Piscean, and would rather evade a subject altogether than have a painful confrontation. As he has Mercury in Aries, under provocation he would lash out. Judging from the fact that Saturn makes no more than three aspects and that he has no Capricorn planets, I would say that guilt is not something he's accustomed to living with. Furthermore, his Neptune squares your Moon, giving him the notion that he's doing you a favor when he avoids sensitive topics; mistaken or not, he really believes you couldn't handle it. He underestimates your Capricorn perseverance. Encourage him to take a chance in confiding in you; appeal to the gambler in him. If you should actually prove a disappointment—which I doubt—there's plenty of time later for him to withdraw into his shell.

My future husband is initiating a housekeeping contract. You wouldn't believe how much is included: like, if I do the dusting, he'll make us bookcases in his carpentry shop, and if I wash the linens, he'll rearrange the furniture. It seems fair that for every chore I do, he does one; but the whole business of putting it down on paper bothers me.

I think that the problem with this contract is that the chores you're to do have to be done over and over again, while the bookshelves stay done and the furniture stays put. Your attitude toward housekeeping, as shown by your fourth house, is more casual. Jupiter is conjunct Venus here, and in the spontaneous and egalitarian sign Aquarius. He, on the other hand, has Mercury (contracts!) conjunct Saturn in the fourth house in the sign Libra, and can negotiate these details from now until the cows come home. You can expect a great deal of discussion before a fairer arrangement will be worked out. Suggest, instead, dividing the house in half: you take full responsibility for the bathroom and the bedroom, for instance, and leave the kitchen (except for *shared* cooking detail) and living room to him. Of course, if he wants to do *all* the cooking, why not give in. . . .

When my husband and I were first married, we made a deal: if we had a son, he would have my husband's surname; if a daughter, she'd have my surname. We now have a son, age seven, and a daughter, age one. *I'm constantly annoyed by slight acquaintances who know my daughter has my name who say, "Didn't the man marry you and give the baby a name?" It's insulting because of the assumptions that a) he did me the favor of marrying me, while the reverse could just as well be true (we both feel lucky!), and b) his is the only name which counts. I can give the baby a name with prestige too!*

You have a Leo ascendant, hence a strong sense of self and the value of a name of your own. As Aquarius is on the cusp of the seventh house (the house of the general public as well as that of marriage) you would have an unusual marriage (in the context of the current norm for the time and place in which you live) and can expect those reacting to you to be visibly disturbed as well as disturbing. Your Sun and Moon in Aquarius are in the seventh house and square Mars in the tenth, so the defensive reactions of others would hurt you more than they should. The most important thing seems to have been resolved: peace within the family (your fourth and seventh houses are your most harmonious). You can afford to be more relaxed and patient with those whose thinking hasn't caught up with yours yet. Educating the public on a one-to-one basis, as the opportunity arises, is a valuable contribution your experience qualifies you to make. Enjoy it!

What bewilders me is why my sister should exhaust me the way she does. She's nine years older than I am (I'm twenty-five) and has a bit more going on in her life than I have in mine. Why, after a day of sitting at a desk where little happens, should I be so tired just listening to my sister talk on the telephone?

The mystery of why people either exhaust other people (regardless of the day's activity or lack of it) or pep them up has to do with electromagnetic blending. Add the planets you have in Fire and Air signs, and those in Earth and Water—in your case, four and six, respectively—and compare them to the same figures for your sister's chart. If the other person's Fire plus Air total varies from yours by more than one, you are indeed likely to feel exhausted (your sister's totals are eight and two). Were her Fire-Air total three, four, or five, she would stimulate you instead. This has nothing to do with liking; there are more Moon aspects between your charts than any other kind of energy, and these are harmonious. The caring, the willingness to tune in, is there. Don't worry about it.

*I am fifteen and have been doing really well in school. My problem is
my parents. They keep pushing me to go out on dates—blind dates, or
just going to parties by myself—because "you never know who you're
going to meet." The social things I arrange for myself are mostly group
get-togethers with both boys and girls, and little or no pairing up. I
would be perfectly happy if I could only be left alone: my friends feel
similarly. We all want to go to college and have professions, so we don't
have too much time for heavy involvements. Another trouble is that I
always get A's, so I can't even say to my parents, "I would have gotten
an A if only you hadn't backed me into that hideous blind date." It's
really awful: as long as I'm single, my mother is going to push me into a
search for someone no matter what I want! Must my needs always come
last?*

Your mother's chart shows her to be strongly Cancerian: the Sun (in
the twelfth house), ascendant, Moon, and Pluto. The last three, in close
conjunction, give enormous depth to her feeling for her family. In
addition, remember that she came of age at the height of the postwar
baby boom, and the propaganda took hold in her when she was young
and vulnerable. Women's liberation was revived too few years ago to put
up an equal fight with the life-style she was brought up to embrace. The
Cancer emphasis in her chart gives above-average tenacity.

In your chart, Neptune in late Libra is in the twelfth house, which
makes you look forward to better conditions in and as a result of college.
It also makes you dream of being left alone. Neptune sextile Pluto in Leo
in the tenth house (the mother) does indeed indicate that your ambitions
can best be furthered by socializing in groups until you personally feel a
strong desire to pair off with someone. If your mother doesn't respond
to level-headed, matter-of-fact reasoning from you regarding your
desire to use your time to best advantage and do justice to your education, try making an ally of someone close to her in age. If a number of
such people—an aunt, a teacher, a guidance counselor—try to convince
her of the sanity of your present course, it's likely she'll see your way and
express more support. You have harmonious aspects for career prominence (specifically writing, teaching, radio or TV journalism) and should
be encouraged to develop your talents.

*My consciousness-raising group is interested in astrology, and we
were talking about which sign would be the most liberated for a man*

and which would be the most chauvinistic. I for one am thinking of sampling the whole zodiac for research purposes, if not fun! What do you think?

I'm thinking of doing the same myself! And if any woman wants to send me the data of her own special certifiable chauvinist (or liberated angel), please write me care of my publisher. Meanwhile, a handy field guide garnered from personal experience, client counseling, and general study:

ARIES: The "relationship," such as it is, is over very quickly and is based on sexual attraction. His enthusiasm burns out quickly, which is unfortunate even for those who want platonic friendship from this dynamic individual. No matter how sensational he thinks you are, he's even more excited about the one he hasn't met yet, and the one after that. Hugh Hefner is an Aries. Need I say more?

TAURUS: This man is more patient and kind than Aries. Craving continuity himself, he's willing to take the time to build a relationship. The length of his stay has a lot to do with the satisfaction of his senses. He genuinely likes people and socializing. One of my best professional opportunities came through the intervention of a Taurus man, so I for one think of this sign with fond regard.

GEMINI: This sign is my absolute favorite: Geminis are talkative—though not always communicative—and are fond of books and sharing mental interests. Trust a Gemini to keep the talk flowing, in bed as well as out. As might be expected with the sign of the twins, they're often of two minds: their words are progressive and liberal, especially with those born during World War II, so they'd be ashamed to look you in the eye and tell you your indifference to domesticity disappoints them. Because every adult Gemini's Sun progresses into the next sign, Cancer, Gemini men secretly compare their lovers to their mothers, but cerebral Gemini will never complain if your pie isn't as tasty as good ol' mom's! Schizoid but fun!

CANCER: This one is the most security-minded of the lot, in emotional as well as material terms. He may even go so far as to suggest you move in with him the second time you meet. He loves good music, better food, his mother, and tender loving care in general; when you're sick he's the man most likely to show up with the chicken soup.

LEO: Leo is all heart, and loves the drama of a romantic relationship at its beginning. You may find him narrow-minded about feminism unless you appeal to his well-developed self-interest: if he thinks you're good for plenty of alimony, he may consider other role reversals as well. But don't bank on it. His real kick comes from rescuing damsels in distress who didn't start life with the advantages he had. He likes comfortable, elegant surroundings and luxurious candlelit dinners when he's in love.

VIRGO: If you're on a par with him intellectually he'll probably recognize it and open up to you. He's discriminating, health-conscious (perhaps even a hypochondriac), a perfectionist (don't be surprised if he corrects your grammar), and has impeccable, understated taste. As for chauvinism, he could go either way: one Virgo of my acquaintance encouraged his wife to become a partner in his business. After she divorced him he often stated emphatically that that line of work wasn't suitable for women!

LIBRA: My own experience ran heavily toward Librans until I decided to wall off that particular primrose path. The three I knew had little in common except physical attractiveness, vanity, and a readiness to accept without reciprocation the hospitality I offered. It's quite common for a Libran to boast good looks, whether or not you're listening. They're diplomatic, kind, and have refined tastes. The problem arises if you're a romantic and meet a Libran man out on one of his bed-hopping festivals; his detachment can drive you nuts. The chauvinism or liberality of these "balanced-scale" types will not be obvious, and you'll seldom find extremism and inflexibility here.

SCORPIO: Position desired: horizontal. They dearly love sex and can discuss it interminably, making it a rationale for anything and everything. If you meet one at work and are attracted to him, the best favor you can do yourself is to fight it. Their discretion leaves something to be desired. In a strictly private relationship, too, it can be rough going, since few are above sadistic testing and jokes at your expense. Although you may be fully aware he's just testing, you still have a struggle to keep your self-confidence from going under. He'll either be faithful and possessive or a flagrant chaser. Definitely not for first-timers: you could find yourself sexually addicted to someone you don't even like, and think this is the way it always is.

SAGITTARIUS: He's fun, sports-loving, and generous with time—yours, that is—as well as money. By that I mean he'll happily give you all the time you need to pursue your enterprises, because he needs breathing room himself. If you're a busy woman you may not even mind if he's married. With this one—indeed, with all men—you have to be absolutely honest with yourself about your priorities; if you're not, you're in for trouble. He's honest—relentlessly!

CAPRICORN: A throwback, no two ways about it. At least when he's young. From my observation, he could be the reverse of the Virgo, who starts out liberal and ends up discriminating. The Capricorn seems old and stodgy when young, then favors equality later—after he experiences a painful alimony bite out of his hard-earned paycheck. He can be reassuringly stable and regular in his habits, but may veer off into melancholy from the eternal sameness of it all, or if the woman in his life complains of boredom. Try to avoid dwelling on office problems after hours; a light touch is needed and it's not his strong suit.

AQUARIUS: He's a real idealist, especially approachable if you meet through a mutual cause. Of all the twelve varieties, the Aquarian is the man most likely to become a platonic friend. My own experience has been conspicuously lacking in Aquarians* either in social or client relationships. The only Aquarian man I ever dated was perfectly content to have an occasional dinner and movie together and say good-bye at the theater. No painful silences, and no painful scenes either.

PISCES: He can be tender and lyrical, and is especially willing to put his feelings on paper. The Pisces has a better time with long-distance love; all the better to idealize you. Less evolved Pisceans may be pathological liars or hooked on drugs or alcohol. If he's involved with one of the creative arts, he would be very open-minded about your career, especially if your pay is steady and you don't mind helping him in his struggle to get started. His ESP and interest in the occult may be keen; however, you shouldn't give in to the temptation to view him as a soul mate or reincarnated love simply because you sometimes anticipate one another's thoughts. Enjoy your good times together, but don't leap into self-delusion. Stay on friendly terms with reality.

I am strongly tempted to get a chart reading, but am hesitant because I'm afraid you'd try to change me, as I've never been anything but homosexual. What policy do you have about that?

If your relationships make you happy, I wouldn't dream of depriving you of your pleasure. Sometimes such intense psychological problems arise, however, that the best thing you can do is change partners, or even do without a sexual relationship for a while. I would never presume to tell you what sex your partner should be. After all, heterosexuals certainly don't have a monopoly on happiness.

The man I'm involved with is driving me nuts, but nobody else can equal him when he's at his best. Frankly, after knowing him every other man bores me, and I'm not a good enough actress to hide this fact. The trouble is he abruptly drops out of my life and then surprises me by coming back just when I think I've gotten over him. I'm afraid it'll be that way for the rest of my life—never really having a commitment from

*This is *not* a "Personals" ad. No resumes please.

him and never being able to make one with anybody else. What can I do?

Develop your sense of humor. That isn't meant to be flippant; a sense of humor and a philosophical attitude will help you through just about any ordeal, and your fifth house shows a succession of nerve-racking surprises (Mercury is conjunct Uranus in this house). In addition, this man is an Aquarian (the sign ruled by Uranus!), with his Sun and Uranus in a discordant aspect. The fascination is undeniably strong, but his erratic behavior shows no probability of stabilizing. Whether the man in your life is your Aquarian friend or someone else, the pattern is abrupt —jagged beginnings and breakups. Devote more of your energy and inspiration to your creative work and don't let yourself be turned inside out as a relationship suddenly ends, or seems to. You can survive—and be stronger and happier for it.

Epilogue

You may well ask how I can talk about sexual neutrality and yet be so blatantly pro-woman. What I am trying to do is tip the scales on the side of women, to achieve the balance that should have existed all along. I am striving for an astrology of pure function. The chart is nothing more than the diagram of a specific moment from the perspective of a specific place. All beings, human and otherwise, and all enterprises born at that moment, will have in common the energies interacting as shown.

You cannot tell from the chart—or, if you will, the *moment*—whether the being connected to it by birth is female or male, black or white or red or yellow, or of any particular religious or national affiliation. Therefore, whenever you see separate readings for females or males, or clauses stating that certain signs are better for one sex than for the other, you are perfectly justified in denouncing the product.

A great deal of time, argument, and more argument went into the selection of this book's title. I hesitated to include the word *woman* for precisely the reason set forth above. *Woman's Astrology* is by no means an absolute, but a premise deserving of scrutiny. If this book is of more interest to women than to men, it is primarily in its stress on avoiding sexism, in its devotion to examples of female achievement, and in its inclusion of contemporary realities into the astrological guidance offered. Men, I hope, may also find help and cheer in these pages. Perhaps the most fortunate test of my thesis was the creative process itself, when I succeeded in losing sight of a specific audience. The silhouette I visualized myself addressing was of indeterminate sex.

The practice of astrology as I envision it will deal strictly with the varying strengths of each form of energy, and not with the sex of the person possessing the strengths. It will deal with the assorted *kinds* of relationships we have—romantic, parental, professional—and not with the sex of the people encountered.

Astrology gives us a mixed bag of confidence and humility: the confidence comes from the knowledge of one's own capabilities; the humility from increased knowledge—the more one learns, the more one learns what not to presume.

Knowledge is power, and power is responsibility. The responsibility to help people become their best possible selves is a trust of no small proportion. And I for one never cease to feel that it is a trust to be earned time and time again.

Recommended Reading

Biographies

Gurko, Miriam. *Restless Spirit: The Life of Edna St. Vincent Millay*. New York: Thomas Y. Crowell Co., 1962.

Johnston, Johanna. *Mrs. Satan*. New York: Popular Library, 1967.

King, Billie Jean. *Billie Jean*. New York: Harper & Row, 1974.

Lader, Lawrence, and Meltzer, Milton. *Margaret Sanger: Pioneer of Birth Control*. New York: Dell, 1969.

Mead, Margaret. *Blackberry Winter: My Earlier Years*. New York: William Morrow & Co., 1972.

Thomas, Helen. *Dateline: White House*. New York: Macmillan, 1975.

Tomalin, Claire. *The Life and Death of Mary Wollstonecraft*. New York: Harcourt Brace Jovanovich, 1974.

Self-Help

Bird, Caroline. *Everything a Woman Needs to Know to Get Paid What She's Worth*. New York: David McKay, 1973.

Fast, Julius. *The Pleasure Book*. New York: Stein & Day, 1975.

LaBarre, Harriet. *A Life of Your Own*. New York: David McKay, 1972.

Lakein, Alan. *How to Get Control of Your Time and Your Life*. New York: Peter H. Wyden, 1972.

Phelps, Stanlee and Austin, Nancy. *The Assertive Woman*. San Luis Obispo, Calif.: Impact, 1975.

Seabury, David. *The Art of Selfishness*. New York: Pocket Books, 1974.